AC DC

FOR THOSE ABOUT TO ROCK

AC/DC

FOR THOSE ABOUT TO ROCK

PALAZZO

PALAZZO

First published in 2018 by
Palazzo Editions Ltd
15 Church Road
London, SW13 9HE
www.palazzoeditions.com

A CIP catalogue record for this book is available from the British Library.

ISBN 978-1-78675-039-6

Manufactured in China

2 4 6 8 10 9 7 5 3

Designed by Adelle Mahoney for Palazzo Editions

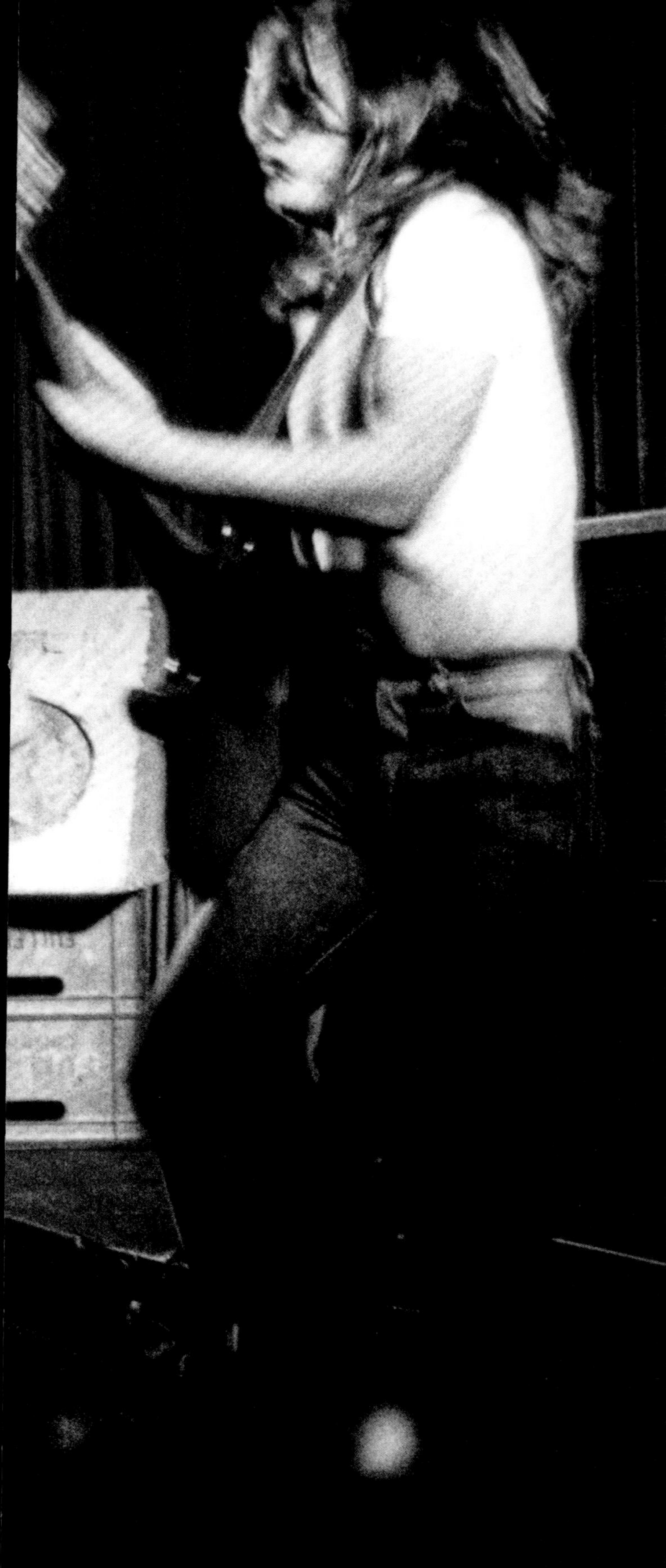

CONTENTS

Previous: **Angus Young in 1988, London**

This page: **AC/DC on stage at the Nashville Rooms, London, as part of their first UK tour in 1976**

NOTE FROM THE AUTHOR

Opposite: **Lead guitarist, Angus Young in 1979. His hyperactive schoolboy routine became a staple of AC/DC's live shows.**

Below: **AC/DC riding the momentum of seventy thousand rock fans at Day on the Green #3 at the Oakland Coliseum, California on July 21, 1979.**

July 21, 1979. On a beautiful summer's day in California, the Oakland Coliseum is filled with seventy thousand rock fans, packed in at pitch level, and lining the curved bleachers around it. At one end of this vast amphitheater is a stage decorated as a jungle scene with two gigantic dinosaur figures at each side and a banner proclaiming: Monsters of Rock. Loud cheers ring out as five skinny, long-haired guys walk out on to the stage and get straight down to business.

The first song starts with throbbing bass, one note repeating, like a racing pulse. The bass player and rhythm guitarist stand back, close to the drummer. The three of them look like clones: jeans, T-shirts, lank hair in their faces. In front of them is the singer, powerfully built, shirtless beneath a cut-off denim jacket, and the lead guitarist, a slight figure, dressed in a schoolboy's uniform complete with cap and tie and a satchel slung across his back.

As he hits the first low notes of guitar, the schoolboy begins to convulse, head twitching, legs shaking. With the first beats of the kick drum, he pulls the cap from his head and tosses it behind him. And as the band locks down into a hard, swinging riff, the little guy is tearing it up across the stage, duckwalking like the

“If you’re lookin’ for trouble, I’m the man to see . . .”

“Live Wire”, AC/DC

Marshall
Marshall
Marshall
Marshall
Marshall
Marshall
Marshall
Marshall

bastard son of Chuck Berry. The singer lets out a scream, bounces on the soles of his feet, and moves to the outer edge of the stage to coolly deliver an opening line loaded with bad vibes: "If you're lookin' for trouble, I'm the man to see . . ."

Out in the audience there are whoops and hollers, hands clapping, girls hoisted on guys' shoulders, arms swaying. The band lays it on thick, a heavy groove. They have this audience by the balls.

AC/DC's time has come. At this event, Day on the Green #3, there are bigger names to follow—Aerosmith and Ted Nugent, all-American superstars—but AC/DC have an irresistible momentum. Their days as an opening act, a cult band, are about to end.

It has been a long, hard road to here. Years of graft, sweating it out, from the pubs and clubs of the band's native Australia, where bottles are thrown if a crowd can smell blood, to bigger stages in Britain and America. The years on the road have honed AC/DC into the most electrifying rock 'n' roll band in the world, and at Day on the Green, they prove it.

In the first song, "Live Wire," the energy comes off them in waves. It is the sound of Chuck Berry and Little Richard and The Rolling Stones jacked up to maximum volume and intensity. The three guys at the back—Malcolm Young on rhythm guitar, Cliff Williams on bass, and Phil Rudd on drums—work away like a machine. The singer, Bon Scott, has a voice as tough as leather, the swagger of a gunslinger, and tattoos of a hardened criminal, effortlessly in control, the epitome of rock 'n' roll cool. The schoolboy, Angus Young, kid brother to Malcolm, is the lightning rod for the band's high-voltage attack, a blur of movement, wiggling his scrawny ass as he boogies, jerking his head violently as he wrings out a solo, and leaping high into the air in the song's frenzied climax.

By the start of the second song, "Problem Child," Bon has his jacket off, already slick with sweat, as the band delivers the knock-down-drag-out riff. The bludgeoning continues with "Sin City." A brand new song, "Highway To Hell"—the title track from the album that is released the following week—has the feel of an anthem.

"Bad Boy Boogie" has Angus stripping down to his shorts in the middle of the song, and playing a manic solo in a trance-like state. There is respite, of a sort, as the band ease into a slow blues number, "The Jack," in which Bon sings of the things he has picked up from sleeping around. Then they are back at full throttle with the deliriously hard and fast "Rocker." With more demanded, they give that audience one last beating with the thuggish assault of "Dog Eat Dog"—Angus rolling around the stage, legs kicking, guitar howling, before the big finish.

"Thanks!" Bon yells, his fist raised as the band walks off. The taste of victory is sweet for a man who has turned thirty-three just a few days earlier. This moment has been a long time coming. He has dreamed of it since he first sensed the power of rock 'n' roll as a teenager.

In the summer of 1979, AC/DC are rising fast. And Bon Scott knows, at last, he has it made . . .

Left: **AC/DC in 1978, on their way to becoming the most electrifying rock 'n' roll band in the world.**

It's a Long Way to the Top

"Early on, we always thought we'd be lucky if we got past the first week."

Angus Young

There was hard-earned wisdom in the words that Bon Scott wrote in "It's A Long Way To The Top (If You Wanna Rock 'n' Roll)," the song that kicked off AC/DC's second album *T.N.T.* For when Bon finally made it as a rock 'n' roll singer, it was the culmination of many years' graft, busting his balls for little or no money. If ever a rock star was a working-class hero, it was Bon.

He was born Ronald Belford Scott on July 9, 1946 in Kirriemuir, a small town in Scotland. His father, Charles, nicknamed Chick, worked in the family bakery, and met his wife, Isabelle, known as Isa, at a dance in Kirkcaldy. They married in 1941 while Chick was on leave from the British army during World War II. The Scotts' first son, Sandy, died after nine months, but Ron, as his mother always called him, was a healthy lad, and fiercely independent. "He used to never come home from school," Isa recalled. "He'd just go off with his little mates." He also loved watching his father play drums in a traditional pipe band that marched in the town square every Saturday, and would mimic the old man by banging on a cookie tin.

In 1952, after Isa had given birth to another boy, named Derek, Chick Scott moved his young family to Australia, tempted by the prospect of a better life. They settled in Sunshine, a blue-collar district of Melbourne, and here, young Ron began honing his drumming skills on a kit bought by his parents. But after four years in Melbourne, the family moved again, traveling one thousand, seven hundred miles to Fremantle, a port town twelve miles south of Perth. At ten, Ronald still had a strong Scottish accent, and his new school classmates quickly picked up on it, nicknaming him "Bonnie Scotland." Later shortened to Bon, the name stuck.

Like his dad, the teenaged Bon played drums for a pipe band but quickly lost interest in the formal disciplines of both the band and school, which he left at fifteen to work as a farm hand. By this point, the rock 'n' roll age was in full swing. Bon grew his hair long, got his first tattoo, fell in with a gang of rockers and began making sporadic appearances on stage at local dance events, cocky enough to jump up and sing the new rock 'n' roll hits such as Little Richard's "Long Tall Sally."

Bon found it easy getting girls, but on one occasion this got him into serious trouble. At a dance hall, he took a young girl outside to fool around a little. When they returned to the dance, Bon was challenged by a gang of youths and a fight broke out. The cops arrived and Bon fled the scene in a friend's car, but was quickly apprehended and later charged with unlawful carnal knowledge and giving a false name to the police. He was sent to a young offenders' institute for nine months. It was a wake-up call. During those months, Bon vowed to clean up his act. He also decided that rock 'n' roll was his future.

In Perth, he joined his first band, The Spektors, in which he doubled as singer and drummer. What the band earned was not enough to pay the rent, so Bon worked as a postman, a job he continued doing until 1967, when he and other members of The Spektors merged with those of another Perth group, The Winstons, to form a new act named The Valentines.

This gave Bon a first fleeting taste of stardom. He switched to full-time singer, sharing the spotlight with co-lead vocalist Vince

Previous: **Bon Scott, lead singer of AC/DC 1974–1980**

Right: **An engraved stone slab in Kirriemuir, Scotland, UK, serves as a permanent memorial to Ronald Belford "Bon" Scott, singer of rock band AC/DC.**

Lovegrove. "It wasn't because I wanted to be up front," Bon later said. "It was because the singer used to get more chicks." And as a bubblegum pop act, The Valentines attracted plenty of young women to their shows. After the band relocated to Melbourne they made their debut single in "Every Day I Have To Cry," a song written by American soul singer Arthur Alexander and previously recorded by the Bee Gees in 1965, before their first international success. Two subsequent singles from The Valentines—"She Said," released in 1967, and "My Old Man's A Groovy Old Man" in 1969— were written by Harry Vanda and George Young, leaders of the most popular Australian group of the late sixties, The Easybeats. In October 1969, The Valentines were the support act for The Easybeats at a concert in Melbourne. In all of this was the first connection between Bon and Harry and George. Five years later, their lives would become inextricably linked. And for Bon, in those years, there would be good times and bad.

As the sixties ended, he sensed that the game was up for The Valentines. Having moved base again, this time to Sydney, the band eventually broke up on August 1, 1970, leaving Bon free to join a new and very different group named Fraternity, in which there was a more serious, modern-thinking mindset in tune with the new rock era. An early Fraternity gig in Sydney had them opening for one of Bon's heroes, Jerry Lee Lewis, The Killer. In December 1970—just a few months after the band formed—they recorded their debut album for Adelaide-based label Sweet Peach, cutting the whole thing inside fourteen hours. In the following month, the band found a new home near Adelaide, a hippie commune set in seven acres of bushland, where Bon enjoyed the rural lifestyle, and where, during one of many house parties, he

Above left: **Before AC/DC, Bon Scott's first, fleeting, taste of stardom was with The Valentines. He is seen here seated, second from the left.**

Above right: (L–R) **Stevie Wright, Harry Vanda, Dick Diamonde, Henry "Snowy" Fleet and George Young of The Easybeats pose for a group portrait in Germany, 1967**

met Irene Thornton. Bon was in a bedroom sucking another girl's toes when Irene first stumbled upon him, but within months he and Irene were living together at the commune.

Fraternity's debut album, named *Livestock*, was released in 1971, and was for Bon a radical departure from the pop music of The Valentines. In the album's title track were echoes of The Doors and The Rolling Stones; in the six-minute "Raglan's Folly," shades of psychedelia and progressive rock. On January 24, 1972, Bon and Irene were married, shortly before Fraternity headed to the UK to promote their second album, *Flaming Galah*—its title an Aussie expression for a person of great stupidity, the music more earthbound than before, with a pronounced blues influence illustrated by opening track "Welfare Boogie." However, on the other side of the world came a rude awakening for Bon and the band.

In the London district of Finchley the band rented a house large enough to accommodate them and their partners. What had not been anticipated was the lack of opportunity for gigs in the UK. A short tour of Germany sustained them for a while, but as the money ran out, tensions rose, two members of the band quit, and in a desperate last roll of the dice they took on a new name, Fang, in an attempt to fit in with the glam rock stars of the time, such as Slade and Sweet. Doggedly, the band remained in the UK until April 1973, when they gigged on the south coast opening for another glam rock act, Geordie. One of those gigs, in Torquay, would stick in Bon's memory. As he later recalled, the singer in Geordie was brilliant, rolling around on the stage, screaming his head off. It was, Bon said, the best Little Richard impersonation he'd ever seen. What Bon did not know then was that the guy had been rushed to hospital after the show, suffering appendicitis. The singer's name was Brian Johnson.

In May, Bon and the band returned to Adelaide, broke and disillusioned. Bon was forced to take a job loading trucks at a fertilizer plant to make ends meet. He began drinking heavily and arguing constantly with Irene. The marriage was only eighteen months old when she told him she'd had enough. Bon got drunk, rode off on his motorcycle, crashed into an oncoming car and ended up in a coma for three days. Irene helped nurse him back to health, but the marriage, like the band, was over. In the last days of 1973, Bon Scott, at the age of twenty-seven, was out on his own: no wife, no band, nothing but a nagging feeling that his dream of being a rock 'n' roll star was slipping away.

Meanwhile, in Sydney, a new rock band was just getting started. It was on New Year's Eve, 1973 that this band, named AC/DC, played its first

Left: **In 1973, Bon Scott toured the UK with his last venture before AC/DC. Fang were opening act for another glam rock band—Geordie—whose lead singer was none other than Brian Johnson** (far left).

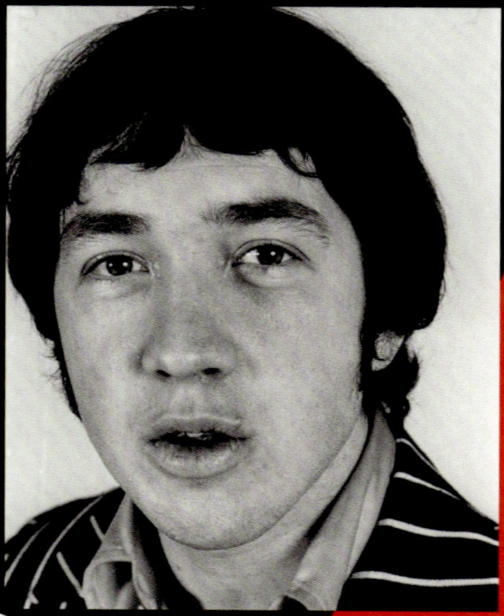

Above left: **George Young, songwriter and older brother of Malcolm and Angus**

Above right: **Fats Domino served as an early introduction to rock 'n' roll for the Young brothers.**

Left: **US rock musician, Little Richard—an early musical influence on both Malcolm and Angus**

Opposite: **Alex Young, also known as George Alexander, was part of the band Grapefruit, pictured here at the band's press launch on January 19, 1968. Back row from left: Brian Jones, Donovan, Ringo Starr, John Lennon, Cilla Black, and Paul McCartney. Seated from left: George Alexander, Pete Swettenham, Geoffrey Swettenham, and John Perry.**

official gig at Chequers, a famous nightclub where Frank Sinatra had once performed. The band featured brothers Malcolm and Angus Young on guitars, Colin Burgess on drums, Larry Van Kriedt on bass, and Dave Evans as singer. What they played that night was a mixture of rock 'n' roll standards, including Chuck Berry's "School Days," a couple of Rolling Stones songs, and a slow, trippy number from The Beatles' *Abbey Road*—"I Want You (She's So Heavy)." Dave Evans was flashy, with a certain swagger about him, but AC/DC's leader was Malcolm Young. He and Angus had a backstory similar to Bon's, as immigrants born in Scotland to William and Margaret Young. And one of their elder brothers was none other than George Young.

It was a big family that William and Margaret had raised in Glasgow, where William worked as a spray painter in the city's shipbuilding industry. The couple had eight children: Steven, born in 1933; one daughter, also named Margaret, born in 1936; John in 1938; Alex in 1939; William in 1941; and George in 1946. The last two to arrive were Malcolm on January 6, 1953, and then Angus on March 31, 1955. The family home was in a housing project in Cranhill, in the east of the city. It was a poor neighborhood, and times were hard, but the home was filled with music that Margaret, the sister, introduced to her brothers—mostly jazz and blues, and also the early rock 'n' roll of Little Richard, Fats Domino, and Chuck Berry. Alex was first to make music a career, playing bass and saxophone for singer Tony Sheridan, who had previously been backed by a then unknown Liverpudlian group, The Beatles. George Young, then still in his teens, was inspired by Alex's example and began making plans of his own.

In 1963, everything changed. In search of a better life, the Young family emigrated to Australia, settling in Sydney. At the time, Malcolm was ten, Angus eight, and both had already started to learn guitar; Malcolm with a cheap acoustic bought by his mother, Angus starting out on a banjo.

George, aged sixteen, was way ahead of them. Within a year of the family's arrival in Sydney, he formed a band with two Dutchmen, bassist Dingeman Vandersluys, known as Dick Diamonde, and guitarist Johannes Vandenberg, aka Harry Vanda, and two Englishmen, singer Stevie Wright and drummer Gordon "Snowy" Fleet. And this band, The Easybeats, took off like a rocket. Their first single, "For My Woman," flopped in early 1965, but by May of that year a second single, "She's So Fine," hit number one in Australia. The group's popularity among teenage pop fans was such that it was equated to Beatlemania, and dubbed "Easyfever." George and Harry were the principal songwriters, and George's powerful rhythm guitar was at the core of The Easybeats sound; a precursor to what Malcolm would create as the heartbeat of AC/DC. In 1966 came the biggest hit of The Easybeats's career—an international hit, "Friday On My Mind." When the band played their debut British show at London's Saville Theatre in November 1966, they had members of The Beatles and The Rolling Stones in

"The sound of Chuck Berry's guitar is everything. It's not clean, it's nasty."

Angus Young

the audience. In the following year, The Easybeats toured in Europe as opening act for the Stones. Meanwhile, Alex Young was hired as a songwriter in London for The Beatles' Apple Publishing group, and was part of the band Grapefruit, so named by John Lennon.

For Malcolm and Angus, both still in school, it was mind-blowing to have older brothers as rock stars. Their father's wish was for them to learn what he considered a proper trade, but by this point their minds were set on music.

In 1968, the year that Malcolm left school, Harry Vanda presented him with a Gretsch Jet Firebird guitar, which would become his signature model. In turn, Malcolm gave his Hofner guitar to Angus. Both were self-taught musicians for whom Chuck Berry was a primary influence, as he was for rock 'n' roll as a whole. As Angus told me in that 1991 interview: "As a kid, I was never one for the Cliff Richard thing with the tennis racket. I was more interested in getting my fingers round the guitar neck, because when I was little—I'm little now, but I was little, little—getting a hand around the neck was a big thing. The sound of Chuck Berry's guitar is everything rolled into one: it's blues, it's rock and roll, and it's got that hard edge to it. To me, that's pure rock 'n' roll. It's not clean, it's nasty."

For The Easybeats it was a fast but short ride. In 1969, with their popularity waning, the band split, and George and Harry returned to London to develop a new career as a songwriting and production team, billed as Vanda and Young. At the same time, back in Sydney, Malcolm was devouring the music of the British blues rock explosion: the early Fleetwood Mac featuring guitar genius Peter Green, and John Mayall and the Bluesbreakers, featuring another emerging guitar hero, Eric Clapton. Malcolm was also blown away by The Who's "My Generation," the Stones' "Jumpin' Jack Flash," and The Beatles' "Get Back."

After leaving school, Malcolm worked in various jobs, as a storeman and repairing sewing machines. By seventeen he was an accomplished lead guitarist. His first band of any real note was Beelzebub Blues, later known as Red House, a covers band playing

Guitar geniuses, Peter Green (above left) **of Fleetwood Mac and Pete Townshend** (above right) **of The Who heavily influenced Malcolm Young.**

Opposite: **Chuck Berry's guitar playing was a source of inspiration for young Angus.**

songs by heavy rock acts including Black Sabbath, The Animals, and Cream. Malcolm was also a big fan of Marc Bolan and T. Rex.

In 1971 he joined a band that had relocated to Sydney from Newcastle. Strangely, they called themselves The Velvet Undergound—a name which had already been made famous in the late sixties by the New York art-rock group fronted by Lou Reed. The band that Malcolm joined, as lead guitarist, played a wide array of songs, from Deep Purple to George Harrison's "My Sweet Lord."

Angus, meanwhile, had his own group, Kantuckee. By this point he had grown his hair long and was into much the same bands as Malcolm: The Animals, The Yardbirds, and bluesmen such as Buddy Guy. A guitarist he admired greatly was Jeff Beck, formerly of The Yardbirds. When Angus left school he worked in a butcher's shop and as a printing apprentice. With the money he earned he bought a Gibson SG guitar, as played by Pete Townshend of The Who and Leslie West of Mountain. Kantuckee, like Malcolm's band, played covers—plenty of Mountain songs and others by Hendrix, Beck, and American power trio Cactus. Angus also attended many Velvet Undergound gigs, and Kantuckee's first paid engagement was opening for Malcolm's

Above: **Brothers Malcolm Young** (seated, left) **and Angus Young** (right)

band at a club in Batemans Bay, a few hours from Sydney.

In 1972 The Velvet Undergound was renamed Pony—inspired by "Ride On A Pony," one of many Free songs they played. But before that year was out, Malcolm quit, and Pony split soon after, following a brief period with Dave Evans as singer. Malcolm put a new band together with ex-Velvet Undergound/Pony bassist Mick Sheffzick and a drummer, Colin Burgess, who was a fairly big name on the Australian rock scene as a former member of the successful group The Masters Apprentices. At this stage, Malcolm was not thinking about getting Angus in the band, which was still unnamed. Equally, Angus was doing just fine with his own group, which had been rechristened Tantrum, and had recorded a few demos with George Young and Harry Vanda, featuring original songs such as "The Kantuckee Stomp." It was only after Malcolm had found a new bassist in American-born Larry Van Kriedt, and then enlisted Dave Evans as singer, that he asked Angus if he wanted in. According to Malcolm, this idea met with some resistance from Dave Evans. The two brothers had a fiery relationship that led many, their father included, to question the wisdom of them being in a band together. But when Angus said yes, that was that.

The band had yet to settle on a name when they played together live for the first time at The Last Picture Show club in Sydney in December 1972. There are differing versions of how they came to be known as AC/DC. The most common story is that the Youngs' sister, Margaret, noted the initials on the back of a sewing machine or vacuum cleaner, but as Malcolm once stated in an interview with *Go Set* magazine: "George's wife Sandra thought it was a good name for a group." Whatever the true origin, it was a name with gay connotations, but the brothers had no reservations about that. To them, AC/DC suggested electricity, and power.

The band's first year was one of slow and steady progress, out of public view and under the tutelage of George Young. In these early stages, as the band began honing their sound—a no-frills blend of hard rock 'n' roll, blues, and boogie—Malcolm and Angus had not yet developed clearly defined roles as rhythm and lead guitarist. They simply played whatever felt right. And before they started on AC/DC recordings, they were involved in a Vanda and Young project under the name of the Marcus Hook Roll Band. Marcus Hook never existed. Nor, in any conventional sense, did the Roll Band. It was simply an invented name for a studio project which had begun a year or two earlier with ex-Pretty Things bassist Alan "Wally" Waller. The resulting album was named *Tales Of Old Grand-Daddy*. Malcolm played rhythm guitar on every track. Angus's contributions were minimal and undocumented.

According to George, this record was merely "a joke," recorded while all except teetotal Angus were "rotten" drunk. The music was low-grade pub rock, with only "Silver Shoes and Strawberry Wine" indicative of Vanda and Young's pop nous. The album was released in 1973, only in Australia. But over time it would take on a significant historical value. "It's the first thing Malcolm and Angus did before AC/DC," George said.

It was in January 1974, just a few days after the official debut show at Chequers, that the first AC/DC recordings were completed at EMI Studios in Sydney, with Vanda and Young at the controls. Among the songs cut in that session were "Rockin' In The Parlour," "Rock 'n' Roll Singer," and a swinging number entitled "Can I Sit Next To You, Girl." After the event, Larry Van Kriedt's bass parts were re-recorded by George Young. A week after the recording session, Colin Burgess was fired on the spot after collapsing on stage during another show at Chequers. Burgess later claimed that his collapse was the result of someone spiking his drink. Whatever the truth was, his dismissal suggested a ruthless streak in the Young brothers, and soon after, Van Kriedt was also fired.

Replacements quickly arrived in bassist Neil Smith and drummer Noel Taylor, both acquired from rival Sydney group Jasper. The new-look AC/DC played residencies in local hotels and began working into their live set extended versions of "Jumpin' Jack Flash" and "Baby, Please Don't Go," the latter a traditional blues song, popularized in the 1930s by Delta bluesman Big Joe Williams and again in the sixties by Van Morrison's group Them.

A defining moment for AC/DC arrived in April when the band appeared at an open-air concert in Sydney's Victoria Park. It was at this show that Angus performed for the first time in the schoolboy uniform for which he would become famous. Until that point, the band had worn regulation blue jeans and T-shirts on stage, save for Evans, who favored colorful glam rock threads. Malcolm had felt that the band needed a stronger visual identity. Angus was not so sure. It required some persuasion from Malcolm to get Angus up on stage in the uniform he had worn at Ashfield Boys High School. But it still fitted him: at nineteen, Angus was the same skinny short-arse he had been four years earlier. And for this show, the whole band dressed up: Malcolm in a white jumpsuit, Dave Evans in a red-and-white striped jacket and red stacked heels.

Speaking to me in 2003, Malcolm thought back to the conversation he had with Angus backstage at that show, as a nervous Angus got into uniform: "The first time he put it on he said, 'Do you think they'll kill me out there?' I said, 'You'd better jump around a bit!'" Angus did that all right. He was high on adrenalin. As he said to me in 1991: "I think the first time I wore the uniform was the most frightened I've ever been on stage. But I had no time to think, thank God. I just went straight out there."

The audience at Victoria Park reacted with a mixture of amusement and bewilderment at the sight of this hyperactive, scrawny little kid who looked as if he was playing truant as he played that guitar like Chuck Berry on amphetamines. But this was a hard act to pull off when the band returned to bread-and-butter gigs in pubs and clubs, where the clientele did not take kindly to anyone appearing to be taking the piss. As Angus told me: "The crowd's first reaction to the shorts and stuff was like a bunch of fish at feeding time—all mouths open. So I never stopped moving. I reckoned if I stood still I'd be dead. I had just one thing on my mind: I didn't want to be a target for blokes throwing bottles. I thought, if I stand still I'm a target. In some of the pubs we played there was that much scrapping going on, you were behind the amps!"

"George's wife Sandra thought it [AC/DC] was a good name for a group."

Malcolm Young

Thinking back, Angus also commented, "Early on, we always thought we'd be lucky if we got past the first week." But in the summer of 1974, AC/DC's career was rapidly gaining momentum. As Malcolm sought to strengthen the band, Neil Smith and Noel Taylor were fired and replaced by bassist Rob Bailey and drummer Peter Clack. In June 1974, AC/DC signed a record deal with Albert Productions. Then on July 22, 1974 came the release of the band's debut single: "Can I Sit Next To You, Girl," backed with "Rockin' In The Parlour." The A-side was very much in the glam rock vein, sung by Dave Evans with a cocksure sneer. It was a minor hit,

"The **first** **time** I wore the **uniform** was the **most** **frightened** I've ever been **on stage.** I had **no time** to think, I just went straight **out** **there.**"

Angus Young

and the band followed it with a headline tour in clubs before a run of theater shows opening for the guy from the original Velvet Underground, Lou Reed. It was during this tour with Reed that two fundamental changes occurred in AC/DC. The first came at a show in Perth, when Malcolm decided that from that point he would play rhythm guitar and Angus lead. The second was the deterioration in the relationship between Dave Evans and the Youngs, a rising tension that escalated into brawling. The singer was on his way out.

Bon Scott just happened to be in the right place at the right time. And it was his old friend from The Valentines, Vince Lovegrove, who brought Bon into contact with AC/DC. In 1974 Lovegrove was working as a concert promoter, and as a favor had hired Bon to run errands. Unknown to Bon, Vince knew that AC/DC were looking to replace their singer, and had recommended Bon. Vince suggested that Bon check out the band at Adelaide's Pooraka club, but Bon didn't like what he'd heard about the band—that they had a "poofy" singer who dressed in satins and stacked heels, and a teenage guitarist who wore a schoolboy's uniform on stage. Bon dismissed them as "a gimmick band." Nevertheless, he went to the show, and—Evans aside—was impressed by what he saw. When the gig was over, Bon went backstage and got talking to Malcolm and Angus. They told him they were looking for a new singer, and only half-jokingly suggested that Bon was too old to cut it. "I took the opportunity," Bon later said, "to explain to them how much better I was than the drongo they had singing for them!"

A few days later, Malcolm and Angus snuck away with Bon to a rehearsal space where they tried out a couple of tunes. What the brothers heard in Bon's voice was all the raw power and attitude that their music demanded of a singer. Bon was offered the job on the spot, and within a couple of weeks AC/DC were back on stage at the Pooraka with Bon as their new singer. In the dressing room before they went on, Angus watched amazed as Bon sank two bottles of bourbon, snorted lines of cocaine and speed, and smoked a joint before declaring, "Right, I'm ready!" Bon wore a pair of Irene's old knickers on stage—proving, in the most literal sense, that he had the balls for the job. He performed with a manic energy that night, some of which could be attributed to nerves, especially as Bon must have sensed that this could be his last chance. "He said," Angus recollected, "that it made him feel young again."

Bon had found the perfect rock 'n' roll band in AC/DC, and everything he had ever dreamed of was about to come true.

Opposite: **Angus Young in full schoolboy kit performing live in Victoria Park, Sydney**

Following: (L–R) **Malcolm Young, Angus Young, and Bon Scott of AC/DC in 1975**

DC

Send Us the Little Guy in the Shorts!

"All you can do is play—and pray! You put your head down and hope a bottle doesn't come your way."

Angus Young

DANG
KEEP

The effect that Bon Scott had on AC/DC in the early days was something that Angus Young told me about in 1991. "Bon joined us pretty late in his life," Angus said. "But that guy had more youth in him than people half his age. That was how he thought, and I learned from him."

What Angus also remembered with affection was the way Bon would act as a protective influence over him, the older and wiser man looking out for the kid who was still in his teens. "Bon used to say to me, 'Whatever I do, you don't.' Oh, I had a few wild nights over the years, but most of the time everyone else was having them for me. Because of the schoolboy uniform, some women have tried to mother me—they think I'm cute because I'm so short. But playing has always been the thing for me. I never really looked beyond the next gig. In the early days, all my mates used to say to me, 'You must be meeting loads of girls . . . ' Well yeah, I used to meet plenty of girls, but none of them used to want to go home with me. Some women would come up and make . . . er, bold statements, but I don't know why. There's nothing sexy about a schoolboy, is there?"

In truth, Angus was not, at nineteen, some green little kid. He played the schoolboy on stage, and while he was and would always remain teetotal, he smoked like a chimney. But to Angus and the other members of AC/DC, Bon was an old hand at this game who had been around the block and knew how to handle what came with the territory. Around AC/DC, as with any rock 'n' roll band, there was the booze, drugs, and women. There was also the rough crowd the band would draw in pubs and clubs around the country in those early days, the spit-and-sawdust joints where the booze flowed, and violence inevitably followed. As Angus explained to me: "Some of the places we played were worse than toilets, let me tell you. When I was at school and there was a dance with a band, it was always a band like Van Halen, an American high school band. You know, the guy with the long blond hair wiggling his hips. In the pubs we played in, in front of that hot, sweaty, beer-swilling crowd, you couldn't even hope to do that. This was the kind of audience you couldn't even tune your guitar to. If you bust a string, that was it. Sometimes you finished with just two strings, because there was no way they were going to put up with a couple of minutes of you fixing the guitar. I remember one night I said to the rest of the band, 'I'm not going out there.' The police couldn't get

Previous: **Angus Young** (second from left) **and Bon Scott** (second from right) **backstage with female fans on August 24, 1977 at the Palladium in New York City**

Left: **AC/DC:** (L–R) **Phil Rudd, Angus Young, Mark Evans, Malcolm Young, Bon Scott**

in the place. There was some madman running around inside the hall with a meat cleaver, chopping into the people! And the front row was all bikers. I said, 'They just want blood!' You looked out and it was just like murderers' row, and the look on their faces is like, 'Send us the little guy in the shorts!'"

Angus laughingly brought to mind a night when he was too scared to go on stage until he was given some assistance from his big brother. "Suddenly I just felt a boot and I was on," he chuckled. "And there's this deathly silence. All you can do is play—and pray! You put your head down and hope a bottle doesn't come your way. That became part of my stage act. I learnt to duck and keep moving." And there was another early gig that Angus remembered for what it said about Bon's character. "People used to get a good laugh out of how we arrived at a show in those days," he said. "We had an old bus with no brakes. It went all of three times! One night we were playing a pub somewhere, Bon walked in, went up to the mic and said, 'Listen, if you wanna see a show tonight, we need about twelve of you to come and help us push our bus!' Then Bon wanted to iron his jeans. He said his other pair had oil and grease on them. So he got an iron from the bus, went over to the bar, pushed everyone's drinks out of the way, took his jeans off right there in this packed pub and done his jeans."

Right: **Bon "The Likeable" Scott**

Opposite: **Original lyrics by Bon Scott for "She's Got Balls"**

Angus once described Bon, with no little admiration, as "the dirtiest fucker I ever knew." As he told *MOJO* in 2000: "When I first met him he couldn't even speak English. It was all 'fuck,' 'cunt,' 'piss,' 'shit.'" But the man was such a charmer, the classic loveable rogue, that people were drawn to him wherever he went.

"We used to call him 'Bon The Likeable.' We could be somewhere you'd never expect anyone to know him and someone would always have a bottle of beer for him."

Angus Young

"We used to call him 'Bon The Likeable,'" Angus recalled to me. "We could be somewhere where you'd never expect anyone to know him, and someone would walk up and say 'Bon Scott!' and always have a bottle of beer for him." Most important of all, Bon was one hell of a rock 'n' roll singer who, Angus said, "molded the flavor of AC/DC."

In November 1974, within a few months of Bon joining the band, they entered Albert Studio in Sydney to record their debut album, with George Young and Harry Vanda as producers. The whole album was cut inside six days, between gigs, and they named it—in tune with the band's name—*High Voltage*. At this time, the band's line-up still included Rob Bailey on bass and Peter Clack on drums, but in a sign of what was to come, Bailey's contribution was limited, with both Malcolm and George playing bass on various tracks, and Clack reportedly played on just one song—their hard and fast take on "Baby, Please Don't Go"—with all other tracks recorded using a session drummer, Tony Currenti.

Of the seven original songs on the album, all were co-written by the Young brothers and Bon, save for "Soul Stripper," credited solely to Malcolm and Angus, and developed from an earlier number named "Sunset Strip" that was originally written with Dave Evans. What the band nailed on "Soul Stripper" was a rhythmic tension that gave it a mesmeric quality, and in a new set of lyrics, Bon cast himself in the unlikely role of victim—with the mind games of a manipulative woman messing with his head. Another key track was "Little Lover," a priapic blues number that Malcolm had first written in his early teens and was originally titled "Front Row Fantasies." Bon brought a whole new dimension of sleaze into the mix, with reference to a girl who left a damp patch on her seat, leaving the singer to wonder if it was cola.

The song that best represented the band was the first that Bon wrote with them, a song with a title that spoke volumes about where they were at and where they were headed—"She's Got Balls." It had a heavy swing, based around a meaty riff from Malcolm, while the title and lyrics were in the style that would become Bon's signature. As Angus told me: "'She's Got Balls' was about his (Bon's) first wife. Bon could conjure a story from anything." And the title of the song was not an insult: quite the opposite. There

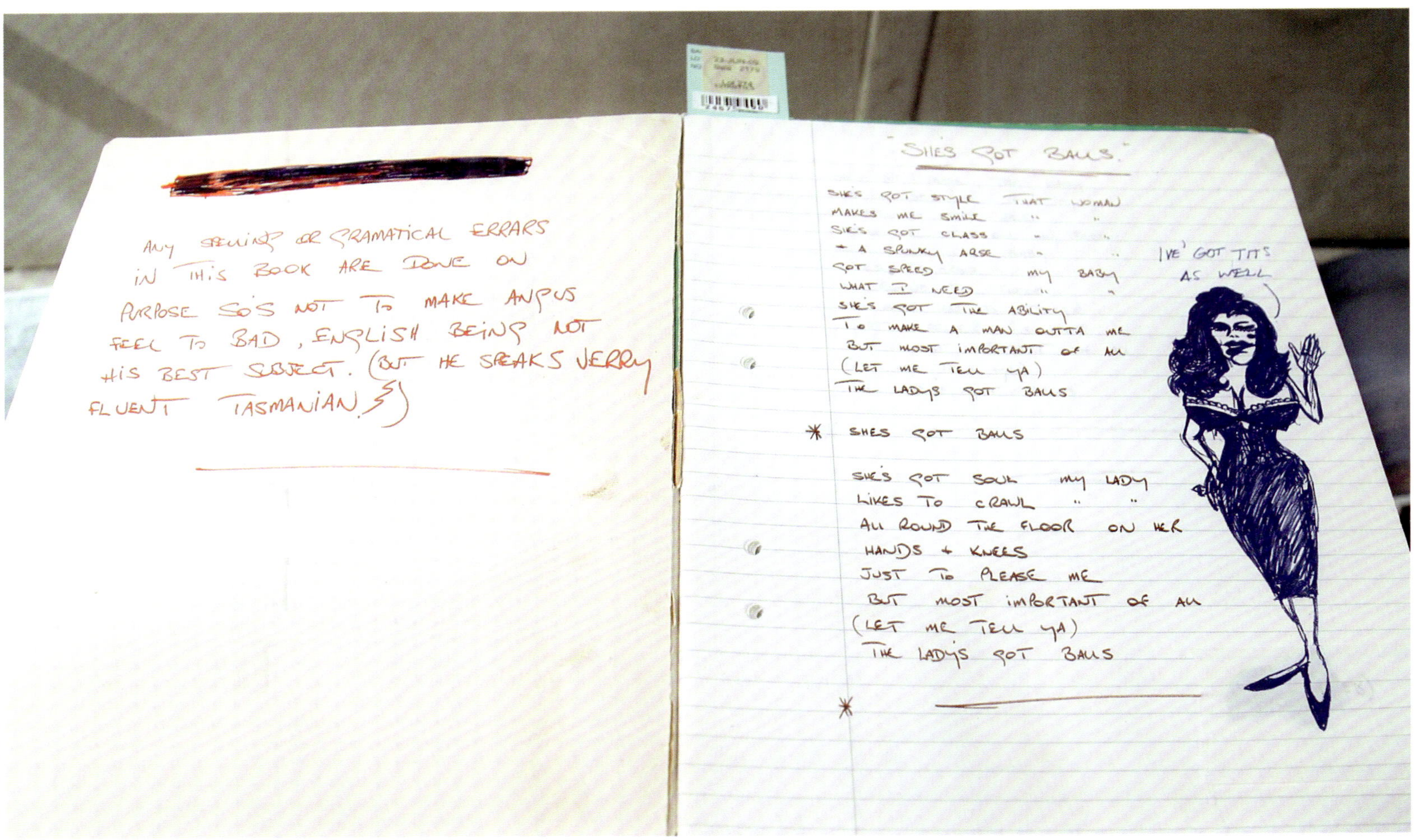

was genuine fondness in this tribute to Irene, a woman, he noted, with "funk" and "spunk."

There was, however, one track on the album that seemed out of place and out of character—"Love Song." Again, it was developed from an earlier track written by Malcolm and Dave Evans, originally titled "Fell In Love" and never recorded by the band. It was later suggested that Bon's romantic lyrics for "Love Song" were written while he was in Fraternity. Whatever the truth, it was a style to which he and the band were not suited.

With the album in the can, the band briefly worked with a new drummer, Russell Coleman, but in the first weeks of 1975, they found the right man for the job. Phil Rudd, born in Melbourne on May 19, 1954, was, like the Young brothers, a self-taught musician. Among his primary influences were Ringo Starr, Small Faces' Kenney Jones, and most of all Simon Kirke of Free and Bad Company, whose simple, groove-based approach really spoke to Rudd.

It was in the group Buster Brown that Rudd had built his reputation alongside Gary "Angry" Anderson—a squat, stocky singer who could belt it out like Bon—and bassist Geordie Leach, both of whom went on to form Rose Tattoo, one of Australia's greatest rock bands. Rudd had been fired from Buster Brown before he auditioned for AC/DC, but one audition was all it needed for the Young brothers to know they'd got their man. Bon, who knew a thing or two about playing drums, sealed the deal.

Another important development came when AC/DC left Sydney to take up residence in Melbourne, which had a thriving rock scene unlike any other city in Australia. It was in Melbourne that Michael Browning, a major figure on that scene, became AC/DC's manager. For Malcolm and Angus, it was the first time they had lived outside of their parents' home. Browning installed the whole band in a communal house in St Kilda. The fact that this was a red-light district was entirely apposite.

The *High Voltage* album was released on February 17, 1975, with a cover symbolic of the band's crude sense of humor: a cartoon of an electrical substation with a small dog pissing up against it. This was not a classic debut of the kind that Led Zeppelin and Black Sabbath made at the dawn of the heavy rock age, or that several American groups made in the early seventies, among them Lynyrd Skynyrd, and Montrose. Moreover, as a purely domestic release, *High Voltage* made no impact in the wider world. What it did was get the ball rolling, and fast.

Shortly after the album's release, the band hired a new bassist, Paul Matters, but he was sacked within a few weeks. As a result, it

Below: **Australian band Buster Brown, featuring Phil Rudd** (front center), **Australia, 1974. Rudd joined AC/DC in 1975. Also notable here is singer Angry Anderson** (second left).

Opposite: **AC/DC bassist, Mark Evans joined the band shortly after the release of *High Voltage*.**

XXXX

Right: **AC/DC:** (L–R) **Malcolm Young, Mark Evans, Bon Scott, Angus Young, Phil Rudd**

"I'd say to Malcolm sometimes, 'You know I don't think Bon can stand up, let alone sing.' But he'd surprise you. He'd last the whole night, although he'd fall down at the end."

Angus Young

was with George Young playing bass that they recorded a brand new song at this time, a song that shared its title with the new album: "High Voltage." It was too late to add it to the album, but the song was a doozy, their first genuine anthem, with a chorus that was a defining statement: "High voltage rock 'n' roll."

It was right after this song was recorded, in March, that AC/DC found a new bassist in Mark Evans. Born in Melbourne on March 2, 1956, Evans was a year younger than Angus, and had limited experience. But he was a perfect fit, a happy-go-lucky kind of guy who played straight, no bullshit. With Evans in place, the band at last achieved a level of stability. But in the same month that Evans joined, there was another lucky escape for Bon. Two years after the motorcycle crash that had nearly killed him, Bon was still a loose cannon. In Melbourne he was visiting a girlfriend and her sister, both of whom worked as hookers, and were heroin addicts. Bon had never tried smack, but when they offered to get him high the temptation was too great to resist. He took the hit, keeled over, and turned blue. Paramedics arrived just in time to save his life. After that, Bon vowed to stick to what he knew—booze, weed, a little coke.

It seemed to the other members of the band that Bon had an almost indestructible constitution, however much he put away before, during, and after a show. As Angus said to me in 1992: "I'd say to Malcolm sometimes, 'You know, I don't think Bon can stand up, let alone sing.' But he'd surprise you. He'd last the whole night, although he'd fall down at the end."

If Bon's arrival had made AC/DC the band that Malcolm and Angus had always wanted it to be, their second album truly defined their style. The riffs had more meat on the bones, Rudd and Mark Evans formed a rock-solid rhythm section, and Bon was really coming into his own as a singer and lyricist of rare distinction.

The album was again recorded at Albert Studios and produced by Vanda and Young. It was named *T.N.T.*, and the bulk of the recording was laid down in July 1975, and what it represented was a huge leap forward from the first album. This was

Opposite: **Buddy Guy** (left) **and Muddy Waters** (right). **Angus Young had been in thrall to the blues since he was a kid.**

Left: **Bon Scott's arrival made AC/DC the band that Malcolm and Angus had always wanted.**

Below: **Pete Way of UFO became a good friend of Bon Scott.**

immediately apparent in the opening track, "It's A Long Way To The Top (If You Wanna Rock 'n' Roll)," with an electrifying staccato riff, Bon singing with complete authority, and the song ending with him playing a solo on bagpipes, having never played them before, and only then on the insistence of George Young.

It was George who suggested they write a song with the chord progression: A, C, D, C,—and from this came the album's title track, a bruising number with a hooligan mentality in its gang chant of "Oi! Oi! Oi!" "Live Wire" was full of menace: a throbbing one-note bass line, guitars easing in slowly, the hiss of a hi-hat pushing it along, and then everything locking together in a riff as mean as they come, with only a brief moment of levity in Bon's exclamation, "Stick this in your fuse box!" "Rocker" channeled Chuck Berry in 2 minutes, 46 seconds of blistering ramalama, with Bon creating his own mythology in the opening line: "I'm a rocker, roller, right-out-of-controller." There was also a version of Berry's 1957 classic "School Days," Bon yelling the immortal refrain—"Hail, hail, rock 'n' roll!"—with the conviction of a true believer. There was "Rock 'n' Roll Singer," a killer boogie with Bon's funniest fuck-you: "Gonna be a rock 'n' roll star. Yes I are!" The song "High Voltage" was included on this album, as was a remake of "Can I Sit Next To You, Girl," which took on a far more decadent feel once Bon had got his teeth into it. And the song that became the most durable, an AC/DC classic and live staple, was the pre-AIDS STD blues "The Jack."

AC/DC had delved into blues with "Little Lover." They went deeper on "The Jack," in which a brilliant, filthy lyric from Bon employed poker as an extended sexual metaphor. This was also a true story. Bon was well versed in this subject: on first-name terms with the staff in his local VD clinic. As Angus told me: "'The Jack' was written about a night when some woman did some bed-hopping. First she went with Phil and during the night she crawled into Bon's bed. The next night we played a pub in Melbourne. This girl went to see a doctor and when she came back she handed a bill to Phil. The doctor had diagnosed a social disease. Phil said, 'The cheek of it! I got no fucking disease.'

During that night's show we did a slow blues song and Bon got the lighting guy to turn a spotlight on this girl's table. Bon said, 'I'd just like to inform you that you gave the doctor's bill to the wrong guy.' Bon had a lot of trouble with diseases on the road. There was a song in the musical *West Side Story* called 'Maria.' Bon used to take the piss out of it. Instead of singing, 'I've just met a girl named Maria,' he'd say, 'I just got a dose of gonorrhea.'"

Right: AC/DC relaxing during a photoshoot for "Jailbreak"

"The Jack" was also played out as a joke on the album, the track ending as if played to a hostile club audience. Over the sound of booing and catcalls, Bon exclaimed: "Thank you! Glad you enjoyed the show!"

The *T.N.T.* album was released on December 1, 1975, and made number two on the Australian chart. Its success confirmed AC/DC as the nation's leading hard rock act. At a time when Led Zeppelin, Deep Purple, and Black Sabbath were still the reigning masters of heavy rock, Australia now had heroes of its own. On every level, AC/DC had raised their game with *T.N.T.* It was Malcolm and Angus whose riffs gave these songs such power, and Bon whose voice and words gave added depth—what Angus called "flavor." Angus recollected to me: "Bon called himself a toilet wall graffitist. He was full of compliments about himself!" Pete Way, the bassist for British hard rock band UFO, who would become a close friend of Bon's, said simply: "Bon was a bloke who lived what he sang about." Across the whole of this album, Bon sang from the heart. There was in "It's A Long Way To The Top (If You Wanna Rock 'n' Roll)" the story of his own personal struggle, and in "Rock 'n' Roll Singer" the yearning of his teenage dreams. And whatever story he was telling—acting tough in *T.N.T.* and *Live Wire*—he was always believable, his voice weighted with experience.

However, even as Bon's dreams were coming true, he still had days when the rock 'n' roll lifestyle rang hollow. Earlier in 1975, in a letter to his estranged wife, Irene, he wrote: "I'm going through a fucking funny period at the moment. I like to be touring all the time just to keep my mind off personal happenings . . . become a drunkard again. Right now I'm just lonely." For all his bravado, there was another side to Bon that was hidden from all but a few of his closest friends, guys like Bruce Howe, with whom Bon talked of a longing for something more than an endless string of one-night stands; of having kids and buying a place out in the country where he could escape the madness of the rock 'n' roll life.

Adding to this dichotomy was the fact that in December 1975,

HIGH VOLTAGE

AUSTRALIA ONLY

Released: February 17, 1975
Recorded: November 1974 at Albert Studios, Sydney, Australia
Label: Albert Productions
Producer: Harry Vanda, George Young

All tracks written by Angus Young, Malcolm Young and Bon Scott, except where noted.

SIDE ONE
"Baby, Please Don't Go" (Big Joe Williams)
"She's Got Balls"
"Little Lover"
"Stick Around"

SIDE TWO
"Soul Stripper"
"You Ain't Got A Hold On Me"
"Love Song"
"Show Business"

PERSONNEL
Bon Scott—lead vocals
Angus Young—lead guitar
Malcolm Young—rhythm guitar, backing vocals, bass guitar, lead guitar on "Little Lover," "Soul Stripper," You Ain't Got A Hold On Me," and "Show Business."
George Young—bass guitar, rhythm guitar, backing vocals
Rob Bailey—bass guitar
Peter Clack—drums on "Baby, Please Don't Go"
Tony Currenti—drums on all other tracks
Harry Vanda—backing vocals
Additional personnel: Chris Gilbey—art direction

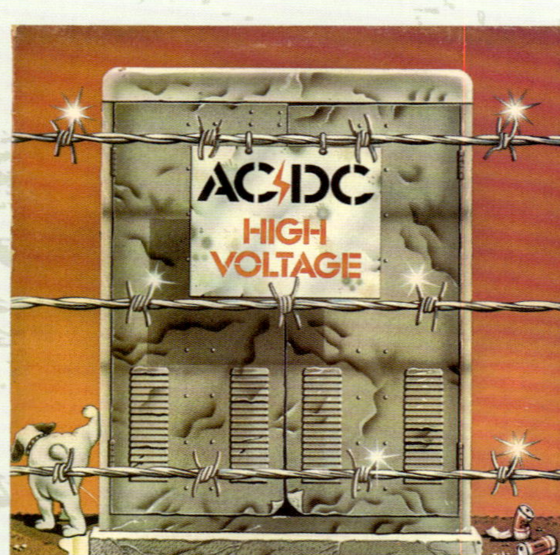

Originally released on Albert Productions only in Australia, *High Voltage* has never been reissued by another label in this format. The international version of *High Voltage,* which was issued on Atlantic Records in 1976, has a different cover and track listing, with only "She's Got Balls" and "Little Lover" included. "Baby, Please Don't Go," "Soul Stripper," "You Ain't Got A Hold On Me," and "Show Business" were later released on *'74 Jailbreak* in 1984. "Stick Around" and "Love Song" were released on *Backtracks* in 2009.

AC/DC had signed a worldwide deal with Atlantic Records, the legendary label that was home to Led Zeppelin and Yes, and so many of America's greatest jazz and soul artists, including Ray Charles, Aretha Franklin, and Otis Redding. To launch AC/DC on the global stage, Atlantic proposed a debut international release incorporating the best material from *High Voltage* and *T.N.T.* In addition, a trip to the UK for the band's first shows outside of Australia—for Bon and the Young brothers, a return home.

Their last act of 1975 was to cut a brand new song, "Jailbreak," Bon's tale of a killer in prison, working on a chain gang and plotting his escape, its drama matched by a taut, jarring riff. As Angus brought to mind in 1992: "Bon had a great way of telling stories, and 'Jailbreak' was a tale of desperation." According to George Young, the singer was so drunk when he recorded "Jailbreak," and put so much into his performance, that he passed out on the studio floor. That was Bon—giving it everything he had, whatever it took.

"Bon was a bloke who lived what he sang about."

Pete Way, UFO

T.N.T.

AUSTRALIA ONLY

Released: December 1, 1975
Recorded: March–April, July 1975 at Albert Studios, Sydney, Australia
Label: Albert Productions
Producer: Harry Vanda, George Young

All tracks written by Angus Young, Malcolm Young and Bon Scott, except where noted.

SIDE ONE
"It's A Long Way To The Top (If You Wanna Rock 'n' Roll)"
"Rock 'n' Roll Singer"
"The Jack"
"Live Wire"

SIDE TWO
"T.N.T."
"Rocker"
"Can I Sit Next To You, Girl" (Young, Young)
"High Voltage"
"School Days" (Chuck Berry)

PERSONNEL
Bon Scott—lead vocals, bagpipes on "It's A Long Way To The Top (If You Wanna Rock 'n' Roll)"
Angus Young—lead guitar
Malcolm Young—rhythm guitar, backing vocals
Mark Evans—bass guitar on: "It's A Long Way To The Top (If You Wanna Rock 'n' Roll)," "Rock 'n' Roll Singer," "The Jack," "Live Wire," "T.N.T.," "Rocker," "Can I Sit Next To You, Girl" and "School Days"
Phil Rudd—drums, percussion on "It's A Long Way To The Top (If You Wanna Rock 'n' Roll)," "Rock 'n' Roll Singer," "The Jack," "Live Wire," "T.N.T.," "Rocker," "Can I Sit Next To You, Girl," and "School Days"
George Young—bass guitar on "High Voltage"
Tony Currenti—drums on on "High Voltage"

T.N.T. is the only Australian AC/DC studio album for which there is no international counterpart. However, "It's A Long Way To The Top (If You Wanna Rock 'n' Roll)," "Rock 'n' Roll Singer," "The Jack," "Live Wire," "T.N.T.," "Can I Sit Next To You, Girl" and "High Voltage" are included in the 1976 international release of *High Voltage*. The other two tracks—"Rocker" and "School Days"—are featured as part of *Dirty Deeds Done Dirt Cheap*'s international version (1976/1981) and the *Bonfire* box set released in 1997.

KODAK SAFETY FILM
JAIL
THE
22
18
U627
23
19

Lock Up Your Daughters

"What I think AC/DC are going to do to heavy metal is crack it and tilt it sideways."

Phil Sutcliffe

In the early weeks of 1976, AC/DC were back inside Albert Studios, cutting tracks for their third album. As the band worked on this new material, both the *High Voltage* and *T.N.T.* albums had been certified triple gold in Australia. Meanwhile, Atlantic Records had prepared the first album for international release—an album that was also titled *High Voltage*, although seven of the nine songs were drawn from the original *T.N.T.* This was scheduled for April, to coincide with the band's first live dates in Europe—beginning with a UK tour as the opening act for Back Street Crawler, the group led by former Free guitarist, Paul Kossoff. But on March 19, during a flight from Los Angeles to New York, Kossoff, one of the great guitar players of his generation, died as a result of a pulmonary embolism, caused by intravenous drug use.

Previous: **AC/DC photoshoot at Shepperton Studios, UK, 1976**

Below: **AC/DC were due to open for Back Street Crawler but when the band's guitarist, Paul Kossoff (pictured) died during a flight from Los Angeles to New York, the tour was canceled, leaving AC/DC uncertain of when their first UK gig would be.**

Opposite: **AC/DC with manager, Michael Browning** (center)

With that tour canceled, AC/DC would head to London uncertain of when the first gig would come. Despite this, they had the album finished—its title, *Dirty Deeds Done Dirt Cheap*—and spirits were high as they bid farewell to their home crowd with a show at the Bondi Lifesaver club in Sydney on March 27. Reportedly, it was during this show that Angus first performed a party piece that would become a regular occurrence at AC/DC gigs—the guitarist pulling down his shorts and baring his ass to the audience during "The Jack."

Within days of the band's arrival in London there was trouble. One evening, Bon returned to a pub in Finchley where he had once served behind the bar during the time he spent in London with Fraternity. He became embroiled in a fracas and was knocked out cold after one local man smashed a pint glass over his head. On the following day, during a band photo shoot, the singer wore sunglasses to conceal two black eyes. On a darker note, it was also rumored that during those first days in the city, Bon was hospitalized following a drugs overdose. If there was a warning in what had happened to Paul Kossoff, it was lost on Bon.

There was also tension within the band as they kicked their heels in London, itching to get on with the business of playing live, but soon they had a venue and a date locked in. AC/DC would make their UK debut at The Red Cow, a pub in Hammersmith, on April 23. One of the few people who witnessed this event was Malcolm Dome, who was at the time a student, and later went on to become a rock journalist who interviewed Bon Scott several times in the late seventies. What he saw that night in AC/DC and their singer was unforgettable.

"I knew a little about the band before the gig," Dome says. "I had heard the Aussie albums, and I'd read a small story about them in *Sounds*. There was a bit of a buzz about them—this new Australian

Jane Birkin

band that suddenly appeared. What I was expecting was a pub rock band—an energetic, fun rock 'n' roll band.

"The Red Cow was an old-school boozer. It was very bare inside, with the venue room at the back, which could hold maybe a hundred people. AC/DC played two sets that night. For the first set there were about thirty people in the audience, but the band didn't seem to care about that. They really went for it. It was an electrifying performance. Their whole attitude was: We're going to entertain every goddamn one of you, we'll make sure you never forget us, and you'll bring your mates next time. And the reaction from everyone there was just, bloody hell!

"Angus was a live wire, jumping all over the place, on the stage and off. Bon was just so cool and charismatic. Angus and Bon really were a great double act. They were both such characters and they complemented each other. They never got in each other's way. You could feel that Bon was very much pushing Angus to the front—to get all the attention. And the other three were so bloody good—just an incredible rhythm section.

"They played nine or ten songs. The power in 'It's A Long Way To The Top' and 'High Voltage' was phenomenal. And as soon as they finished, Bon walked off the stage and straight to the bar. He'd taken his shirt off during the show and didn't bother to put it back on. He just put a towel around his neck and

Left: **AC/DC in London, 1976**

Below: **Punk bands, such as the Ramones, were springing up all over. AC/DC found themselves repeatedly described in the British music press as punk rock, a term to which Malcolm especially took offence.**

strolled up to the bar and said to a few people standing there, 'Right, who wants a drink?' It was a case of, 'I'm buying you all a drink and I expect you to buy me one back.' Which was fair enough. I talked to him. He was really affable, very happy to be in England, and very much Bon the bon viveur. He was great."

Left: **Malcolm Young with pre-gig beer and cigarette, 1976**

Opposite: **AC/DC performing on stage, Nashville Rooms, London, May 27, 1976**

In the hour between the band's two sets at the Red Cow, many who had witnessed the first set rushed out to a phone box to call their friends and tell them they had to see this band. The audience had doubled by the time AC/DC were back on stage. "There was a real buzz in the room," Malcolm Dome says. Word of mouth was spreading fast.

It was also that night that Bon was reunited with Margaret "Silver" Smith, a former girlfriend from Australia. She and Bon had been lovers in 1971, while Bon was in Fraternity. When the affair ended, Silver left Australia, and by 1976 had wound up in Kensington, West London. They had not kept in touch, and Silver had never heard of AC/DC before she went to the Red Cow to see what she had heard was an up and coming band from Australia. As they took to the stage, she was stunned to see Bon fronting the band. And when they met again after the gig, Bon was smitten.

In the months that AC/DC were based in London that summer, the band lived together in digs in Barnes in South London. But not Bon. He moved in with Silver. This did not sit well with the Youngs. To them, Silver spelled trouble. She was a well-known figure on the rock scene who mixed with stars such as UFO, Thin Lizzy, and

"The record company wanted to market us as a punk band. We told them to fuck off!"

Malcolm Young

newly appointed Rolling Stones guitarist Ronnie Wood. She was also using heroin. But whatever the Youngs thought or said, Bon was his own man. The company he kept was his business.

On April 30, a week after the first show at the Red Cow, the new version of the *High Voltage* album was released in the UK and Europe. The US release followed on May 14. The band went on to play a residency at the Marquee, the famous Soho club where so many legendary rock acts had performed—Jimi Hendrix, Led Zeppelin, the Stones, Pink Floyd, The Who. One of those Marquee shows was reviewed by *Melody Maker*'s Harry Doherty, who stated: "They're a good boogie band, with apparently no pretensions about being anything else. Judging from the wild reaction of their audience, they could slip comfortably into Status Quo's shoes."

Certainly, there were similarities between AC/DC and Quo, in the heavy boogie numbers they played, with Malcolm Young a rhythm machine like Quo's Rick Parfitt. What the members of AC/DC could never understand was why their band was repeatedly described in the British music press as punk rock.

Although it was not until the end of 1976 that punk became front-page news in Britain's tabloids, with the *Daily Mirror*'s famous headline: "THE FILTH AND THE FURY!" in reaction to the Sex Pistols swearing in a live TV broadcast, the rise of punk was in full swing by the time AC/DC made it to London. In February, the Pistols had set the tone for what was to follow when guitarist Steve Jones declared in the *NME*: "We're not into music. We're into chaos." The Pistols' riotous early gigs had increased their notoriety. All across the country, punk bands were springing up. On the very day that AC/DC played at The Red Cow, a defining album was released—the debut by the leading American punk group, The Ramones. And in June, when AC/DC set out on a nationwide UK tour, promoted by *Sounds*, the magazine hailed them as an "outrageous Aussie punk-rock combo."

This did not sit well with Malcolm Young, who was already fuming after a meeting with the PR department at Atlantic Records. Speaking to me in 2003, Malcom said: "When we first came to England in '76, the record company wanted to market us as a punk band. We told them to fuck off!" Malcolm also recalled other heated exchanges from that time. "You'd get these punks having a go at us," he said. "And Bon would go, 'You shut up or I'll rip that fucking safety pin out of your fucking nose!'"

Yet despite Bon's distaste for punk fashion, there was a similarity between AC/DC and the early punk bands. This was an era in which some of the biggest rock acts were making music on a grandiose scale far removed from the down-and-dirty rock 'n' roll that AC/DC dealt in. Led Zeppelin's 1976 album *Presence* began with the ten-minute odyssey "Achilles Last Stand" in which Robert Plant sang of Atlas holding up the heavens. Queen had a number one hit with the operatic rock magnum opus "Bohemian Rhapsody." This was also the golden age of progressive rock, in which Pink Floyd, Yes, and Genesis made arty concept albums, and

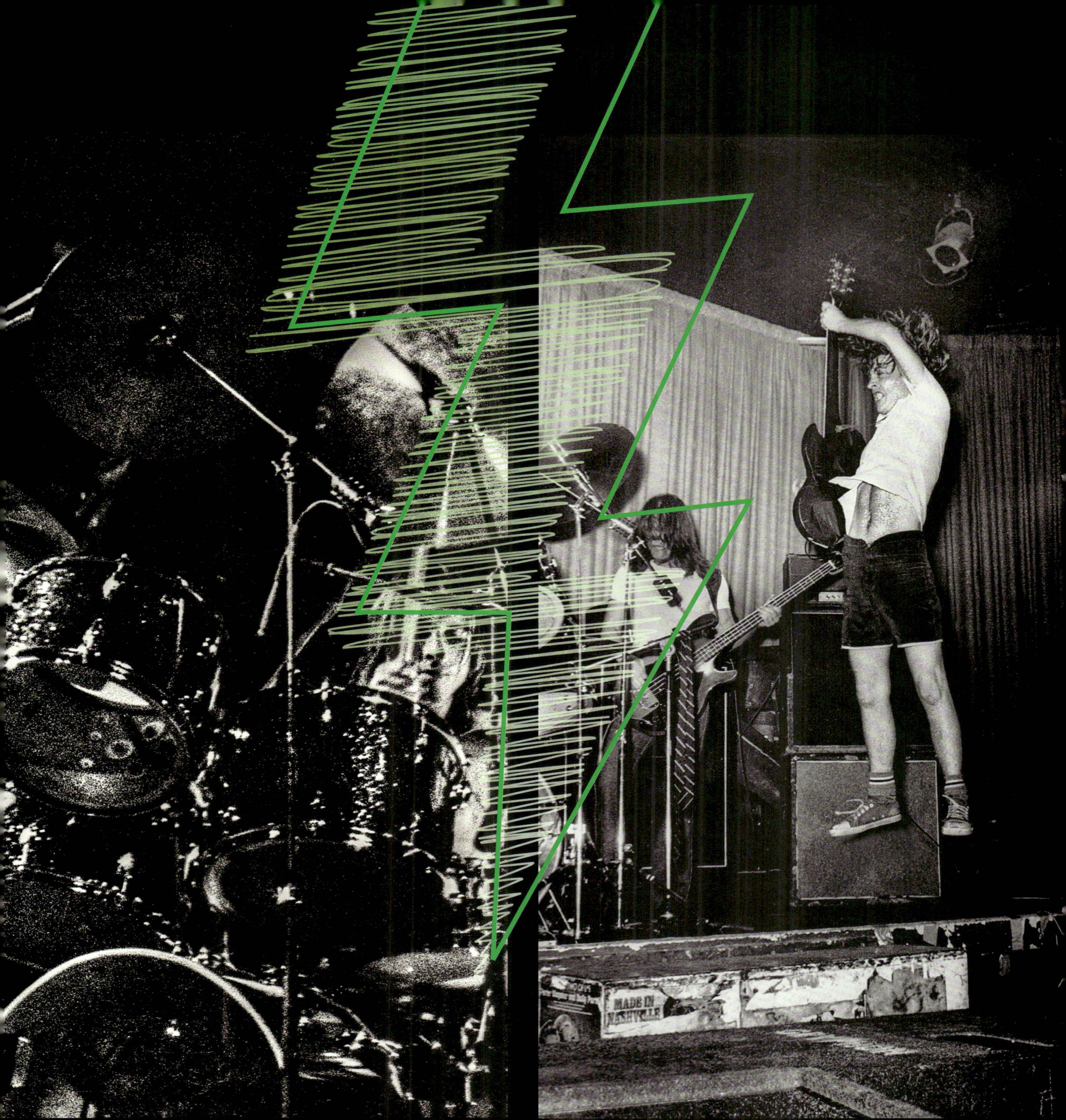
MADE IN
NASHVILLE

Previous page left: **Angus Young and Bon Scott performing on stage at the Lyceum Theatre, London, July 7, 1976, during the Lock Up Your Daughters tour**

Previous page right: **Mark Evans and Angus Young** (jumping) **performing live on stage on the band's first UK tour**

Above: **Many fans were drawn to Bon Scott, including music journalist Phil Sutcliffe who described him as: "Like a pirate, sort of leathery and macho."**

Opposite: **Mark Evans** (left) **and Bon Scott** (right) **at a WEA Records press event, London, 1976**

former Yes keyboard maestro Rick Wakeman, famed for wearing a cape on stage, had in 1975 performed his album *The Myths And Legends Of King Arthur And The Knights Of The Round Table* at London's Wembley Arena as a theatrical extravaganza on ice.

AC/DC was not the only hard rock group playing more down-to-earth stuff in 1976. There was Thin Lizzy, Status Quo, Bad Company, Aerosmith, and Lynyrd Skynyrd. Yet no other band had the streetwise sensibility of AC/DC, the energy and attitude. As Malcolm Dome puts it: "Punk was just beginning to rear its head and it was the antithesis of the so-called dinosaur rock bands, so people saw AC/DC as a raw, high-energy rock 'n' roll band. And that fitted with punk."

The band's *Sounds*-sponsored tour kicked off at Glasgow's City Hall, in the city where the Young brothers were born. It was named the Lock Up Your Daughters tour after a line from the song "T.N.T." It ran from early June to July, at the height of the long hot summer of 1976, when the UK baked in record high temperatures, as lawns turned to dust and the country slowed to a crawl. The June 12 issue of *Sounds* carried a major feature in which the tour was billed as "a rampage across Britain under the *Sounds* banner," and tongue-in-cheek questions were raised: "Are we doing the right thing? Are schoolboys the future of rock 'n' roll?" The headline was in reference to Angus Young's manic stage persona: THE FASTEST KNEES IN THE WEST.

This feature, by Geoff Barton, was a detailed portrait of the band and their lifestyle. Barton met up with the band at the house in Barnes before traveling with them in a van to a gig at a club called the Porterhouse in Retford, Nottinghamshire. In his description of the house, you could almost smell the place: "Cosy, if cluttered—cigarette butts and half-finished drinks are strewn liberally about its interior." His description of the five band members equally vivid: "The first thing that strikes you about the band is their smallness—they're all around five feet four inches; the second is their fresh-faced and bright-eyes appearances. On closer inspection, however, you find that, although the skin is smooth enough, it looks a good deal older than it should: the eyes are glazed more than shiny. On the road wear and tear, without a doubt. Bon Scott, the oldest and most well-worn of the five."

The show in Retford drew an audience of around a hundred people. The songs they played that night included "Live Wire," "The Jack," "High Voltage," and a version of "It's A Long Way To The Top (If You Wanna Rock 'n' Roll)" featuring Bon on bagpipes. Most evocative of all was the way in which Barton described Angus on stage, his frenzied antics at the climax of the show: "He begins rushing up and down like a lightning streak—as the music gathers speed, so it acts as a series of electrical stimuli to the young lad. Ultimately, he falls to the floor and there, still holding his instrument, turns a full circle, crab-like, on his back in the grime, twitches violently, and then hits the final note of the evening with such force you expect the stage to cave in and see the whole band disappear in a cloud of dust."

The Lock Up Your Daughters tour ended at London's Lyceum Theatre on July 7, and ahead of the band's appearance at the Reading Festival on August 29, another *Sounds* writer, Phil Sutcliffe, predicted big things for AC/DC—only this time, there was no reference to punk rock. "What I think AC/DC are going to do to heavy metal," Sutcliffe wrote, "is crack it and tilt it sideways." Describing AC/DC as "a completely physical rock 'n' roll experience," he stated: "The two Youngs' music is like a forge in a black night beating heat and energy together into something almost beautiful it's so strong. And Bon Scott's lyrics, well, they got balls." In this feature there was also a comment from Bon that would become famous. "They say to me are you AC or DC?" Bon said. "And I say, 'Neither, I'm the lightnin' flash in the middle.'" Phil Sutcliffe's support for the band would prove hugely influential, and he, like so many others, was immediately drawn to Bon. As he recollected, "Bon was so eccentric and yet so down-to-earth. On stage he was like a pirate, sort of leathery and macho, but in a comic way. Wherever he was, he made people feel good. And he attracted girls because he was a load of fun—you could tell that girls thought, what a laugh it would be to roll around in bed with him."

In the event, AC/DC's performance at the Reading Festival on August 29 did not turn out as they had hoped. With the bill that day topped by two of America's biggest hard rock acts, Ted Nugent and Black Oak Arkansas, it seemed like the perfect set-up for AC/DC, but when they played, in the early afternoon, the audience was dampened by a steady drizzle, and slow to react. The band was in the middle of "The Jack" when the audience became distracted. As Angus told the story to me in 1991: "The real showstopper was when some blonde girl walked real slow across the photo pit right in front of the stage and thirty thousand eyes went with her. Malcolm says to me, 'You gotta do something to get the crowd's attention back!' So I dropped my trousers."

This was only a minor setback. In September the band headed out on a nineteen-date European tour, with a few dates opening for Ritchie Blackmore's Rainbow. In October, with the track "High Voltage" released as a single, AC/DC returned to the UK for a major headline tour, which included a prestigious show at London's Hammersmith Odeon on November 10. And in the same month came the release of *Dirty Deeds Done Dirt Cheap*—in two different versions, one for Australia, one for Europe.

The Australian album cover had a cartoon of Bon and Angus in a pool room, Bon with an outsized forearm like Popeye the Sailor, and Angus flicking a V-sign like the punk rockers that AC/DC so despised. In Europe, the artwork was by Hipgnosis, the company that designed iconic covers for albums such as Pink Floyd's *The Dark Side Of The Moon* and Led Zeppelin's *Houses Of The Holy*. The image created by Hipgnosis for *Dirty Deeds Done Dirt Cheap* was of a no-tell motel and a cast of people—businessman, biker, schoolgirl, granny—all with eyes blacked out. It was an image powerfully evocative of the sleazy music within.

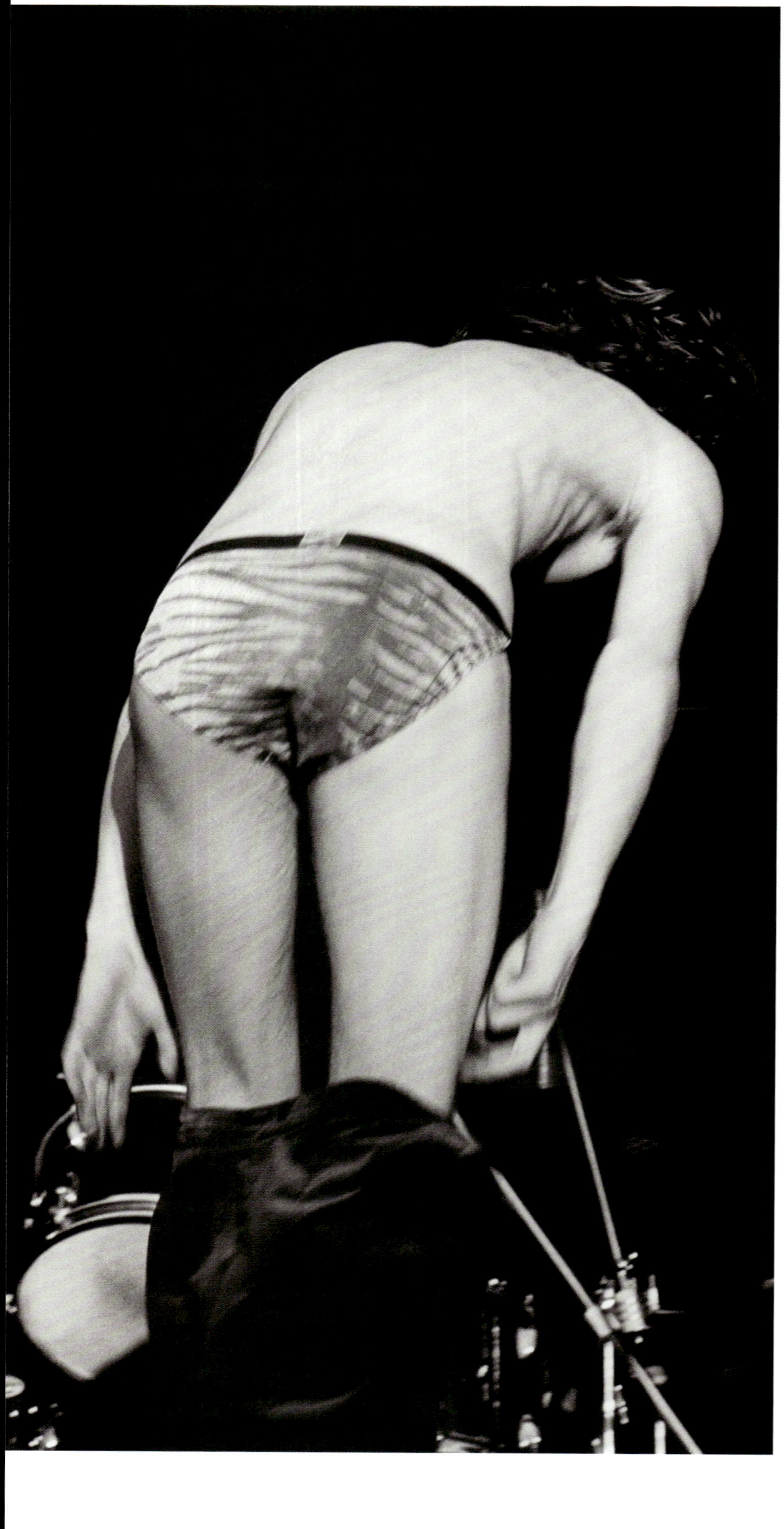

"Bon did say he wrote 'Problem Child' for me, but I never owned a knife like it says in the song. Just having a guitar was bad enough."

Angus Young

The two versions of the album also had different track listings. Australians got "Jailbreak," previously a single, and "R.I.P. (Rock In Peace)," a rowdy song with a simple message: in Bon's words, "Fuck off while I'm playing." In Europe these two tracks were replaced by a new version of "Rocker," originally from the *T.N.T.* album, and "Love At First Feel," which had a filthy groove to match its title.

On what was once memorably described as AC/DC's most "deviant" album, the title track was destined to become an anthem and a part of AC/DC live sets for decades to come—with a badass riff and Bon reveling in the role of contract killer, with various means of disposal: concrete shoes, cyanide, T.N.T. . . . The theme of "It's A Long Way To The Top (If You Wanna Rock 'n' Roll)" was picked up again in "Ain't No Fun (Waiting Round To Be A Millionaire)," as Bon indulged himself in the classic poor boy's fantasy—to make it rich in a rock 'n' roll band. As he explained in an interview: "It takes a long time to make enough money to be able to fuck Britt Ekland." "Big Balls" was one long, extended joke, delivered by Bon in a comical posh accent, the band playing as if stumbling drunk, and ending with a chorus of "Bollocks! Knackers! Bollocks! Knackers!". "Squealer" was the sordid tale of Bon's struggle to seduce a nervous virgin, played out over an insistent riff. "There's Gonna Be Some Rockin'" was as low-brow as its title, a simple boogie shuffle with lyrics about a rock 'n' roll show—the kind of stuff they could have written in their sleep.

There was one song on the album in which the band, and Bon in particular, dug deep. In the melancholy blues "Ride On," the singer, who so loved to brag about all the women he'd had, instead reflected upon the loneliness of a life on the road. The band played it subtly, with Angus pulling out a solo rich in emotion. "Ride On" is AC/DC's greatest blues number, and the one song above all others in which Bon Scott really bared his soul.

There was also on this album the song in which Bon paid tribute to Angus with a tongue-in-cheek dedication. As Angus told me in 1991: "Bon did say he wrote 'Problem Child' for me, but you know, I never owned a knife like it says in the song. My dad took my knife off me when I was four. Just having a guitar was bad enough, I suppose. But yeah, Bon summed me up in two words!" I suggested to Angus that Bon could have used one word. "That's right," he laughed, "with four letters!"

Opposite: **Angus Young on stage at the Reading Festival in the UK on August 29, 1976**

Above: **Bon Scott at the Hordern Pavilion, Sydney on December 12, 1976**

When AC/DC finished their UK tour in Oxford on November 15, it was mission accomplished. In seven months the band had worked their way up from the Red Cow to the Hammersmith Odeon, and the *Dirty Deeds Done Dirt Cheap* album was selling well. In America though, it was a different story. At a time when FM radio was dominated by soft rock stars such as Fleetwood Mac, The Eagles and Peter Frampton, and when the breakout hard rock act was Boston, whose smash hit "More Than A Feeling" was a masterpiece of melodic sophistication and sonic perfection, *Dirty Deeds Done Dirt Cheap* was so raw, so rough around the edges, that senior figures at Atlantic Records considered it commercially unviable. As a result, the company refused to release the album in the US.

Adding insult to injury was the review from *Rolling Stone* magazine in December 1976 of the one AC/DC album that Atlantic had released in America—*High Voltage*. Writer Billy Altman stated: "Those concerned with the future of hard rock may take solace in knowing that with the release of the first US album by these Australian gross-out champions, the genre has unquestionably hit its all-time low."

There was even a suggestion that in this period Atlantic were pressing the band to change singer. Bon, it was said, was too idiosyncratic in his approach, his slurry voice difficult for Americans to understand. There was more disappointment for AC/DC on their return to Australia in late 1976 for a tour that stretched into January 1977. The band, buoyed by their success in the UK, wanted to call this the Little Cunts Did It tour. In the end it was named The Giant Dose of Rock 'n' Roll. But there were dates on that tour when venues were half empty. One show in Tasmania reportedly drew around sixty people. After the *Dirty Deeds Done Dirt Cheap* album had reached number four on the Australian chart, this was a real kick in the balls. The broad consensus in Australia was that AC/DC had been away too long, too busy trying to make it in the UK. And whatever people called it—forgetting your roots, selling out—it fueled resentment.

For AC/DC it had been a year of highs and lows. What they knew for sure was that the next album would either make them or break them.

HIGH VOLTAGE

INTERNATIONAL RELEASE

Released: April 30, 1976
Recorded: 1974–1975, Albert Studios, Sydney, Australia
Label: Atlantic
Producer: Harry Vanda and George Young

All tracks written by Angus Young, Malcolm Young, and Bon Scott except where noted.

SIDE ONE
"It's A Long Way To The Top (If You Wanna Rock 'n' Roll)"
"Rock 'n' Roll Singer"
"The Jack"
"Live Wire"

SIDE TWO
"T.N.T."
"Can I Sit Next To You, Girl" (Young, Young)
"Little Lover"
"She's Got Balls"
"High Voltage"

PERSONNEL
Bon Scott—lead vocals, bagpipes on "It's A Long Way To The Top (If You Wanna Rock 'n' Roll)"
Angus Young—lead guitar
Malcolm Young—rhythm guitar, backing vocals
Mark Evans—bass guitar on "It's A Long Way To The Top (If You Wanna Rock 'n' Roll)," "Rock 'n' Roll Singer," "The Jack," "Live Wire," "T.N.T.," "Can I Sit Next To You, Girl."
Phil Rudd—drums on "It's A Long Way To The Top (If You Wanna Rock 'n' Roll)," "Rock 'n' Roll Singer," "The Jack," "Live Wire," "T.N.T.," "Can I Sit Next To You, Girl."
George Young—bass guitar on "Little Lover," "She's Got Balls," "High Voltage."
Tony Currenti—drums on "Little Lover," "She's Got Balls," "High Voltage."

Additional personnel
Michael Putland—cover photo

"Little Lover" and "She's Got Balls" were previously released on AC/DC's first Australian album *High Voltage* in February 1975. The rest were previously released on the band's second Australian album, *T.N.T.*, in December 1975.

DIRTY DEEDS DONE DIRT CHEAP

Released: September 20, 1976
Recorded: December 1975–March 1976, Albert Studios, Sydney, Australia
Label: Albert Productions
Producer: Harry Vanda, George Young

AUSTRALIAN RELEASE

All songs written by Angus Young, Malcolm Young, Bon Scott.
Cover art: Kettle Art Productions

SIDE ONE
"Dirty Deeds Done Dirt Cheap"
"Ain't No Fun (Waiting 'Round To Be A Millionaire)"
"There's Gonna Be Some Rockin'"
"Problem Child"

SIDE TWO
"Squealer"
"Big Balls"
"R.I.P. (Rock In Peace)"
"Ride On"
"Jailbreak"

A modified international edition was released on Atlantic Records on December 17, 1976 with a different cover by Hipgnosis—the company that had also designed iconic covers for albums such as Pink Floyd's *The Dark Side Of The Moon* and Led Zeppelin's *Houses Of The Holy*. However, Atlantic Records in America rejected the album, and it was only released there in 1981.

INTERNATIONAL RELEASE

(Excluding US)

All tracks written by Angus Young, Malcolm Young, Bon Scott.
Cover art: Hipgnosis

SIDE ONE
"Dirty Deeds Done Dirt Cheap"
"Love At First Feel"
"Big Balls"
"Rocker"
"Problem Child"

SIDE TWO
"There's Gonna Be Some Rockin'"
"Ain't No Fun (Waiting 'Round To Be A Millionaire)"
"Ride On"
"Squealer"

PERSONNEL
Bon Scott—lead vocals
Angus Young—lead guitar
Malcolm Young—rhythm guitar, backing vocals
Mark Evans—bass guitar
Phil Rudd—drums
George Young—bass guitar on "There's Gonna Be Some Rockin'"

AC/DC Is a Four-Letter Word

"We were kind of alike—ratty little guys with attitude. They were cocky Australians and we were cocky Southern rebels!"

Gary Rossington, Lynyrd Skynyrd

Previous: **Guitarist Angus Young shows off his trademark energy on stage.**

Right: **Bon Scott hoists guitarist Angus Young on his shoulders at a gig in February 1977 in Hollywood, California.**

After the *Dirty Deeds Done Dirt Cheap* album had been rejected by Atlantic in the US, and after disappointing ticket sales on their latest Australian tour, the band had a lot to prove. They would do so with an album of searing intensity and bludgeoning power. It was conceived as what Angus called simply "a fucking good guitar album," and at its heart were four songs that would become cornerstones of the band's live set for decades to come—"Hell Ain't A Bad Place To Be," "Bad Boy Boogie," "Whole Lotta Rosie," and the title track, "Let There Be Rock."

It was the album with which all doubts about AC/DC were obliterated. The album that took them to the next level. And it was achieved without a trace of compromise.

No way were AC/DC going to polish up their act for the American market. What Atlantic Records had signed was a balls-out rock 'n' roll band, and that was what they were going to get with "Let There Be Rock." From the get-go, the remit from Vanda and Young was to capture the energy of the band's live performance—to get that lightning in a bottle. To this end, the album was recorded as live, with the band playing together, full-tilt, and if the best takes had imperfections, then no matter.

This much was evident throughout the album: in the first few seconds of "Go Down," in which the band were heard warming up before being counted in by Bon, and then, with the first big power chords, came a wail of feedback; in "Hell Ain't A Bad Place To Be," where the guitars were plainly out of tune; and in "Overdose," which began in shambolic fashion, a false start and a bum note, before the Young brothers locked into a groove. In this sense, *Let There Be Rock* was as raw as any of the great punk albums of 1977.

On what was a make-or-break album for the band, "Go Down" was a ballsy choice as the opening track, with the way it eased down from driving boogie into a loose, funky jam, as Bon and Angus played call-and-response with mock-orgasmic wailing. It was a song about blow jobs, after all. There was a heavier vibe in "Dog Eat Dog," as Bon's grim meditation on the fight for survival was hammered home with brute-force aggression from the band. The title track was a riotous rock 'n' roll sermon inspired by Chuck Berry's "Roll Over Beethoven"—essentially the creation myth of rock, for which Bon cribbed lyrics from a Bible bought in a

"Bon liked his women in all shapes and sizes and Rosie wasn't no skinny little puppy."

Angus Young

Sydney bookstore. In the recording of this song, cut live off the studio floor, the momentum in the band's performance was such that George Young refused to stop Angus mid-solo when his amp overheated and caught fire.

"Bad Boy Boogie," its title self-explanatory, was a classic rebel-without-a-cause song that was developed on stage into a showcase for Angus's guitar-hero pyrotechnics. "Overdose" was a tale of sexual obsession, not drugs, built around a riff of hypnotic power. There was more of Bon's vulgar humor in "Crabsody In Blue," another dirty blues track, essentially "The Jack" Part II, the subject of which was laid out in that punning title. "Hell Ain't A Bad Place To Be" had one of Malcolm's greasiest bump-and-grind riffs, and from Bon a witty story of a bad girl who gave him the runaround, spending his money and, worst of all, drinking his booze. And to finish, there was "Whole Lotta Rosie." With its explosive staccato intro and runaway-train refrain, it was the song in which that searing intensity and bludgeoning power hit peak levels, and in Bon's lyric was the most famous story he ever told.

It was written in tribute to a heavyweight groupie in Melbourne with whom he had grappled in 1975, and as with all good rock 'n' roll stories, many of the details vary according to whoever was telling it.

Angus Young told me in 1991: "Rosie was a lady from Tasmania. A big girl. Bon met her one night when he went off on a midnight walk. He went past this sleazy old motel and Rosie stuck her head out of a window and yelled out, 'Ooh, Bon Scott!' Now, Bon had had a few drinks that night . . . He liked a drink, but the drink done a bit of distortion, if you know what I mean. Bon went into the motel and Rosie and her friend dragged him off to bed. Bon done his duty, so to speak. He didn't remember much of what went on, but he did remember pretending to be asleep and hearing Rosie whispering to her friend, 'That's twenty-seven this week!' Bon liked his women in all shapes and sizes and Rosie wasn't no skinny little puppy."

Malcolm Young revealed a little more to me in 2003. He was a part of the story, and the other witness to what happened: "I saw her," he laughed. "We were in a Travelodge in Melbourne in the heart of the red-light area, and we were broke. Bon told

Opposite: **Bon Scott in 1977**

Below: **"Rosie," the leading lady in Bon Scott's most memorable story as told in the song "Whole Lotta Rosie"**

"Geezer was in the bar, crying in his beer. I was giving him no sympathy. He pulled out this silly flick knife. Ozzy walked in. He goes, 'You fuckin' idiot, Butler—get to bed!'"

Malcolm Young

me there were two females who were gonna cook us some food, a big fat bird and a little skinny one. It was one night I never got drunk, thank Christ. But poor old Bon, this big mama just jumped on him and had him on a single bed. The other bird's sitting there, really ugly, and I said, 'I'm just going for a pee'—and I left. Bon said it took him half an hour to get out of the bed, and when he was getting over her she grabbed him again."

For his part, Bon said that he succumbed to Rosie's heavy embrace partly out of a strange notion of gallantry—a man had to do, what a man had to do—and partly because, as he explained, "She'd have broken my arm if I'd refused." Certainly, it was a song that spoke volumes about the man who sang it. Most rock stars would have been too vain to tell such a story, but not Bon. He reveled in it.

With the album completed, the band played a few dates in Australia and then headed straight back to the UK in February for a tour that kicked off at Edinburgh University on February 18 and included a date at the Rainbow Theatre in London's Finsbury Park on March 11.

They were still promoting the *Dirty Deeds Done Dirt Cheap* album, but in London the audience got a taste of what was to come with three heavy-hitters from *Let There Be Rock*: "Dog Eat Dog," "Bad Boy Boogie," and "Whole Lotta Rosie." The UK tour was just finishing when the new album was released in Australia on March 21—with a US release to follow in June, and the UK and European release delayed until October. In Australia, the album cover was a grainy black-and-white shot of hands on a guitar

Above: **AC/DC live on stage at the Kursaal Ballroom, Southend-on-Sea, UK, March 19, 1977. Keith Morris's photographs of this gig would later be used on the album cover of *Let There Be Rock*.**

Opposite: **Geezer Butler** (top) **and Ozzy Osbourne** (bottom) **of Black Sabbath**

neck—not the hands of Angus or Malcolm, but of a friend of theirs.

It was in April that AC/DC began the *Let There Be Rock* tour in Europe, with a bunch of headline shows and twelve dates opening for British heavy metal legends Black Sabbath. This came at a troubled time in Sabbath's career. Their 1976 album, *Technical Ecstasy*, was their first to peak outside the UK top ten, and in the US it stalled outside the top fifty. Tensions within the group, exacerbated by cocaine and alcohol, would soon lead to singer Ozzy Osbourne leaving Sabbath to go solo. Amid this turmoil, the last thing they needed was an opening act as shit-hot as AC/DC. In addition, while Ozzy later said that he and Bon hit it off—two larger-than-life characters and hardened boozers—there was no such camaraderie between Malcolm Young and Sabbath's bassist Geezer Butler. Following a show in the Swiss capital of Zurich, there was an incident in a hotel bar in which it was reported that Malcolm pulled a knife on Butler. Malcolm gave a very different version of the events of that night when he retold the story to me in 2003. "It was the other way around," he said. "That was when we were all larrikins. We were staying in the same hotel and Geezer was in the bar, crying in his beer, 'Ten years I've been in this band, ten years—wait till you guys have been around ten years, you'll feel just like us.' I said, 'I don't think so.' I was giving him no sympathy. He'd had too many and he pulled out this silly flick knife. As luck would have it, Ozzy walked in. He goes, 'You fuckin' idiot, Butler—get to bed!' Ozzy saved the day and we sat up all night with him."

Below: **Bassist Cliff Williams, who replaced Mark Evans, performing at The Palladium in New York City, August** 24, 1977

Opposite: **Lynyrd Skynyrd, 1977: (L–R) Ronnie Van Zant, Gary Rossington, and Allen Collins**

The last date of this tour, in Gothenburg in Sweden on April 22, turned out to be the last that Mark Evans played as a member of AC/DC. A rift had developed between him and Angus, and with this there could be only one outcome. Once the band had returned to London from Sweden, Angus and Malcolm informed manager Michael Browning that the bassist had to go. Evans was fired on May 3, and promptly returned to Australia, where he joined a new band named Finch.

Within a few weeks, Cliff Williams was appointed as the new bassist in AC/DC. Born on December 14, 1949, in Romford, Essex, Williams was raised in Liverpool and had moved to London in his teens, where he experienced hard times. At one point he was sleeping rough on the streets. He then took whatever jobs were available—tough work in demolition—before he finally got his break in the music business in 1970 with rock group Home. They made the album *Pause For A Hoarse Horse* in 1971, and in the same year they supported Led Zeppelin. Later they opened for other big names, including the Jeff Beck Group, Mott The Hoople, and Slade, but after their 1973 concept album *The Alchemist* flopped, the band split when guitarist Laurie Wisefield left to join the successful Wishbone Ash. In the following years, Williams worked as a session musician and launched a new group named Bandit, but he already had a sense that this was going nowhere when he got the call from AC/DC. He passed the audition in June, and just in time: the band's first US tour began in July, and before that they were booked into a rehearsal space in Sydney to work on new material.

On July 25, *Let There Be Rock* was released in the US, with two significant changes from the original Australian version. First, a new cover—a photo of the band on stage, dimly lit yet atmospheric, as if they were playing under storm clouds, with Angus the focal

point, guitar held high, and Bon off in the shadows, a menacing presence. What this cover also featured, for the first time, was the AC/DC logo that would become famous throughout the world—jagged, in blood-red lined with yellow. The other change was in the album's track listing, with the grubby joke song "Crabsody In Blue" replaced by an alternate take of "Problem Child." In this there was an echo of Atlantic's rejection of the *Dirty Deeds Done Dirt Cheap* album, but it was only a minor detail.

The sessions in Sydney produced three new songs, a couple of bruisers—"Kicked In The Teeth" and "Up To My Neck In You"—and one that was a little funkier, "Touch Too Much." The band's last job before heading to America was the filming of a promo video for the song "Let There Be Rock." They had fun with it. Playing up to the sacrilegious theme of the song, the video was shot in the Surry Hills Kirk Gallery church, with Bon dressed as a priest, complete with dog collar, and Angus as a choirboy crowned by a wobbly halo. Bon injured himself when jumping from the altar at the climax of the song, tearing ligaments in one ankle. A holier man than he might have believed this was divine retribution. However, nothing so trivial as a bad ankle was going to prevent Bon and AC/DC from getting to America. This was the birthplace of rock 'n' roll and the blues, the home of their heroes: Chuck Berry, Little Richard, Elvis, Muddy Waters. Now AC/DC were set on battering the Americans into submission just as they had the British.

Their onslaught on the US began on July 27 in Texas, where they supported the Canadian band Moxy at the wonderfully named Armadillo World Headquarters theater in Austin. There had been panic within the AC/DC entourage in the hours leading up to the show—nobody had seen Bon since he disappeared the previous night with a bunch of Mexican guys. But with just thirty minutes to go before showtime, Bon was delivered to the venue in the Mexicans' pickup truck, a little worse for wear after partying with them for the best part of twenty-four hours. And once he got up on stage, he just rolled through it as AC/DC's visceral rock 'n' roll connected with a rowdy Texan audience. The first gig on American soil was a success, and when they moved on to Jacksonville, Florida on August 6 for a co-headline show with REO Speedwagon, the city's most famous rock band were in attendance. Lynyrd Skynyrd were the standard bearers for Southern rock, a soulful blend of boogie, blues, country, and heavy rock 'n' roll. With anthems such as "Free Bird" and "Sweet Home Alabama," Skynyrd had become one of the biggest acts in America. In AC/DC, these Southern boys found kindred spirits.

"Jamming with those guys was so cool. We had a blast."

Gary Rossington, Lynyrd Skynyrd

As Skynyrd guitarist Gary Rossington said to *Classic Rock* magazine: "We all loved AC/DC. That band had so much energy. We were a guitar band so we loved guitar players, and Angus, you don't get no better than that. So after the show we got to meet 'em backstage and had a few drinks—you know how it goes. With all bands there's a rivalry, but when we met those guys we really hit it off. We were kind of alike—ratty little guys with attitude. We were really the same kind of band. They were cocky Australians and we were cocky Southern rebels!"

That night, Rossington invited the members of AC/DC to his home, along with Skynyrd bassist Leon Wilkeson. They all sat out by the river that ran through Rossington's land, drinking and talking until the sun came up. The following day, the two bands, twelve guys in all, got together for a jam session at Skynyrd's practice room. Rossington was not able to recall exactly what went down, due to the amount of booze that was sunk, but he was fairly sure they played "Sweet Home Alabama." "Jamming with those guys," he said, "was so cool. We had a blast. Those were some good times." Rossington also spoke of the bond between Skynyrd's singer Ronnie Van Zant and Bon Scott. "Ronnie and Bon had a great mutual respect," he recalled. They were great storytellers. Everybody could relate to their lyrics. The way they both wrote was so simple and yet so cool."

AC/DC traveled from coast-to-coast on that tour, opening for Foreigner and Santana, and for blues legend Johnny Winter, a hero to Angus. Strangely, the band that had hated being aligned to punk rock in London was pitched into New York City's punk scene with two gigs on the same night, August 24. At the Palladium they supported local heroes The Dictators, one of the seminal punk groups. Hours later they were at the famous club CBGB, the spiritual home of punk, opening for power-pop band The Marbles.

Five days later, AC/DC were on the other side of America, playing the first of three dates at the Whisky a Go Go, the Los Angeles club where many of the great American groups of the late sixties had made their name, including The Byrds and The Doors. For AC/DC's LA debut, only eighty people showed up, but among them were three major rock stars—Iggy Pop, Aerosmith singer Steven Tyler, and Gene Simmons of Kiss. For the second and third shows, the place filled up. For subsequent gigs at the Old Waldorf in San Francisco, AC/DC were pulling eight hundred people a night.

When the US tour finished in Miami on September 7, *Let There Be Rock* had peaked at 154 on the *Billboard* chart. But AC/DC were fully committed to the long haul. They would return to America after tours of Europe in September and the UK in October.

It was on October 7 that *Let There Be Rock* was released in the

Opposite top: (L–R) **Angus Young, Bon Scott, and Malcolm Young on August 24, 1977, performing at the Palladium in New York City**

Opposite bottom: **On the same night they also performed at the famous CBGB club in New York.**

Below: **Def Leppard, 1979 (L–R): Joe Elliott, Rick Savage, Pete Willis, Rick Allen, and Steve Clark**

UK, and a review in *Sounds* by Phil Sutcliffe was right on the money. "AC/DC are a four-letter word band," he stated. "So it's just as well I first heard *Let There Be Rock* in the bath: very handy for washing my mouth out with soap. Because I could hardly [deleted] usually believe the [deleted] audacity of the mother [deleted], the sheer [deleted] simplicity and [deleted] directness of the little [deleted]. They [deleted] me totally." Sutcliffe noted a subtle shift in the band's music, as illustrated in longer songs such as the title track. "A greater sense of space and tension to the straight power they have always had in abundance." He felt that Vanda and Young had succeeded in capturing that lightning in a bottle. "You know what AC/DC do live. Blow roofs off. Destroy walls. Steamroller the debris into a fine powder. Well, this is the first time I've heard them pack all of that into a record." And his review concluded with a salute to Bon: "Ten years older than the rest of the band, he remains a maverick kid in his heart and head. Nobody could match the crass earthiness of his tributes to old acquaintances like 'Crabsody In Blue' and 'Whole Lotta Rosie.' They broke the master after they pressed Bon Scott."

The UK tour began on October 12 at Sheffield Polytechnic. In the audience were the five members of a young local rock band named Def Leppard. As Leppard's singer Joe Elliott recollected: "The band [Def Leppard] had only been together a few months, so that gig was like a bonding moment for us." It was also during this tour that the members of AC/DC were devastated by news from America concerning their friends in Lynyrd Skynyrd. On October 20, Skynyrd's chartered plane crashed near Gillsburg, Mississippi, leaving six people dead, including Ronnie Van Zant, guitarist Steve Gaines, and his sister Cassie, a backing singer for the band.

Ahead of AC/DC's second US run there was some downtime, a brief respite from the road. Bon traveled to Paris with girlfriend Silver Smith to visit Ronnie Wood while The Rolling Stones were recording the *Some Girls* album at the city's Pathé-Marconi studios. It was on that visit to Paris that Bon first met the French rock band Trust. He sat in with them in a studio as they recorded a version of AC/DC's "Love At First Feel," to which they added new lyrics in French and a new title, "Paris By Night."

On their return to America in mid-November, AC/DC supported Canadian trio Rush, a hard rock band of a very different kind, with long and complicated songs, intellectual lyrics, a strong progressive rock influence, and a penchant for wearing silk robes on stage. Following that were dates with UFO, who played straight-up hard rock and had in Michael Schenker

Below: **American rock group Cheap Trick:** (L–R) **Robin Zander, Bun E. Carlos, Tom Petersson and Rick Nielsen**

a guitar hero to rival Angus. The guys in UFO also liked a drink as much as Bon did. A close friendship between Bon and UFO's Pete Way developed over many a long night. On December 7, when AC/DC returned to New York City, they took a break from regular gigs by performing to a small audience at Atlantic Studios. The performance was broadcast live over Radio WIOQ in Philadelphia, and a promotional-only album was later distributed to radio stations nationwide, titled *Live From The Atlantic Studios* and featuring "Live Wire," "Problem Child," "High Voltage," "Hell Ain't A Bad Place To Be," "Dog Eat Dog," "The Jack," "Whole Lotta Rosie," and "Rocker."

The tour continued for another two weeks with shows opening for Aerosmith, Kiss, Blue Oyster Cult, and pomp rockers Styx, plus a few co-headline gigs with another up-and-coming band, Cheap Trick, from Rockford, Illinois, whose 1977 album *In Color* was one of the best of that year, a power-pop classic, and whose guitarist Rick Nielsen later called AC/DC "the best rock band, bar none, that I've ever heard."

The last show was with Kiss on December 21 in Pittsburgh. AC/DC then headed home to Australia for Christmas. Nineteen seventy-seven had been a good year for them, with *Let There Be Rock* a dynamite record, and America finally waking up to the band. The next year would be even better, as AC/DC laid down not one, but two of the greatest rock 'n' roll albums ever made.

LET THERE BE ROCK

AUSTRALIA

Released: March 21, 1977
Recorded: January–February 1977, Albert Studios, Sydney, Australia
Label: Albert Productions
Producer: Harry Vanda, George Young

All tracks written by Angus Young, Malcolm Young and Bon Scott.

Cover art concept and photography: Colin Stead

SIDE ONE
"Go Down"
"Dog Eat Dog"
"Let There Be Rock"
"Bad Boy Boogie"

SIDE TWO
"Overdose"
"Crabsody In Blue"
"Hell Ain't A Bad Place To Be"
"Whole Lotta Rosie"

INTERNATIONAL

Released: July 25, 1977
For the original vinyl release, in all markets other than the USA, Canada, and Japan, "Crabsody In Blue" was featured instead of "Problem Child." This cover also features the now world-famous AC/DC logo for the first time.
Art direction: Bob Defrin
Cover photography: Keith Morris

SIDE ONE
"Go Down"
"Dog Eat Dog"
"Let There Be Rock"
"Bad Boy Boogie"

SIDE TWO
"Overdose"
"Problem Child"
"Hell Ain't A Bad Place To Be"
"Whole Lotta Rosie"

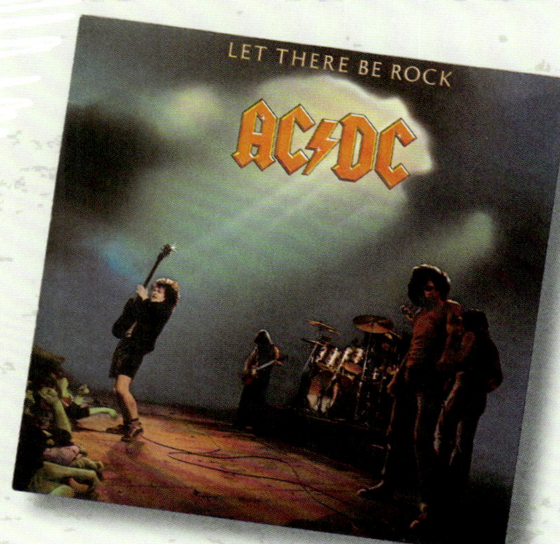

PERSONNEL
Bon Scott—lead vocals
Angus Young—lead guitar
Malcolm Young—rhythm guitar, backing vocals
Mark Evans—bass guitar
Phil Rudd—drums, percussion

If They Want Blood...

"It was the magic show. One night, guitars out of tune, feedback, singer farting, whatever."

Angus Young

Just as James Brown called himself the hardest working man in show business, so AC/DC worked as hard as any rock band of the late seventies. The pace was relentless as they jumped off the *Let There Be Rock* tour straight into the recording of the next album, *Powerage*.

Only this time, there was a little more involvement from Atlantic Records, and specifically from the man who had signed the band, Phil Carson. Carson made it known that he wanted a more accessible AC/DC album, something more geared towards the American market, and to this end he pushed hard for the inclusion of a song he felt had hit potential, "Rock 'n' Roll Damnation," with its rollicking groove and hooky refrain. The band had other catchy numbers in "Gimme A Bullet" and "What's Next To The Moon," the latter featuring a wickedly funny lyric from Bon with references to Superman and Casey Jones. There was also an anthem in the gambler's song "Sin City." But the rest of the material had all the raw power and hard edges of *Let There Be Rock*.

The two tracks demoed in Sydney in June 1977 were piledrivers: "Up To My Neck In You" an all-out assault on the senses, "Kicked In The Teeth" as brutal as its title implied, begun with a howl of indignation from Bon about a two-faced woman before the band slammed into a fast and furious melody. Another song dating back to '77 was "Riff Raff," reportedly first worked on during the *Let There Be Rock* sessions, and one of the most electrifying songs the band ever recorded—full-throttle, take-no-prisoners stuff. In stark contrast was the slow-burning "Cold Hearted Man," with a sense of foreboding in its creeping tune and Bon's story of a mysterious loner with ice in his eyes. For Bon as a lyricist, there were two songs of gritty authenticity. "Down Payment Blues" was not a blues song in the conventional sense, but over a grinding riff he laid out the harsh realities of all the years he had spent living hand-to-mouth. While in "Gone Shootin'," AC/DC's funkiest song, he sang of his doomed relationship with a junkie girlfriend, possibly in reference to Silver. The devil was in the details: how the girl never made it past the bedroom door, and how he stirred his coffee with the same spoon that she used for cooking up heroin.

The *Powerage* album was recorded mostly at night, with the band starting around eight o'clock and working till dawn. After eight weeks it was finished, allowing for a couple of weeks off before a UK tour started at Hanley Victoria Hall on April 27. Due to popular demand, the tour was expanded from eight shows to twenty-four. And on April 30, the band rolled into the Glasgow Apollo for a show that would go down in history.

A live album from AC/DC had been mooted for a year or two, partly in reaction to Atlantic's proposal for a best-of album, an idea that was quickly dismissed by the band. Much better, they

Previous page: (L–R) **Bon Scott, Cliff Williams, Angus Young, Phil Rudd, Malcolm Young, 1978**

Right: **The Glasgow Apollo, UK, where AC/DC recorded their first live album on April 30, 1978**

Opposite: **Angus Young and Bon Scott on stage at the Glasgow Apollo wearing Scotland football kit**

thought, to cut a live record. AC/DC were at their best on stage, and in the 1970s the live album was a defining statement for major rock acts such as Deep Purple, with *Made In Japan*, The Allman Brothers Band with *At Fillmore East*, Led Zeppelin with *The Song Remains The Same*, Kiss with *Alive!* and Peter Frampton with the multi-million-selling phenomenon *Frampton Comes Alive!* For AC/DC there was no better place to record a live album than Glasgow, the city where the Young brothers had been born. The Apollo was known for its rowdy audiences. Status Quo had recorded there for the 1977 album *Live!* What was captured on *Live!*—the interaction between band and audience, the heated atmopshere—was what AC/DC got on the night of April 30,1978.

"It was the magic show," Angus later said to me. "One night, guitars out of tune, feedback, singer farting, whatever." This was only the third date of the tour, but the band, so road-hardened and well-drilled, was like a machine. They opened with "Riff Raff" and played two other tracks from the forthcoming album: "Rock 'n' Roll Damnation" and "Gimme A Bullet." The rest of the set list was by this point pretty much set in stone: "Problem Child," "Hell Ain't A Bad Place To Be," "Bad Boy Boogie," "Dog Eat Dog," "The Jack," "High Voltage," "Whole Lotta Rosie," "Let There Be Rock," "Rocker." For the encore, the whole band emerged wearing Scotland football shirts—this at a time when the nation was gripped by over-optimistic football fever ahead of the 1978 World Cup tournament in Argentina, in which the Scottish team would be cheered on by the traveling Tartan Army. The audience was loudest during the intro to "Whole Lotta Rosie," in which a chant of "Angus! Angus!" accompanied the opening jabs of guitar—a chant that would echo down the years at every AC/DC show. Although other gigs on this tour were recorded, the band, and Angus especially, knew that the tapes from Glasgow had everything they needed.

At Newcastle's Mayfair club on May 5, *Sounds* writer Phil Sutcliffe marveled at the progress the band had made since he first saw them on stage at the Marquee in London two years previously. "Angus's lead playing becomes cleaner and more authoritative," he stated. "The whole band turns the screw relentlessly towards an optimum tightness which hopefully they will never reach because it will prove entirely too much for the human cranium. The result is an endless sequence of satisfying riffs, 'Hell Ain't A Bad Place To Be,' 'High Voltage' and the new one, 'Riff Raff.' Bon smiles most of the time with a kind of lascivious relish at how good everything is." Sutcliffe also noted that Angus had a new set of teeth: "an elegant row of even ivories that wouldn't look out of place in the mouth of Donny Osmond." In this small detail was something bigger. "It appears to be the only way in which AC/DC have made any concession to the imminent probability of becoming 'stars'," Sutcliffe wrote. "Pretentiousness in their music or their

Opposite: **Bon Scott performing live on the *If You Want Blood* UK tour at the Coventry Theatre in the UK, November 8, 1978**

Below: **Music journalist Phil Sutcliffe noted that the only concession the band made to becoming stars was Angus's improved teeth; their music remained unpretentious.**

conduct is so alien to them that I'm sure it will always be impossible. They are shaping up as the next generation's Status Quo, a rock 'n' roll touchstone."

Powerage was released in Europe and the US on May 5, and in Australia two weeks later. In the UK it made number twenty-three, and while reviews at the time were positive, it was many years before the album was recognized as a classic. While Malcolm Young felt it was "the most underrated" album of the band's career, for Keith Richards—whose rhythm playing in The Rolling Stones was such an inspiration to Malcolm—*Powerage* is the best record AC/DC ever made. "I love it," he said. "It's just great songs. The whole band means it, and you can hear it. It has spirit. That's what I love about recording. It's not just the sounds—you can actually capture a spirit. Timeless."

In the month after *Powerage* was released, AC/DC had their first hit single when "Rock 'n' Roll Damnation" reached number twenty-four on the UK chart. In this, Phil Carson's instincts were proven right. It was followed by the band's first appearance on

Above: **Music promoter Bill Graham** (left), **organizer of Day on the Green #3, and Eddie Van Halen** (right) **performing at the event in 1978**

the UK's biggest music show, *Top of the Pops*, after which Angus went on a promotional trip to Australia, where he ended up jamming on stage at the War And Peace club in Sydney with Phil Rudd's former bandmates in Rose Tattoo, blasting out a version of Little Richard's "Keep A Knockin'." Angus then joined the rest of the band in Miami for a two-week break ahead of a sixty-three-date tour of the US.

The first dates were on the East Coast, opening for Alice Cooper, the legendary rock showman who had recently been sectioned to a sanitarium in an effort to cure him of alcoholism. At his lowest ebb, Cooper was drinking so much whiskey every night that in an effort to clean out his system he would breakfast on warm Budweiser to induce vomiting. Bon Scott, for all the bad mornings he had, was still a functioning alcoholic.

In the US, sales of *Powerage* remained modest. The album peaked at number 133 on the *Billboard* chart. It was as a live act that AC/DC were making waves. After the Alice Cooper gigs, they supported Aerosmith, whose guitarist Joe Perry was blown away by the power of AC/DC's performances. As he recalled to writer Murray Engleheart: "They reduced the elements of rock 'n' roll to the basics and they didn't pull any punches."

On July 13, when Aerosmith and AC/DC played at the Los Angeles Forum, a fifteen-year-old kid named James Hetfield was in the audience. Three years before Hetfield would become a founding member of Metallica, he was witnessing his first rock concert, and it had a profound effect on him. "I was a big Aerosmith fan," Hetfield recollected to me in 2008. "But I had no idea that AC/DC was that cool. Going to a big arena rock concert was a pretty eye-opening experience, just the whole feel: the lights going out, the anticipation, the crowd, the smells. Every sense was just soaking it in. I remember smelling this very strange smell at the gig. I didn't know much about pot but . . . learned kind of quickly! I went with my older brother, and I remember him pointing at Angus and saying, 'That little guy running around was annoying!' But I wanted to be the guy up there on the stage."

Ten days after the LA show, AC/DC again shared a stage with Aerosmith at one of the biggest events on the American rock circuit. Day on the Green was an annual series of shows held at the eighty thousand-capacity Oakland Coliseum in California, and organized by the influential promoter Bill Graham. Since its inception in 1973, Day on the Green had featured landmark performances from superstars such as The Grateful Dead, and Crosby, Stills, Nash & Young. In 1977, there were seven concerts spread through the summer, with headline acts including Fleetwood Mac, The Eagles, Peter Frampton, and Led Zeppelin—the latter performing for what would be the last time in America. In 1978, there were five shows. The first, billed as Day on the Green #1, was a mellow affair featuring The Beach Boys, Linda Ronstadt, and Dolly Parton. The second was more of a rock 'n' roll event, with Steve Miller, Bob Seger, and Ronnie Montrose, while the third, Day on the Green #3, on July 23, was hard rock from top to bottom, starring Aerosmith, Foreigner, guitar hotshot Pat Travers, a new band out of LA called Van Halen, and, opening the show, AC/DC.

Their stage time was a shock to the system. As Angus revealed to me: "We were on at ten-thirty in the morning and most of us hadn't even been to bed!" But they had a good friend in Bill Graham, who loved the band, and had done all he could to hype them up on local radio before the day. As a result, the stadium was close to full as

Below: **James Hetfield of Metallica who was inspired by AC/DC after seeing them perform live when he was 15 years old**

"I had no idea that AC/DC was that cool. I went with my older brother, and I remember him pointing at Angus and saying, 'That little guy running around was annoying!' But I wanted to be the guy up there on the stage."

James Hetfield, Metallica

"In Cleveland, they blew us off the fucking stage. Angus was unbelievable."

Gary Moore, Thin Lizzy

Previous: **Angus Young and Bon Scott get swept away by fans and media at The Oakland Coliseum 1978, California, USA.**

Opposite: **AC/DC at the Hammersmith Odeon, London, May 1978**

Below: **Gary Moore** (left), **guitarist with Irish rock band Thin Lizzy,** and (right) **French hard rock group Trust:** (L–R) **Moho Schemlek, Nono Krief, Bernie Bonvoisin, Yves Brusco, and Kevin Morris**

AC/DC readied themselves backstage. It was in these moments that Bon and Angus—sharp-witted even at that early hour—made the joke that would become the title of AC/DC's live album. As Angus said to me: "This guy from a film crew got hold of me and Bon and asked what kind of show it was gonna be. Bon said, 'You remember when the Christians went to the lions? Well, we're the Christians!' Then the guy asked me and I said, 'If they want blood they're gonna get it!'"

When the band hit the stage, they were amazed at the size of the audience. "Eighty thousand people turned up!" Angus told me with a laugh. Equally amazed, as he watched from the wings, was the guitar player with the band that was on next. Eddie Van Halen later told VH1.com: "I was standing on the side of the stage thinking, 'We have to follow these motherfuckers?'"

AC/DC's triumph at Day on the Green #3 was followed by more dates in the US with Aerosmith, Rainbow, and Ted Nugent. On September 2 they were back in Oakland for Day on the Green #5,

headlined by Nugent. The bill also featured Blue Oyster Cult and local heroes Journey, with AC/DC moved up one slot, and Cheap Trick opening. For the remainder of that month, there were shows with Blue Oyster Cult, UFO, and Irish rockers Thin Lizzy, whose guitarist Gary Moore later told writer Murray Engleheart of a fierce rivalry between Lizzy and AC/DC. "In Cleveland, they blew us off the fucking stage," Moore said. "They fucking killed us that night." Moore also described AC/DC as "a great band," and as a tribute from one guitar hero to another, he said simply, "Angus was unbelievable."

When AC/DC's US tour ended on October 3, with a last show with Aerosmith, the *Powerage* album had sold two hundred thousand copies—more than the combined sales of *High Voltage* and *Let There Be Rock*. Then, just three days after the band had completed a European tour, on October 13, came the live album—

> **"We were all big drinkers, and Bon would have a double Jack Daniel's for breakfast."**
>
> **Pete Way, UFO**

POWERAGE

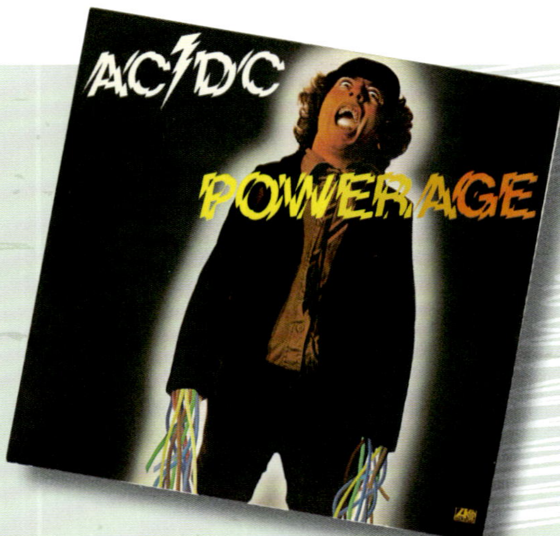

Released: May 5, 1978
Recorded: January–March 1978, Albert Studios, Sydney, Australia
Label: Atlantic
Producer: Harry Vanda, George Young

All tracks written by Angus Young, Malcolm Young and Bon Scott.

SIDE ONE
"Rock 'n' Roll Damnation"
"Down Payment Blues"
"Gimme A Bullet"
"Riff Raff"

SIDE TWO
"Sin City"
"What's Next To The Moon"
"Gone Shootin'"
"Up To My Neck In You"
"Kicked In The Teeth"

EUROPEAN LP RELEASE

SIDE ONE
"Rock 'n' Roll Damnation"
"Gimme A Bullet"
"Down Payment Blues"
"Gone Shootin'"
"Riff Raff"

SIDE TWO
"Sin City"
"Up To My Neck In You"
"What's Next To The Moon"
"Cold Hearted Man"
"Kicked In The Teeth"

PERSONNEL
Bon Scott—lead vocals
Angus Young—lead guitar
Malcolm Young—rhythm guitar, backing vocals
Cliff Williams—bass guitar, backing vocals (all tracks except "Cold Hearted Man")
Phil Rudd—drums

Additional personnel
Mark Evans—bass guitar (on "Cold Hearted Man")
Bob Defrin—art direction
Jim Houghton—cover photography

Powerage was the first album to feature Cliff Williams on bass guitar. It was also the first album to have the same cover for both Australian and international releases, although there were differences in track listings.

If You Want Blood (You've Got It). What Angus called "the magic show" from Glasgow sounded incendiary on record—from the first frenzied notes of "Riff Raff" through to the hell-for-leather rampage of "Rocker." *If You Want Blood* is now widely acknowledged as one of the greatest live albums of all time, and its cover, like its title, was powerfully symbolic of a band that gave everything they had on stage: Angus Young speared through the chest by his guitar, his mouth, chin, and white school shirt stained red, Bon leering over him, eyes glazed. On the back cover, Angus lay prone on stage, the headstock and half the neck of the guitar sticking out from his bloodsoaked back. It was a cover that Angus described to me as "tongue-in-cheek," but on a deeper level, the album's title had added significance for Bon.

Interviewed in 1978, he confessed: "I've been on the road for thirteen years. Planes, hotels, groupies, booze, people, towns: they all scrape something from you." At this point he was putting away a bottle of scotch a day. As Pete Way later said, "We were all big drinkers, and Bon would have a double Jack Daniel's for breakfast. He always went for it. I remember Angus saying to me once, 'Y'know, Bon's been drunk three times today. He got up, got drunk, went back to bed, got up, got drunk. He did that three times.'"

The European tour included a show at Le Stadium Paris with, at Bon's invitation, his friends in Trust as the support act. On the UK tour that followed, a gig at Essex University in Colchester was filmed for the BBC series *Rock Goes To College*. This humble venue was a world away from the Day on the Green, with just a few hundred people squeezed in, and the band confined to a small stage. But AC/DC played every show, big or small, at the same high intensity, and in this performance the energy levels were off the scale as the band hammered out "Live Wire," "Problem Child," and "Let There Be Rock," with Angus in perpetual motion, tearing across the stage, and Bon shirtless and slick with sweat yet as cool as a rock 'n' roll singer could be.

The tour ended with two sold-out shows at the Hammersmith Odeon, as *If You Want Blood* peaked on the UK chart at thirteen. In the US it reached 113. By early December, the band were back in Australia and working on a new album at Albert Studios with Vanda and Young. It appeared as if it was business as usual, but in the making of this album there would be major changes in the way that AC/DC operated.

Powerage was not the hit that Atlantic Records expected, and as the pressure was building, the band would part from three of the guys who had been instrumental in getting them this far. For Malcolm and Angus, it would mean breaking family ties. But they had fired people before. They knew how show business worked. It was a game like any other. When you play to win, someone has to lose.

IF YOU WANT BLOOD (YOU'VE GOT IT) LIVE ALBUM

Released: October 13, 1978 (Europe)
November 21, 1978 (North America)
November 27, 1978 (Australia & New Zealand)
Recorded: April 30, 1978 at the Apollo, Glasgow, Scotland
Label: Atlantic
Producer: Harry Vanda, George Young

All tracks written by Angus Young, Malcolm Young and Bon Scott.

SIDE ONE

"Riff Raff" (from *Powerage*)
"Hell Ain't A Bad Place To Be" (from *Let There Be Rock*)
"Bad Boy Boogie" (from *Let There Be Rock*)
"The Jack" (from *T.N.T.*)
"Problem Child" (from *Dirty Deeds Done Dirt Cheap*)

SIDE TWO

"Whole Lotta Rosie" (from *Let There Be Rock*)
"Rock 'n' Roll Damnation" (from *Powerage*)
"High Voltage" (from *T.N.T.*)
"Let There Be Rock" (from *Let There Be Rock*)
"Rocker" (from *T.N.T.*)

PERSONNEL

Bon Scott—lead vocals
Angus Young—lead guitar
Malcolm Young— rhythm guitar, backing vocals
Cliff Williams—bass guitar, backing vocals
Phil Rudd—drums

Additional personnel

Mike Scarfe—sound (MHA Audio)
Bob Defrin—art direction
Jim Houghton—cover photography

The Promised Land

"It was the first sniff that things were really going to happen for us."

Cliff Williams

In the first weeks of 1979, Malcolm and Angus Young had to make one of the toughest decisions of their lives. Atlantic Vice President Michael Klenfner had flown to Sydney to meet the band and hear the new material they had been working on with Harry Vanda and George Young. What Klenfner heard disappointed him. He wanted more than just another rough-and-tumble rock 'n' roll record like *Let There Be Rock* and *Powerage*. He wanted to hear songs that could get to radio in America, and there was nothing of that in the demos that George Young played to him.

George and Harry knew how to make a hit record. They had done so in the past with The Easybeats, and in early 1978 they had, as producers, a worldwide hit with Australian singer John Paul Young's *Love Is In The Air*, a disco-influenced pop number that had cruised into the US top ten. But with AC/DC it was different. They saw the band as Malcolm and Angus saw it—raw rock 'n' roll, plain and simple.

Something had to give. Malcolm and Angus were fiercely resistant to the idea of changing producers. More than that, George was family, and Harry too in a broader sense. Perhaps that was part of the problem: that George and Harry were too close to the band to see a way forward as Michael Klenfner did. For AC/DC to get to the next level, Klenfner believed that a new producer was needed, and eventually, after consultation with George, it was agreed with Malcolm and Angus. This was tough on George and Harry. Hard, too, for Malcolm and Angus. And while this turned out to be the right call, the first producer enlisted by Atlantic was not a good fit.

Eddie Kramer came with a big reputation and a proven track record. Born in South Africa, he made his name as a young recording engineer in the late sixties, working on one of The Beatles' most famous songs, "All You Need Is Love," on The Rolling Stones' psychedelic album *Their Satanic Majesty's Request*, and on the three groundbreaking works by The Jimi Hendrix Experience—*Are You Experienced*, *Axis: Bold As Love*, and *Electric Ladyland*. Kramer also served as engineer for Led Zeppelin on the classic albums *Led Zeppelin II*, *Houses Of The Holy* and *Physical Graffiti*, and as a producer he cut the breakthough album for Kiss—the live double *Alive!*—plus their studio records *Rock And Roll Over* and *Love Gun*.

In February 1979, Kramer began working with AC/DC at Criteria Studios in Miami. It was there that the band created the song that would become the new album's title track, "Highway To Hell," with a killer stop-start riff reminiscent of Free's "All Right Now"—a riff which, in Malcolm's words, "stuck out like a dog's balls." For all that, it quickly became apparent that Kramer and the band were not on the same page. It was Malcolm Young who called an end to the sessions, and the timing could not have been better.

Previous: **AC/DC in 1979**

Opposite: **Angus Young at a photo session in Paris France, 1979**

AC/DC's manager Michael Browning was sharing an apartment in New York City with an up-and-coming producer, Robert John Lange, nicknamed "Mutt." A South African expat like Kramer, Lange had enjoyed his first success in 1977 with the debut album by Irish punk band The Boomtown Rats, which made the top twenty in the UK. By 1978 he was on a roll, with a big hit for pop-rock act City Boy in "5.7.0.5." and the Rats' second album, *A Tonic For The Troops*, yielding the number one single "Rat Trap." Michael Browning presented Lange to Atlantic as the perfect candidate for the AC/DC job—a guy with a feel for hard rock music and a shrewd pop sensibility. Lange was promptly hired, even if this meant that the band's Japanese tour, scheduled for March, was canceled at considerable expense.

Instead, the band set to work with Lange in London. First, they rehearsed and fine-tuned the songs in a low-rent practice space with a dirt floor and a kerosene heater to take some of the bite out of the winter chill. For the recording of the album they moved to Roundhouse Studios in Chalk Farm. What Lange got out of the band was exactly what Atlantic had demanded—a straight-up, no-bullshit, hard-rock record that was true to AC/DC's roots, but with a cleaner edge.

On previous albums, Vanda and Young had recorded the band in all its ragged glory. What they had on *Highway To Hell* was a producer with a more hands-on approach. On the simplest level, Lange worked on the basics. As Def Leppard's Joe Elliott said to me: "A lot of the stuff that AC/DC did with Vanda and Young has great energy, but the tuning on the guitars is fucking terrible. The *Highway To Hell* album is like the Vanda and Young stuff in tune." In addition, Lange applied his pop smarts to AC/DC in a subtle fashion. As an accomplished singer in his own right, Lange contributed backing vocals to lift the choruses. He also got the very best out of Bon Scott. Lange made AC/DC sound better, without cutting off their balls.

This was immediately apparent in the very first song on the album, that thumping title track. Its name came from Angus, who was asked to describe the band's grueling 1978 tour and replied bluntly, "It's a fucking highway to hell." Bon ran with it in a lyric that raised two fingers to the so-called moral majority, and became a defining statement of devil-may-care rock 'n' roll attitude from a legendary hell-raiser. The route-one chorus was pumped up by Lange into a noise to raise the dead. And in the home run came a moment of pure abandon from Angus, as he slid his fingers down the frets to create a noise as thrilling as anything that his hero Chuck Berry had conjured up before him.

Previous page: **AC/DC performing live on the *Highway To Hell* tour at The Long Beach Arena, California, USA, on September 10, 1979**

Opposite: **AC/DC manager Peter Mensch** (far left) **with Bun E. Carlos** (second left) **and Robin Zander** (second right) **of Cheap Trick, and Bon Scott** (far right) **of AC/DC playing pool during the *Highway To Hell* tour in Nürnberg, Germany, September 1, 1979**

Below: **AC/DC at Oakland Coliseum, Oakland, California, July 21, 1979**

It was with "Touch Too Much," a song that was first demoed in 1977, that Lange really honed the band's sound for radio. The funky riff was twanged instead of hammered; the chorus punched through with Lange's vocals high in the mix with Bon's. While the lyrics were vintage Bon, as he eulogized a woman with a body like Michelangelo's Venus, but with arms. What Joe Elliott heard in "Touch Too Much" was the kind of song that he wanted to create with Def Leppard and with Mutt Lange. As Joe told me: "I thought it was the best song on the album. And it's funny, because as Mutt said to me later, AC/DC couldn't stand 'Touch Too Much.' They thought it was too poppy. But I loved the sound of it and the pace of it. If they'd done that song with Vanda and Young they'd have spoilt it, played it too fast."

In a similar vein was "Girls Got Rhythm," one of the raunchiest songs the band ever recorded, the backseat rhythm that Bon referred to replicated in a bouncing riff. There were big hooks and dirty grooves in "Shot Down In Flames" and "Get It Hot;" the former a song in which Bon, for all his swinging-dick machismo, could admit that even he got blown out sometimes, the latter an

ode to cruisin' and boozin' that had the singer taking a swipe at the big-nosed king of schmaltz, Barry Manilow. There was also a cool, almost laidback vibe to "Love Hungry Man," another song that the band considered too lightweight.

Equally, there were some really heavy numbers on the album. Heaviest of all was "Walk All Over You," started at a crawl, with Phil Rudd ratcheting up the tension before the band blasted into high gear. Again, the chorus was huge. Fastest was "Beating Around The Bush," a white-knuckle ride with Bon sounding like he was foaming at the mouth, and another echo of an old rock classic in a riff like Fleetwood Mac's "Oh Well" played at double speed. There was piss and vinegar and a wild energy in the song they named after their live album, "If You Want Blood (You've Got It)," in which Bon expanded upon the joke he made at Day on the Green about Christians being thrown to the lions. The album ends on a sinister note with "Night Prowler," a tense, creepy blues song wherein Bon adopted the persona of a murderous villain. Angus never played a better blues solo than the one on "Night Prowler." And for all the grisly imagery in the lyrics, the song ended with a weird joke, as Bon quoted mock alien language from seventies sci-fi sitcom *Mork & Mindy*: "Shazbot! Nanu nanu!"

Years later, "Night Prowler" would come back to haunt the band, when the song was linked to American serial killer Richard

"A lot of the stuff that AC/DC did with Vanda and Young has great energy, but the tuning on the guitars is fucking terrible."

Joe Elliott, Def Leppard

Ramirez, an AC/DC fan who was dubbed in the media as "The Night Stalker." But it was not this song that raised concern at Atlantic once the album was completed in the spring of 1979. It was the title track that had the suits worried. As Angus Young said to me: "As soon as we called the album *Highway To Hell*, the American record company immediately went into a panic. With religious things, I thought everywhere was like Australia. There, they call them Bible-thumpers, and it's a limited species, very limited! Christianity was never a popular movement. It's that convict background!" In America, where Christian morality was more entrenched, *Highway To Hell* was a controversy waiting to happen. Nonetheless, it was in America that the big push for the album began on May 8, with the first of fifty-three dates in which AC/DC opened for their old friends UFO.

The announcement that followed this tour on July 1 gave another indication of the Young brothers' steely determination to drive the band on to greater success. Just as Vanda and Young had been passed over in favour of Mutt Lange, so Michael Browning was dismissed as AC/DC's manager as the band signed with American company Leber-Krebs, whose clients included high rollers such as Aerosmith and Ted Nugent. A key figure in this deal was Peter Mensch, who had first sensed the potential in AC/DC during their 1978 tour with Aerosmith, on which Mensch served as tour accountant. On the insistence of Malcolm and Angus Young, Mensch was installed as AC/DC's manager within the Leber-Krebs organization, and was based in the band's adopted hometown, London. And it was there that *Sounds* writer Phil Sutcliffe met again with Angus and Bon in early July at a Holiday Inn.

During the interview with Sutcliffe, conducted in the early afternoon, Bon was so drunk he could barely string together a coherent sentence. The tone of Sutcliffe's feature was mostly humorous. Published in the last week of July, it carried a headline that made joking reference to the core values at the heart of the band's new album: "More Songs about Humping and Booze." However, in one observation that Sutcliffe made of Bon, there was a chilling prescience: "Oddly enough," he wrote, "there does seem to be some truth in Angus, of perhaps the whole band, having taken Bon in hand in almost fatherly fashion although he's much the oldest of them at thirty-three. Bon remains the one they feel they have to keep an eye on."

Meanwhile, the wheels kept turning. In mid-July, the band continued their US tour as support to Cheap Trick, whose live album *At Budokan*, recorded at the famous arena in Tokyo, had given them a breakthrough top ten hit. On July 21, AC/DC returned to Oakland for Day on the Green #3—the 1979 version, where the bill was comprised entirely of Leber-Krebs acts, with Ted Nugent headlining over Aerosmith, and AC/DC positioned above Frank Marino & Mahogany Rush, and St. Paradise.

"This is gonna be one of the biggest bands rock's ever seen. Give us a year or two and we'll sell this place out ourselves."

Bon Scott at New York's Madison Square Garden

Six days later, *Highway To Hell* was released in the UK, where it became the band's first top ten hit outside of Australia. On July 28, they played at another huge event in America, the World Series of Rock show in Cleveland, Ohio, again with Aerosmith and Nugent, plus Journey, and Thin Lizzy. The following month, on August 4, a day after the US release of *Highway To Hell*, AC/DC performed for the first time at New York's Madison Square Garden, opening for Nugent. It was a thrill for the band to be at this famous place where all the biggest stars had played, from Elvis to Led Zeppelin, and where Muhammad Ali had first fought Smokin' Joe Frazier. But in no way were AC/DC overawed by the occasion. Quite the opposite. They had the audience up out of their seats from the get-go, and after their set, backstage, Bon confidently predicted to *Hit Parader* writer Andy Secher: "This is gonna be one of the biggest bands rock's ever seen. Give us a year or two and we'll sell this place out ourselves."

This was no idle boast. With the title track "Highway To Hell" released as a single, AC/DC had at long last got a break with US radio. Also if, as Atlantic had anticipated, the album's title incited America's so-called "moral majority"—as did the cover, a band photograph in which a sneering Angus sported devil horns and, for added effect, a forked tail—the resulting controversy had the members of AC/DC bemused and laughing at the sheer absurdity of it all. As Angus told me in 2003: "In America you had guys in bed sheets

Above: **Angus at the World Series of Rock concert at Cleveland Municipal Stadium on July 28, 1979 in Cleveland, Ohio**

Above: **August 18, 1979 at London's Wembley Stadium. AC/DC open for The Who in front of a crowd of sixty thousand fans.**

Opposite: **Angus Young and Bon Scott live on stage at Wembley Stadium, August 18, 1979**

and placards with prayers on, picketing the gigs. I said, 'Who are they here for?' And they said, 'You!' And we had that thing with 'Highway To Hell'—that if you play it backwards you get these Satanic messages. Fucking hell, why play it backwards? It says it right up front: Highway To Hell!"

For AC/DC, all this fuss about *Highway To Hell* was a joke. And they had the last laugh. As Angus recalled to me: "That was the album that broke us in America."

On August 18, AC/DC were back on familiar ground, in London, as the opening act for British rock legends The Who at Wembley Stadium. The bill also featured punk band The Stranglers and American guitarist Nils Lofgren. The audience of sixty thousand was the biggest that AC/DC had played to in the UK. For Malcolm Young in particular, it was an honour to share a stage with The Who, a band that had lit a fire in him, and millions of other kids, with the youth anthem "My Generation" in 1965. For one critic who witnessed the show, Harry Doherty of *Melody Maker*, it was a defining moment for AC/DC. What Doherty noted in The Who was "an ability to function, no matter how lethargically, while commanding total adulation from their audience." In stark contrast, he wrote of AC/DC: "Good hard rock owes much to hunger. They might be a bit raw at the edges, but they're a tremendously tight unit, chugging along mercilessly. The audience left no doubt as to their partiality for AC/DC. This could be just the break the band needed to finally push their point home to Britain."

From September 5 through to October 21, AC/DC were on the road in America as a significant milestone was reached. *Highway To Hell* became the band's first gold record in the US, with half a million sales. As bassist Cliff Williams said: "It was the first sniff that things were really going to happen for us." AC/DC were no longer just a cult act: that weird band from Australia with the little dude in a schoolboy's outfit for a gimmick. They were shaping up as serious contenders, on the cusp of major success.

On October 26, just five days after the last US date, a UK tour began at Newcastle Mayfair. The support act was the young British band that Peter Mensch was soon to be co-managing—Def Leppard. For Def's singer Joe Elliott, who had just turned twenty,

this tour was an experience he would never forget. As he shared with me: "Two years after we saw AC/DC in Sheffield we were opening for them. It was madness."

The gig that Joe remembers most vividly was the second date of the tour, at the place where *If You Want Blood (You've Got It)*, was recorded. "I was out in the crowd at Glasgow Apollo," he said, "up in the balcony. And when they opened up with 'Live Wire,' the bass pumping, I swear that fucking balcony was moving twelve inches. It was like an earthquake. The people were going so nuts I thought the balcony would collapse. I was watching the audience, soaking up that reaction, and I thought, I want a bit of that! Thinking back, it still makes the hairs on my arms stand up."

On every other night of that tour, Joe and the other members of Def Leppard watched AC/DC's performance from the side of the stage. "As a band we learned a lot from AC/DC on that tour," he said. "The presentation, the high energy. Bon used to talk a lot between songs, and I loved that banter. Communication with the crowd is an integral part of rock 'n' roll, and Bon was a master at it. Sometimes he didn't even have to say anything. He did it with his facial expressions. He was royalty. And I watched to see what he did when he wasn't singing. He had a way of standing in front of the drum riser. Shirt off after three songs, lots of sweat, controlled aggression in the voice. He didn't look like he was trying. He was like a tap—you just turn him on. He was born to do it."

The tour included three nights at London's Hammersmith Odeon, the first of which, on November 1, marked the sixteenth birthday of Def Leppard's drummer, Rick Allen. On November 11, AC/DC headed off to Europe with Judas Priest as support act in place of Leppard, and on December 9 a show at the Pavillon de Paris in the French capital was filmed for the concert movie *AC/DC: Let There Be Rock*, which was scheduled for a theatrical release in 1980. In addition to the live performance, the movie cameras also recorded backstage interviews with the band members, in which Bon admitted, "I drink too much," and laughed off the suggestion that he was a star by joking, "I see stars sometimes." Angus, in his own way as witty as Bon, described AC/DC as a bunch of hooligans. "The band," he said, "I'd hide from them. If I saw them walking down the street, I'd run, you know? Probably liable to kill you."

It was a freak accident that derailed the tour in its final weeks. After a show in Nice on December 15, Bon pulled a muscle in his leg during a drunken play-fight with one of the band's roadies. Although Bon got through a few more gigs in the

Left: **Bon Scott on stage in New York, August 1979. Def Leppard singer, Joe Elliott, learned a lot from the way Bon would banter with the crowd in between songs.**

ATLANTA
79

Opposite: **Angus Young** (jumping) **and Bon Scott on stage at London's Hammersmith Odeon, 1979**

UK, at the Hammersmith Odeon, Brighton Centre, and two at the Birmingham Odeon, his injury forced the postponement of a date at Southampton Gaumont, which was rescheduled for the following month.

Bon headed back to Australia for Christmas to see his parents and look up some old friends. He paid a visit to his ex-wife, Irene, who was six months pregnant. If there was sadness in this for Bon—a vision of how his life might have been if things had turned out differently—there was also a sense of victory in his return to the place where his long journey to rock 'n' roll stardom had begun. *Highway To Hell* was on its way to becoming AC/DC's first million-selling record.

The prediction that Bon had made in August at Madison Square Garden—that AC/DC would be "one of the biggest bands rock's ever seen"— was no pipe dream. He believed it. The whole band did. As did the President of Atlantic Records, Jerry Greenberg, who remembered of this time: "You could really feel that this band was ready to explode."

In that moment, it seemed that nothing could stop them.

HIGHWAY TO HELL

Released: July 27, 1979
Recorded: December 1978, Albert Studios, Sydney, Australia
January–February 1979, Criteria Studios, Miami, Florida
March–April 1979, Roundhouse Studios, London, England.
Label: Atlantic
Producer: Robert John "Mutt" Lange

All tracks written by Angus Young, Malcolm Young, and Bon Scott.

SIDE ONE
"Highway To Hell"
"Girls Got Rhythm"
"Walk All Over You"
"Touch Too Much"
"Beating Around The Bush"

SIDE TWO
"Shot Down In Flames"
"Get It Hot"
"If You Want Blood (You've Got It)"
"Love Hungry Man"
"Night Prowler"

PERSONNEL
Bon Scott—lead vocals
Angus Young—lead guitar
Malcolm Young—rhythm guitar, backing vocals
Cliff Williams—bass guitar, backing vocals
Phil Rudd—drums

Highway to Hell was the first AC/DC album not produced by Harry Vanda and George Young. It became the band's first gold record in the US, with half a million sales. It was also the last album to feature Bon Scott.

"As soon as we called the album *Highway To Hell*, the American record company immediately went into a panic."
Angus Young

Additional personnel
Bob Defrin—art direction
Jim Houghton—cover photography

Death by Misadventure

"When you're young you always feel immortal. But after Bon died, I felt horribly grown up."

Angus Young

KOKO

Previous: **Bon Scott (July 9, 1946 – February 19, 1980)**

Left: **Pete Way, bassist with** UFO, **was one of the last people to see Bon** Scott alive.

Above: **The KOKO music venue in Camden, previously known as** The Music Machine, **where Bon Scott was the night before his death on February 19, 1980**

AC/DC began 1980 on a high. In late January, when Bon Scott returned to London to start working on new songs with Malcolm and Angus Young, he was buzzing. One song, based on a funky, stop-start riff that Malcolm had cooked up during a soundcheck on tour in 1979, had a power and groove so deep in the pocket that Bon was convinced that the next album would be bigger than *Highway To Hell*—that it would sell millions. Bon had told his mother Isa, "This one is going to be it!"

On January 16, the band traveled to France to complete the *Highway To Hell* tour by playing those shows canceled after Bon's injury. There were eight dates in France, and the last two in the UK, at Newcastle Mayfair on January 25, and Southampton Gaumont two days later—the final stop. At this last show the band rolled through a set list that had been worked over and over across the previous eight months into a thing of irresistible force: with "Live Wire" to start, four songs from *Highway To Hell*, and perennial crowd-pleasers such as "Whole Lotta Rosie," "Bad Boy Boogie," "T.N.T.," and "The Jack." The last song they played that night was "Let There Be Rock."

In early February there was plenty for AC/DC to celebrate. As the band scored its first top thirty UK hit with "Touch Too Much," Angus was married in a small private ceremony in London. Bon's love life was more complicated. Although he remained in contact with on-off girlfriend Silver Smith, Bon was dating a Japanese woman named Anna Baba, who had moved into his new flat in Victoria. Bon would start his days with a glass of scotch before setting to work on lyrics for the new songs, but he was restless. He missed the sense of adventure and the momentum of life on the road, and he and Anna were already drifting apart.

In the first week of February, Bon went to see his friends in UFO playing at the Hammersmith Odeon, where a photograph was taken backstage of Bon with UFO's bassist Pete Way. In the same week, AC/DC appeared on *Top Of The Pops* performing "Touch Too Much." Bon wore a black shirt, unbuttoned, the sleeves rolled

"Bon always drank so much. I can't imagine him dying from it."

Pete Way, UFO

up to reveal his tattooed forearms, and mugged to the camera with a knowing expression, but there was something about him—the lines and the pallor in his face—that made him appear older than his thirty-three years.

A few days later, Bon was with Malcolm and Angus at E-Zee Hire studios, close to King's Cross. As Angus discussed with me in 1991: "We started writing the music with Bon on drums. He was a drummer originally. He'd bang away while me and Malcolm worked out the riffs." As a drummer, Bon was not in the same class as Phil Rudd, but he still had his chops. And while the new songs were still works in progress, with no lyrics completed, they all knew they were on to something good. Maybe, as Bon had said, this next record could be the big one.

It was a Monday evening, February 18, when Bon called Silver to ask if she would go with him to see a band at Dingwalls in Camden. He had been drinking and did not want to go out alone, but Silver was not interested. She suggested he go with her friend, Alistair Kinnear, who was at her flat that evening. Bon agreed.

What happened that night has been a source of conjecture for almost forty years. There is only one known witness to the events, and that is Alistair Kinnear, a man whose name is forever linked to the story of AC/DC as the last person to see Bon Scott alive.

Opposite: **Heavy drinking was starting to take its toll on Bon Scott.**

Kinnear's version of events was given in a testimony to police. He stated that he had driven to Bon's flat in Victoria at midnight, and that from there, the pair headed not to Dingwalls, which was by then closed for the night, but to another Camden club, The Music Machine. It was reported that Bon was drinking large whiskies, four measures in a single glass, straight. After a couple of rounds, Kinnear drove back to Bon's place, but when they arrived, Bon had passed out drunk and Kinnear was unable to rouse him. Kinnear then headed to East Dulwich, where he lived in a third floor flat at 67 Overhill Road. Again, Kinnear could not wake Bon. Nor could he lift him out of the car. Instead, Kinnear covered Bon with a blanket and went alone to his flat to sleep. Kinnear claimed that he slept through to the next evening, and that when he returned to the car, at 7.45pm, he saw that Bon was unconscious and had not moved. As Kinnear later stated in an interview with the *London Evening Standard*: "I knew something was wrong immediately."

In the last hours of February 19, 1980, Bon Scott was pronounced dead on arrival at the Kings College Hospital. It was on the following morning that the news reached Angus and Malcolm Young. As Angus solemnly recalled to me in 2003: "We were all living in little shoebox flats all over London. One of Bon's girlfriends called but she was in a panic. I told her not to worry, there's always some rumor going round. Then a Japanese girl rang about it. I got hold of Mal and he'd heard something. Nobody knew for sure. Then our manager told us."

Outside of AC/DC's inner circle, one of the first to learn of Bon's death was Joe Elliott, who was on the afternoon of February 20 at the Top Rank club in Sheffield, where Def Leppard were playing that night. "I will always remember the moment we heard that Bon had died," Joe told me. "We got to the Top Rank to soundcheck and we heard the news from Peter Mensch. It was horrible. Obviously we had a job to do, but we dedicated the gig to Bon—'a good friend of ours passed away last night.' That was how it felt." Def Leppard's performance that night ended with a version of "Whole Lotta Rosie." Joe Elliott never had the chance to pay back the money that Bon had given to him.

The other members of AC/DC were devastated. As drummer Phil Rudd, normally the most taciturn of rock stars, admitted, "It was pretty hard on all of us." Angus Young told me in 1991: "As a person, Bon stared death in the face a lot. The way he said it was, 'One day you gotta go. You gotta be a stiff.' That was just how he talked." What Angus said in another interview revealed something deeper: "When you're young you always feel immortal," he said. "But after Bon died, I felt horribly grown up."

In all the years that followed, a sense of mystery has hung over the death of Bon Scott, as with the deaths of other famous rock stars before him, such as The Rolling Stones' Brian Jones and The Doors' Jim Morrison. The coroner's report on Bon's death cited "acute alcohol poisoning" and stated that no traces of drugs were found in the body. It was declared "death by misadventure." Silver Smith later stated: "No one gave Bon drugs. He could have used any time he wanted, but we wouldn't let him." But another of Bon's closest friends, Pete Way, believes that Bon may have overdosed on heroin. Way was using heroin at that time, and has since claimed that he saw Bon in conversation with a drug dealer on the night of UFO's Hammersmith Odeon show, at which the last known photograph of Bon was taken—he and Way together, just two weeks before Bon's death. Way said that he could not recall ever seeing Bon use heroin, but has suggested that the drug dealer who spoke with Bon at the UFO gig may also have been with Bon on the night that he died. Contrary to the coroner's report, Way said to me: "Bon always drank so much, I can't imagine him dying from it."

Central to the mystery was the disappearance of Alistair Kinnear just three days after Bon died. It was all of twenty-five years later, in 2005, that Kinnear broke his silence in an interview with Spanish journalist Maggie Montalbano. Kinnear said that he had been working as a musician on the Costa del Sol for twenty-two years, and related the same version of the events of February 1980 that he gave to police at the time. "I truly regret Bon's death,"

Above: **Tributes adorn the memorial of Bon Scott in Fremantle Cemetery in Perth, Australia.**

Left: **While Bon Scott** (left) **drank too much, Angus Young** (right) **remains teetotal.**

Kinnear said. In conclusion, he stated: "We should all take better care of our friends, and err on the side of caution when we don't know all the facts."

Among all the rumors, innuendo, and half-truths that have circulated since Bon's death was one bizarre conspiracy theory implicating the Young brothers. As Angus said, disbelievingly: "There was even a story that we poisoned the guy!" What Malcolm Young said on the subject was, foremost, respectful and protective of Bon's memory. "We knew exactly what happened to Bon," he said. "We still haven't told what we know because it's more of a personal thing for Bon. Different rumors . . . they still grow. But we know what went on that night. Bon was let down by a friend. Bon was a big drinker, and that night he went a bit further. But he didn't go drink himself to death, that's for sure. He had too much to live for."

Writer Malcolm Dome, who had seen AC/DC's first ever UK show at the Red Cow in 1976, and had subsequently interviewed Bon a number of times for magazines such as *Record Mirror*, says of the singer's death: "I was shocked, absolutely. I knew that Bon drank too much and took too many drugs, but somehow you really felt he was indestructible. In all the times I met him, he never changed. Bon was such a great bloke. It sounds like a cliché, but he was exactly the way you wanted him to be. I think the truth was that his death was a horrible accident. I don't think there's any more to it than that."

Joe Elliott agrees. As he said to me: "The rumors about Bon's death are all Chinese whispers. It's like the Bible—a good story

Left: **A sculpture of Bon Scott is displayed near the Fishing Boat Harbour in Fremantle, Western Australia.**

Opposite: **Bon Scott pictured in 1976 at Albert Studios**

with hints of the truth in it. After all these years we still can't get the story straight because people remember things differently. I don't know if anyone will ever know the truth. But on the night he died, I imagine that nobody fully realized what was going on. Somebody was too drunk to realize how cold it was outside—'Oh, he'll be fine!' And Bon had been fine every other time he had done this. You only die once. You get away with it every other time."

Perhaps it was inevitable that Bon Scott's life would end as it did, after one drunken night too many. He never lived to see AC/DC become the biggest rock 'n' roll band in the world. As Angus said in a 1980 interview: "Bon really hadn't reached his peak." But if it was a life that ended too soon, it was also a life that was lived to the full.

It was at Bon's funeral—on February 29, in Fremantle, the suburb of Perth where he had grown up—that the surviving members of AC/DC decided their future. Bon's father, Chick, pulled Malcolm Young to one side to offer some words of encouragement and to give his blessing for the band to carry on without his son. It gave them the lift they needed. "Bon would have done the same," Angus has said. "We felt we had his blessing too."

After the funeral, Angus, Malcolm, Cliff, and Phil flew straight back to London. For a few days, they remained in mourning, feeling drained. "We were still real low," Malcolm said. "We weren't snapping out of it." Then, at Malcolm's insistence, he and Angus convened at E-Zee Hire to begin writing again. "It was the two of us," Malcolm recalled. "Pick up the guitars, just for therapy. Maybe that's the way to get through this." They had the two songs demoed with Bon. As Angus shared with me in 1991: "Bon wrote a little of the stuff, a week before he died." And as other songs started to take shape, they began to think about who would sing them.

Speaking to *Sounds* in March 1980, as auditions for a new singer began, Angus acknowledged the problems facing potential candidates. "Bon was a unique character," he said, "and it's difficult for any guy to walk in knowing that Bon's just died and thinking that we're all going to be a bit funny about a new guy singing his songs. That's an added pressure."

It was not going to be easy—for the band, or for the singers who would be trying out. Bon's were big shoes to fill. "He was a very cool dude," Phil Rudd said. "Such a character." To Malcolm Young, Bon was a talismanic figure. "He pulled us all together," Malcolm said. "He had that real stick-it-to-'em attitude. Bon was the single biggest influence on the band." But still, they had to move on. And as Malcolm and Angus got back into a rhythm, with new songs coming together fast, there was a change of mood in the AC/DC camp.

Angus told *Sounds*: "We wouldn't like to have someone who was a Bon imitator. We're looking for something that little bit different. We'll certainly do our best to put out a great album. And if someone walked in tomorrow and clicked, we'd go straight in and record it, because we've basically got all the ideas and songs—it just needs that one missing ingredient."

What Angus did not know at the time was that the missing ingredient—the man who would become AC/DC's new singer—was someone that Bon himself had raved about to Angus years earlier. Sometimes, the truth really is stranger than fiction.

Lost and Found

"My name was on the list up front, but they just couldn't find me. I'd fallen off the end of the world. Nobody knew where I was."

Brian Johnson

Brian Johnson would never forget the day in February 1980 that he discovered that Bon Scott had died. "I remember exactly," Johnson said to me in 2003. "I read it in *The Daily Mail* on my way to work. Bon's death got two fuckin' inches in the paper. I was disgusted."

For Johnson, in 1980, the beginning of a new decade had brought little cause for optimism. He was living in Newcastle in the North-East of England, close to Dunston, Gateshead. And at the age of thirty-two, he believed that his days as a rock 'n' roll star were long gone.

Johnson had a fleeting taste of the big time as the singer for glam rock act Geordie back in the seventies. The band was signed to EMI, home to The Beatles, and had a top ten hit in the UK in 1973 with the rabble-rousing anthem "All Because Of You." At a time when Slade were one of the biggest bands in Britain, Geordie had a similar style and sound, and like Slade's singer Noddy Holder, Johnson could really belt out a tune. What Geordie did not have was the pop genius of Slade's gleefully misspelled hits such as "Cum On Feel The Noize," "Gudbuy T'Jane" and "Coz I Luv You." When Geordie split in the late seventies, after some lean years on the North-East club circuit, Brian Johnson fell on hard times. As he recollected to *Classic Rock:* "I had nothing. I had two kids and a mortgage to pay. I was driving a VW Beetle that was fourteen years old. I was fuckin' skint."

By 1980, he was running a small business in Newcastle, fixing windshields and fitting vinyl roofs on sports cars. He had also recently separated from his wife, and was living at his parents' house. The business was enough for him to make ends meet. To make a little extra, he was performing with a new version of the old band, christened Geordie II. The band's shows had a whiff of cabaret, with comedy routines between songs, but when they rocked out they could still do so with conviction, and among the popular songs they played live was one that always got the place shaking—AC/DC's "Whole Lotta Rosie." He enjoyed the gigs, for what they were worth, but he was no fool. He knew there were few second chances in rock 'n' roll, and had learned it the hard way, having auditioned for Ritchie Blackmore's Rainbow in 1978 following the departure of front man Ronnie James Dio. It was another British singer with a raucous voice, Graham Bonnet, who got the Rainbow job. Time was running out for Brian Johnson. He felt old, past his sell-by date. Little did he know that the oportunity of a lifetime was just days away.

In the aftermath of Bon's death, one package from a fan in Cleveland, Ohio, would prove to be particularly influentual. It contained a Geordie album and a simple note that read: "You've got to listen to this singer." This was not Brian's only endorsement, with Mutt Lange having also told Malcolm Young there was "one

Previous: **Following Bon Scott's death, Brian Johnson joined AC/DC as singer in 1980.**

Right: **Brian Johnson was living in Newcastle fixing windshields when he got the gig as AC/DC's lead singer.**

NEWCASTLE
BROWNS

Geordi
GEORDIE

"I had **nothing.** I had two **kids** and a **mortgage** to pay. I was driving a **VW Beetle** that was **fourteen** years old. I was **fuckin' skint.**"

Brian Johnson

guy you should really listen to." To which Malcolm thought, "That's twice his name's come up . . . " What Malcolm had not remembered at the time was Geordie's tour of Australia in the mid-seventies, for which Albert Productions had provided publicity. And what Angus Young came to realize, after the event, was that this was the singer that Bon had seen doing that brilliant Little Richard impersonation back in 1973, when Bon's band Fang had supported Geordie. Bon had told Angus how great this guy was on that night in Torquay—flat out on the stage, singing his balls off. Bon never knew that Brian had been in agony during that show, his screams and convulsions induced by appenditicis. Bon just thought that this guy was one hell of a rock 'n' roll singer and as Angus told me in 1991: "It was rare that Bon ever raved about anything."

In the early days of March 1980, Brian Johnson's name was placed on a shortlist of potential singers for AC/DC. As Brian told *Classic Rock*: "My name was on the list up front, but they just couldn't find me. I'd fallen off the end of the world. Nobody knew where I was." Among the other names on that list, some were famous, some not. It was later suggested that Malcolm and Angus Young thought of approaching two of the great British rock singers of their time: Steve Marriott, formerly of the Small Faces and Humble Pie, and Noddy Holder of Slade. In the end, neither option seemed right. There were singers back in Australia that seemed a better fit, including Jimmy Barnes from Cold Chisel, and Phil Rudd's old bandmate Angry Anderson from Rose Tattoo. Both had voices as powerful and gritty as Bon's. There was also John Swan, a Scottish singer who, like Bon, used to be a drummer. The similarities did not end there though, as Swan admitted to writer Murray Engleheart: "I don't think they would have been in their right minds to take me, because they would have had another Bon on their hands—I was doing speed, coke, plus I drank 24/7."

Reportedly, two British singers were also in the frame, Terry Slesser and Gary Holton. Slesser was from Newcastle, where Brian Johnson was living, and had previously starred in Back Street Crawler, the band that AC/DC had been scheduled to support in 1976 before the death of guitarist Paul Kossoff. Holton, a Londoner, had been the frontman for the Heavy Metal Kids, a band that had seemed destined for big things in the mid-seventies, their rowdy rock 'n' roll sound similar to the Faces and Slade, with Holton a cocky, charismatic figure. It has been said, by a source who declined to be named, that Holton had an audition for AC/DC but blew it by making a poorly judged joke—telling the band that he could hold his drink better than Bon could.

Holton went on to achieve fame as an actor in the hit TV series *Auf Wiedersehen, Pet*, but

Opposite: **Brian Johnson (left) had already enjoyed a taste of success with glam rock band, Geordie in the seventies.**

he too would end up a victim of the rock 'n' roll lifestyle that had killed Bon. Holton's death in 1985 was attributed to an overdose of morphine. He died at thirty-three, the same age as Bon.

It was at Vanilla Studios in Pimlico, London, that AC/DC held the auditions, and for each candidate a basic remit was laid down.

"When we auditioned singers, they'd say, 'How am I supposed to sing over all this volume?' We said, 'We don't want you to sing—we want you to scream!'" Angus Young recalled. A few of the applicants failed at the first hurdle by suggesting they jam on songs that were unsuited to AC/DC, such as the Deep Purple classic "Smoke On The Water." It was heavy going, but eventually, the band's management located Brian Johnson, and the call was made.

What Johnson remembered was a woman with a German accent informing him that he had been recommended for a job with a major band, and inviting him to London to audition. When Johnson asked for the name of the band, the woman said she was not permitted to tell him. Johnson explained that he was broke, that he was not going to travel all the way to London without knowing who he was auditioning for. He suggested she could at least give him the initials of the band's name. There was a pause. "Okay," she said. "It's A.C. and D.C." As Brian later told me, laughing: "She wasn't the smartest."

At the time, he could not believe his luck. It had been fun to sing "Whole Lotta Rosie" with his old mates in the clubs. The thought of singing that song with AC/DC was mind-blowing.

On the day Brian traveled to London for the audition, the omens were not good. Fearing that his clapped-out Beetle might not carry him far, he borrowed a friend's car, a Toyota Crown, and just a few miles outside Newcastle, he got a puncture. He worked like a maniac to fix the flat tyre and floored the Toyota down the M1. When he arrived outside Vanilla Studios, he was shaking with nerves. For the best part of an hour he sat in a café across the street from the studio, chain-smoking and drinking tea. He tried to eat a pie but could not get it down because the crust was so hard he thought he might break a tooth. Such was his lack of confidence, he wanted to just get up and go home. It took all the guts he had to walk into the studio.

Once inside, he saw a bunch of guys playing pool and mistook them for the band. These were AC/DC's roadies. He spent an hour with them before he realized his mistake and was led through to the rehearsal room, where he was introduced to the band and was immediately put at ease when Malcolm Young gave him a bottle of Newcastle Brown Ale. Brian gulped it down and was relieved to discover that the members of the band were, in his words, "just regular guys."

"The boys had lost a great friend and a great singer. Bon, he was their best pal."

Brian Johnson

Other contenders for AC/DC front man included Steve Marriott (far left), **Noddy Holder** (left), **John Swan** (above left), **the lead singer of Feather, and his step brother, Jimmy Barnes** (above right), **lead singer of Cold Chisel.**

Opposite: **Brian Johnson was not a Bon Scott copy. He had his own working-class style, complete with flat cap.**

Below: **Gary Holton, who later achieved fame as an actor in *Auf Wiedersehen, Pet*, blew his chance to front AC/DC due to a badly judged joke about Bon and his drinking.**

They asked him what song he would like to sing with them. What he chose was Ike & Tina Turner's 1973 hit "Nutbush City Limits"—funky and full of soul, but with a rock 'n' roll edge as dirty and mean as The Rolling Stones at their decadent peak. It was a song that Malcolm and Angus loved, and when Brian sang it with the band, it sounded good. They could feel it, all of them. Next they tried "Whole Lotta Rosie." Brian knew it inside out, and like the subject of the song, gave it all he had. "I got tingles singing Rosie," he later said.

Phil Rudd, for one, was convinced that AC/DC had got their man. When the audition was over and Brian was heading home up the M1, Rudd told the others, "Fuck it—let's have Brian. Let's go!" It took a little longer for Malcolm and Angus to make the decision. A second audition for Brian was arranged, and again, he was late showing up. As the band waited at Vanilla Studios, Brian was elsewhere in London, doing another job—singing an advert for Hoover. The fee was three hundred and fifty pounds, cash, a lot of money back then, especially for a guy who was struggling to make ends meet. Brian figured that if he failed at the second attempt with AC/DC, at least he would be making a little money on the side.

The jingle for Hoover was easy money. When I interviewed Brian for *Classic Rock* in 2009, he remembered every word and sang them to me: "The new high-powered mover from Hoover, it's a little groover!" In his second audition for AC/DC, they ran through a few old numbers, and a couple of the new songs the band had been working on. That night, Brian stayed at a hotel in London, where he spoke with Keith Evans, one of the band's roadies. Evans told him: 'I think you've got it, mate." Brian's reply was cautious: "Nah, I think they're just making their mind up."

He did not speak to Malcolm or Angus before returning to Newcastle.

In the days that followed, there were media reports linking two other singers with AC/DC. Australian magazine *TV Week* proclaimed: "Stevie is just right for AC/DC"—predicting that Stevie Wright, formerly the singer for The Easybeats, was the leading contender. While in the UK, the March 29 issue of *NME*. stated that Allan Fryer was to be AC/DC's new singer. Fryer was at that time a member of Adelaide band Fat Lip. Years later, after he had worked with ex-AC/DC bassist Mark Evans in the band Heaven, Fryer revealed that in 1980 he had gone to Sydney to meet George Young, with whom he recorded vocal tracks for three AC/DC songs: "Whole Lotta Rosie," "Sin City," and "Shot Down In Flames." By the time the *NME* story was published though, Fryer's chance had already gone.

One night in late March, Brian Johnson had been celebrating his father's birthday at his local pub, before returning alone to his parents' home. It was late when the phone rang, and Malcolm Young, dispensing with the usual pleasantries, got straight down

Left: **AC/DC perform on stage with new singer, Brian Johnson**

Opposite: **Brian Johnson was announced as AC/DC's new singer on April 1, 1980.**

to business. "We got an album to do," he said. "We gotta leave in a couple of weeks, so . . . if you're set for it . . . " For Brian, who had been drinking all evening, it took a few seconds for these words to sink in before he asked, "Are you telling me I've got the job?" Malcolm replied matter-of-factly, "Oh, yeah."

At that point, Brian said: "I'm gonna put the phone down. Could you ring again in ten minutes just so I'm sure that it's not somebody takin' the piss?" Malcolm said he would. Exactly ten minutes later, he called back. First came a simple question: "Well, are you comin' or what?" Then a simple answer: "Shit, yeah!"

Moments later, the call was over, and a loud yell of "Whoah! Fuck!" echoed around the house where Brian Johnson stood trembling. He promptly opened the bottle of whiskey he had given as a birthday present to his father, and took a huge swig straight from the bottle. He had never felt so excited in all his life.

On April 1, 1980—just six weeks after Bon Scott's death—AC/DC announced Brian Johnson as their new singer. When Brian broke the news to his younger brother, a die-hard AC/DC fan, there was laughter. His brother thought it was an April Fool's joke. That night, the drinks were on Brian. A few days later, in his first interview as AC/DC singer, Brian spoke to *Sounds* about the challenge ahead of him. "I still don't know quite where I am," he confessed. "All I know is there's a stack of work to do and the rest of the band have still got to find out about me. I'm still scared shitless, really!" It was also a period in which emotions were running high among the other members of the band. As Brian later said to *Classic Rock*: "The boys had lost a great friend and a great singer. They'd gone through all their shit together. He wasn't just a singer in the band, Bon, he was their best pal."

With plenty of material written, final rehearsals for the new AC/DC album were conducted at E-Zee Hire, where the first two songs had been worked on by Malcolm, Angus, and Bon. "When I went in," Brian said, "the guys had some titles for songs but no lyrics. They didn't even know what my lyrics were gonna be like. Literally, they said, 'Can you write some lyrics for us?' I said, 'I'll give it a shot!' A couple of titles came from the lyrics I wrote later on. But it's hard to remember, because it was a blur."

In late April, with nine songs ready, the band flew to the tropical island of Nassau in the Bahamas to record the new album with Mutt Lange again as producer. What happened there was something akin to a miracle. Bon had always said that AC/DC's next album was going to be big. What the band and their new singer created in *Back In Black*—the album made in tribute to Bon—would be bigger than he could ever have imagined.

AC/DC

Rolling Thunder

"***Back In Black*** **saved rock 'n' roll. It was the defining rock record of that time, and it just exploded!"**

Slash, Guns N' Roses

The place where AC/DC created their comeback album could not have been further removed from the cold and grey of London, where they had left behind them the tragedy of Bon's death. They were in Nassau, on the island of New Providence in the Bahamas. What drew the band to Nassau was the caliber of Compass Point Studios, a world-class facility that had been established by the founder of Island Records, Chris Blackwell. According to Tony Platt, the engineer working on this album alongside producer Mutt Lange, it was also beneficial for the band to be in such a remote location, far away from all the distractions of London or Sydney. "That helped to bring everyone together," he said.

Inside the studio, in a haze of cigarette smoke, the first song recorded was the funky number that had been demoed in London back in February with Angus and Malcolm Young on guitars and Bon on drums. They named it "Back In Black," and in its lyrics was a statement of invincibility in which, Malcolm said, they were remembering "the good times" they had with Bon. It was a theme they picked up on again with the other track that Bon had worked on, titled "Have A Drink On Me," its words a drunken toast from Brian to his predecessor. "The whole point of the album," Brian said, "was to celebrate Bon's life."

As Angus revealed to me in 1991, some of the lyrics that Bon had written were used in these songs. Brian also admitted that there were times when he struggled to find the words for a song, when he felt intimidated by all the great stuff that Bon had written before him. "I was a little worried," he said. "Like, who am I to try to follow in the footsteps of this great poet? Because Bon really was a kind of poet." Mostly, Brian stuck to the one subject that was at the core of so much rock 'n' roll and blues music, a subject in which AC/DC were well versed. Many of the song titles were self-explanatory: "Shoot To Thrill," "Let Me Put My Love Into You," "Given The Dog A Bone." Brian had a way with double-entendre, just as Bon had, and some of his best lines were in "You Shook Me All Night Long," in which he enthused about a girl's "American thighs" before delivering the classic punchline: "She told me to come but I was already there".

The biggest challenge for Brian, as a writer, was "Hells Bells." The song's slow, mighty riff—dubbed "ominous" by Malcolm and "mystical" by Angus—called for a heavy opening statement, but Brian was still working on it when the band had arrived at Compass Point. One night, he was sitting alone in his bedroom adjacent to the studio—a no-frills breeze-block cell with just a bed, a table, and a toilet—staring at a blank piece of paper and saying to himself, "I'm fucking running out of ideas here . . . " Then came a moment of divine inspiration. As Mutt Lange entered the room to see how Brian was getting on, a distant rumbling signaled the breaking of a storm over the island. "That's rolling thunder," Brian said. Mutt's eyes lit up: "Write that down!" In an instant,

Previous: **Brian Johnson** (center) **with Angus Young** (left) **and Cliff Williams** (right) **at the Orpheum Theatre, Boston, USA on October 9, 1980**

Opposite: **Brian Johnson in 1980**

Left: **Backstage on the *Back In Black* tour at London's Hammersmith Odeon, November 12, 1980:** (L–R) **Brian Johnson, Malcolm Young, Angus Young, Phil Rudd, Cliff Williams**

ctric lady studios
Roland

LOUGHBOROUGH
AC/DC
HELLS BELL

Above: **Brian Johnson at the Rosemont Horizon, Chicago, Illinois, September 20, 1980. Brian wasn't sure how AC/DC fans would react to him, especially when he was singing the old songs with Bon's words.**

Above left: **Electric Lady Studios in Manhattan, USA, where *Back In Black* received its final, dramatic touches.**

Left: **A custom-made bell from a specialist foundry in Leicestershire in the UK provided the tolling-bell sound that signals the start of "Hells Bells," the opening track on *Back In Black*.**

a downpour of rain was hammering on the roof, so loud that the two men could barely hear themselves speak. Brian wrote: "Pourin' rain . . . " And as a fierce wind howled, he added: "I'm comin' on like a hurricane."

Brian had the song finished that night, complete with the classic Christian-baiting payoff: "If God's on the left, then I'm sticking to the right!"

It was a line worthy of Bon, and as Brian later said, there were moments during the making of the album when he felt as if Bon was watching over him. Speaking to me in 2003, Brian said: "I can't deny it. I feel soft saying it, but there were certain times when I was sitting on me tod in these little recording booths in the Bahamas...Ah, fuck it. I've got goosebumps now, you cunt." Angus said that the whole band sensed a presence around them in these times. As he told *Sounds* magazine in 1980: "We still think Bon's around."

At the end of their fifth week in Nassau, AC/DC had nine tracks in the can. What they had was dynamite. It was also different to what had come before, and not only because the band had a new singer. While the music was anything but subtle, the change in it was. If the essence of AC/DC remained intact—the hard riffing, the heavy grooves—the tone had shifted a little. It was rock 'n' roll, but with more of a heavy metal edge. And what Mutt Lange had begun with AC/DC on *Highway To Hell*—adding a touch of

sheen, while retaining maximum power—was brought into full effect. The sound was huge, and at the highest end of it was Brian Johnson's voice, pushed to its limit.

Some of those nine tracks recorded were as simple as they come: shoot-from-the-hip numbers such as "Have A Drink On Me," "What Do You Do For Money Honey," "Given The Dog A Bone" and the frantic "Shake A Leg." Elsewhere, a little more sophistication came into play—in the title track, with its ticking time bomb intro and twisting riffs, in the slow-burning "Let Me Put My Love Into You," and in "Shoot To Thrill," with its funky breakdown. There was, in "You Shook Me All Night Long," this album's "Touch Too Much"—a rock 'n' roll song made for radio, with its ringing intro, hooky riff, walloping groove, and shout-it-out-loud chorus. In "Hells Bells," with that heavily atmospheric refrain, there was an epic feel, a sense of gravitas that AC/DC never had before.

With all of this, the members of the band believed they had enough, but Mutt Lange, along with key figures at Atlantic Records, felt that the album needed one more track. And once Malcolm and Angus had agreed to it, no time was wasted. They wrote a new song, from scratch, in fifteen minutes: a slow, swaggering boogie number they called "Rock And Roll Ain't Noise Pollution." "I thought it was just gonna be a boozy chuck-away," Brian later revealed to *Classic Rock*. "Mal came up with the title—he said, ''Ere Jonna, we'll call it "Rock And Roll Ain't Noise Pollution."' I thought, eh? There's a great one to fucking rhyme!" In the song's lyrics—inspired by the evangelist preachers that the band had seen on American cable TV channels—was another allusion to the past and the words that Bon had sung in "Let There Be Rock." And in keeping with the fast and loose manner in which the song was written, Brian was instructed to "fuck around" in the song's intro. "Just talk," Mutt told him. As the tape rolled, Brian cracked open a can of beer, lit a cigarette, inhaled deeply, and went into what he called "this Southern preacher thing"—just talking off the top of his head and hailing with missionary fervor the life-affirming

While *Rolling Stone* writer David Fricke (above left) **declared *Back In Black* a "masterpiece," long-time AC/DC supporter and *Sounds* contributor Phil Sutcliffe** (above right) **had reservations, especially about Brian, who he dismissed as a Bon copy.**

Right: **AC/DC on stage in London, 1980, one of six sold-out shows:** (L–R) **Brian Johnson, Malcolm Young, Angus Young, and Cliff Williams**

power of rock 'n' roll. "Honestly," he said, "it was one take. And I never ever thought that it was gonna be on the record."

A rock anthem was born, and with that, *Back In Black* was complete, save for one important detail. With the work in Nassau finished, Malcolm Young traveled to New York with Mutt Lange and Tony Platt to mix the album while the rest of the band headed back to London. Inspiration had often come to Malcolm when he was taking a piss, and so it happened in the bathroom at Electric Lady Studios in Manhattan. It had been decided that "Hells Bells" would be the album's opening track, and as Malcolm stood filling a urinal he realized what the track needed: a tolling bell as the intro, a dramatic flourish.

Tony Platt was promptly dispatched across the Atlantic to record the bell at a grand old English church in Loughborough. It was, Platt said, "a total nightmare." The bell-tower was home to dozens of pigeons that flew from their perches each time the bell was struck. The fluttering of their wings meant that Platt was unable to get a clean recording of the bell's ring. As Malcolm recollected in 2003, laughing at the memory: "Tony Platt spent a whole day trying to shoo these pigeons off." A quick rethink led Platt to commission a custom-made bell from a specialist foundry in Leicestershire. The man who made the bell struck it as Platt's tape rolled. The job, finally, was done.

In the days since the band had returned to London, Brian Johnson had been holed up in a hotel room. There was a lot on his mind. As he would later recall, "I just sat there wondering if I'd done good or bad." His fears were allayed when Malcolm returned from New York with the finished album. "I was knocked out," Brian said. "I couldn't believe it was that good." Angus felt the same. He remembered: "When I first heard it in all its glory, I thought, fuck—it's magic!"

Atlantic Records knew it too. The only problem, as the record company saw it, was the band's idea for the album cover—all black, with the AC/DC logo and album title the only detail. It was suggested by Atlantic that this would not be good for business, but the band would not yield.

As Angus later told me: "The whole *Back In Black* album was our dedication to Bon. That's why the album cover was pure black, and why the album starts with a bell ringing, something somber and different to anything else we'd done."

With the album's release scheduled for July, a world tour was set in place, beginning in late June with six low-key warm-up gigs in Belgium and Holland. For Brian Johnson it was a daunting prospect. He fretted over how AC/DC fans would react to him, especially when he was singing the old songs, Bon's words. The first show—his first show—was on June 29 at the Palais des Expositions (Now the Namur Expo) in the Belgian city of Namur, and in the moments before the band took to the stage, the singer was, as Angus put it, "shitting himself!" As they walked out, something caught Brian's eye—a banner held up in the audience, on which it was written: "R.I.P. Bon Scott. Good Luck Brian." In that instant, all of Brian's anxiety evaporated. "It just lifted me," he said. That night, the band played a set majoring on the new album material. They opened with "Hells Bells," the first of seven tracks from *Back In Black*. The other eight songs performed for the first time without Bon were "Shot Down In Flames," "Hell Ain't A Bad Place To Be," "Problem Child," "Bad Boy Boogie," "Highway To Hell," "Whole Lotta Rosie," "Rocker," and, to finish, "Let There Be Rock." Brian later said of that show: "Maybe I missed a few cues here and there, but we had enough spirit to cover up any mistakes."

Opposite: **Brian Johnson on stage in London, 1980. He won the respect of audiences by singing the hell out of the band's songs.**

For all the pressure that was on Brian in these early gigs, he won the respect of the band's audience by singing the hell out of those songs, and by being his own man. Wearing a flat cap—a sign of his working-class northern English roots—Brian looked very different to Bon, and had a different kind of demeanor on stage, an easy, laddish charm, without that glint of craziness that was always in Bon's eyes. Brian also knew from the start how the band worked on stage, ceding the center ground to Angus just as Bon had done. At one of the shows in Holland Brian realized just how much the fans were rooting for him. He met a guy who had a tattoo of Bon Scott on his arm. "Bon was my hero," the fan said, "but now he's gone I wish you all the luck in the world." Brian later recalled the profound effect these words had on him. "I just stood there shaking," he said.

The band were in North America, in the first week of a major tour, when *Back In Black* was released on July 25. For one British writer who reviewed the album, there were mixed emotions. Phil Sutcliffe had been a supporter of AC/DC since 1976, and had a great affection for the guys in the band, Bon in particular. In his review for *Sounds*, Sutcliffe awarded *Back In Black* four out of five stars, but stated in memory of Bon: "The ecstasy with which I expect to greet a new AC/DC album just wasn't possible this time." Moreover, he dismissed Brian Johnson as a "copy" of Bon. For all that, Sutcliffe concluded: "*Back In Black* remains a genuine, excellent AC/DC album."

Two other leading critics had no such reservations. *Rolling Stone* writer David Fricke declared the album a masterpiece and a milestone in rock. "*Back In Black* is not only the best of AC/DC's six American albums," Fricke wrote. "It's the apex of heavy metal art: the first LP since Led Zeppelin II that captures all the blood, sweat and arrogance of the genre. In other words, *Back In Black* kicks like a mutha." In *Record Mirror*'s review—headlined: "POWER IS RESTORED"—Robin Smith stated: "The resurrection shuffle starts here. Brian was the perfect choice, possessing an almost uncanny feel for the band's songs."

"I couldn't believe it was that good. I thought, fuck—it's magic!"

Brian Johnson on *Back In Black*

In his feature on AC/DC in the July 26 edition of *Record Mirror* Robin Smith began with a poetic line on the making of *Back In Black*: "The ghost of Bon Scott rides with AC/DC." It was a subject that Brian Johnson discussed in depth in his interview with Smith. "Bon is still around and watching," Brian said. "At night in my hotel room I had proof that he was there in some form. I know that he approves of what the new line-up is trying to do. He didn't want the band to split up or to go into a long period of mourning. He wanted us to build on the spirit he left behind."

Back In Black was an immediate hit. Within two weeks of its release, the album was at number one in the UK. The first single, "You Shook Me All Night Long," made the top forty in the UK and US, and the top ten in Australia. In early October, when the band finished touring in North America, the album was certified platinum in the US as it began an incredible thirteen-month residency in the *Billboard* top ten.

It had been a punishing schedule in North America—sixty-four shows in three months—and there was no let-up. On October 19, just eight days after the final US date, the band's UK tour kicked off at Bristol's Colston Hall. Such was the demand for AC/DC that this tour included six sold-out shows in London; three at the Hammersmith Odeon, and three at the Apollo Victoria Theatre. One fan who saw the band at Hammersmith Odeon was Phil Alexander, who went on to become editor of *Kerrang!* and *MOJO* magazines. "I was nervous before that gig," he remembered. "The fans wanted the band to be great. We wished them well. But there was this feeling of uncertainty—what is this new singer going to be like? I thought *Back In Black* was a strong record, but I was still unsure if it would work live. And then, after two songs, there were no doubts. The audience reaction was great from the start, and Brian's personality, the bonhomie, was there straight away. The band was forged in this country, it's where their reputation was made, so there was a sense of empathy in the audience—a sense that this was still our band, and a sense of triumph, for sure, at the end of the show. Somehow, even after the death of Bon, you felt that the band was completely unstoppable."

At this time, the single "Rock And Roll Ain't Noise Pollution" gave AC/DC their biggest UK hit to date, reaching number fifteen. While in America, it was reported that *Back In Black* was selling ten thousand copies a day.

From November 20 through to the early weeks of January 1981, the band played across Europe, with just a short break over Christmas and New Year. Then, after four dates in Japan in early February, came the last and most significant shows of the *Back In Black* tour. A year after Bon Scott's death, AC/DC returned to Australia.

In what was an emotional and triumphant homecoming, AC/DC performed seven shows in Australia, and at the third date in Sydney on February 23 there was a moment that Brian Johnson would remember for the rest of his life. Bon's mother, Isa, was a guest at the show, and afterwards she said to Brian: "Our Bon would have been proud of you, son." For Brian, there could be no greater validation.

The tour ended with two shows at the Sidney Myer Music Bowl in Melbourne. A few days later, when Brian got home to Newcastle, there was another moment to savor. He received his first AC/DC royalty cheque, for thirty thousand pounds. He paid off his mortgage in cash, told the bothersome manager of the building society to never call him again, and, after years of driving old bangers, he finally got himself a flashy motor. As he told *Classic Rock*: "I treated myself to a Chevy Blazer. It was an SUV, one of the first. And I'll never forget, my next door neighbor, he always used to smirk at what I did. He always got a new Cortina every four years. And when my Chevy arrived, I remember him going, 'That's a big daft stupid bloody thing, isn't it?' I went, 'You're jealous mate?' I was dead pleased. It was a big daft stupid thing, but I didn't care. I knew I'd made it."

The resurrection of AC/DC with *Back In Black* was arguably the greatest comeback in the entire history of rock 'n' roll. Out of their darkest hour had come a heroic victory.

The album that turned AC/DC into superstars was exactly as *Rolling Stone*'s David Fricke had described it: "the apex of heavy metal art." Over time, *Back In Black* would be acclaimed as one of the greatest rock records ever made. It was an inspiration to countless rock bands across the years, including world famous acts such as Guns N' Roses, Def Leppard, and Metallica. The album's key songs—"Back In Black," "Hells Bells," "Shoot To Thrill," "You Shook Me All Night Long"—would remain in AC/DC's live set for decades. Most remarkable of all is the sheer scale of this album's success. *Back In Black* is not only the biggest selling rock album there has ever been—bigger than anything by Led Zeppelin, Pink Floyd, The Rolling Stones, or even The Beatles—it is, with more than fifty million copies sold, the second biggest selling album of all time after Michael Jackson's *Thriller.*

For Joe Elliott of Def Leppard, what AC/DC achieved on *Back In Black* was perfection. "That record is never going to get old," he told me. "It's so sonically correct, the sound is so real, it just doesn't date. With *Back In Black*, AC/DC set a precedent for other people to mimic. They took the classic rock 'n' roll instruments and made them sound the best they can sound. You can't make rock music sound better than *Back In Black*. You can't go further than the top."

Joe and the other members of Def Leppard were among the first to hear *Back In Black*. In an echo of what happened

Opposite: **Fans storm the stage and rush towards guitarist Angus Young during a concert in the UK, 1980.**

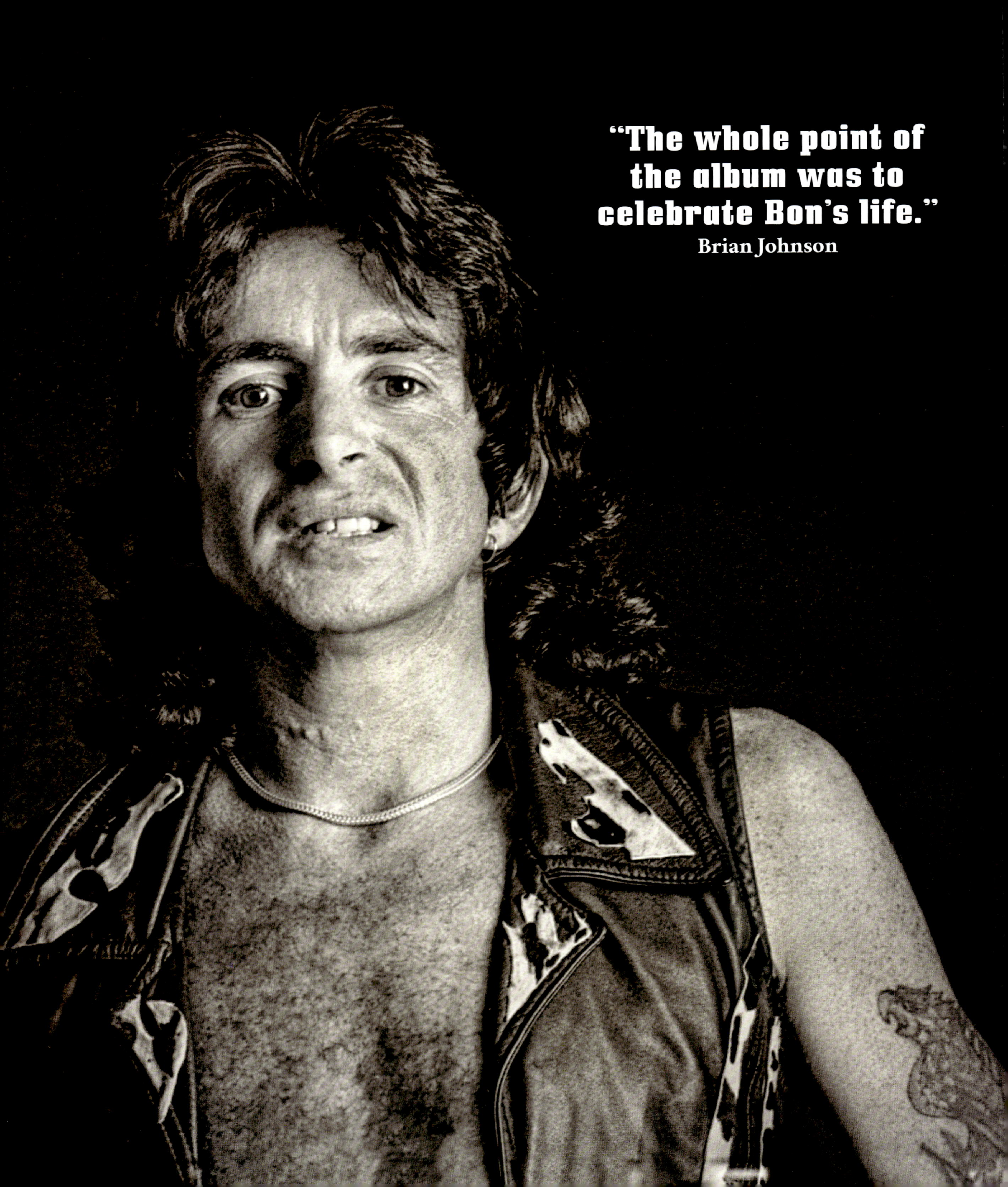

"The whole point of the album was to celebrate Bon's life."

Brian Johnson

Previous: **Angus on stage at Japan's Nippon Budokan in Tokyo where AC/DC played four dates in February 1981, before heading to Australia for the last and most significant shows of the *Back In Black* tour**

Left: **Bon Scott in 1976. *Back In Black* was the band's tribute to him. It's also the biggest selling rock album there has ever been.**

in February 1980—when manager Peter Mensch informed Def Leppard of Bon Scott's death before the news broke in the media—it was Mensch who let Leppard hear *Back In Black* before the album's release. The band were on their first US tour when Mensch boarded their bus with an advance copy of the album on cassette. As Joe later remembered: "When we heard the opening to *Hells Bells* we shat our pants! I thought, fucking hell—this is a bit good. Too fucking good! There was such an anticipation for Brian's first vocal—there's this whole intro, the bell, this slow song—it's not 'Whole Lotta Rosie,' is it? But as soon as he opened his mouth we thought, This works! There wasn't one second when I thought, what are they doing? Probably because I bought Geordie singles when I was twelve and I liked Brian Johnson then."

Certainly, there was truth in a funny line that Joe said to me: "Brian Johnson jumped on a winning horse that was about to cross the finishing line." What he added, in respect to a guy he has known for years, was equally true: "*Back In Black* is Brian's record," he said. "It's just stellar. Brian was the perfect replacement for Bon because he wasn't just a Bon clone. I just wish that Bon could have experienced that kind of success. Not to be a millionaire, but to get up in front of a really big crowd and finish what he started. But if *Back In Black* was a tribute to Bon, it's one of the best tributes ever."

Guns N' Roses guitarist Slash was just fifteen when *Back In Black* was released. Many years later he spoke to me of the impact that it had on him, and of the album as a triumph not just for Brian Johnson and AC/DC but for rock music, period. "*Back In Black* saved rock 'n' roll," he said. "It was the defining rock record of that time, and it just exploded! AC/DC was always a great band, totally genuine. But the miracle of the whole thing was that *Back In Black* was just a great new record, it was still AC/DC. We all missed Bon, but we let him go and at the same time welcomed and embraced Brian."

As Slash concluded: "*Back In Black* is one of the huge Cinderella stories of rock 'n' roll history."

What the band put into that album, on the deepest level, was most powerfully expressed by Malcolm Young: "Because of what we'd all gone through, all these emotions were in play when we were recording *Back In Black*. That's how that album was made. We meant it. It's real. It's coming from within. The emotion on that record—that will be around forever."

BACK IN BLACK

Released: July 25, 1980
Recorded: April–May 1980, Compass Point Studios, Nassau, Bahamas
Label: Albert Productions / Atlantic
Producer: Robert John "Mutt" Lange

All tracks written by Angus Young, Malcolm Young, and Brian Johnson.

SIDE ONE
"Hells Bells"
"Shoot To Thrill"
"What Do You Do For Money Honey"
"Given The Dog A Bone"
"Let Me Put My Love Into You"

SIDE TWO
"Back In Black"
"You Shook Me All Night Long"
"Have A Drink On Me"
"Shake A Leg"
"Rock And Roll Ain't Noise Pollution"

PERSONNEL
Brian Johnson—lead vocals
Angus Young—lead guitar
Malcolm Young—rhythm guitar, backing vocals
Cliff Williams—bass guitar, backing vocals
Phil Rudd—drums
Bob Defrin—art direction

Back In Black is the biggest selling rock album there has ever been. It is also, with more than fifty million copies sold, the second biggest selling album of all time after Michael Jackson's *Thriller*.

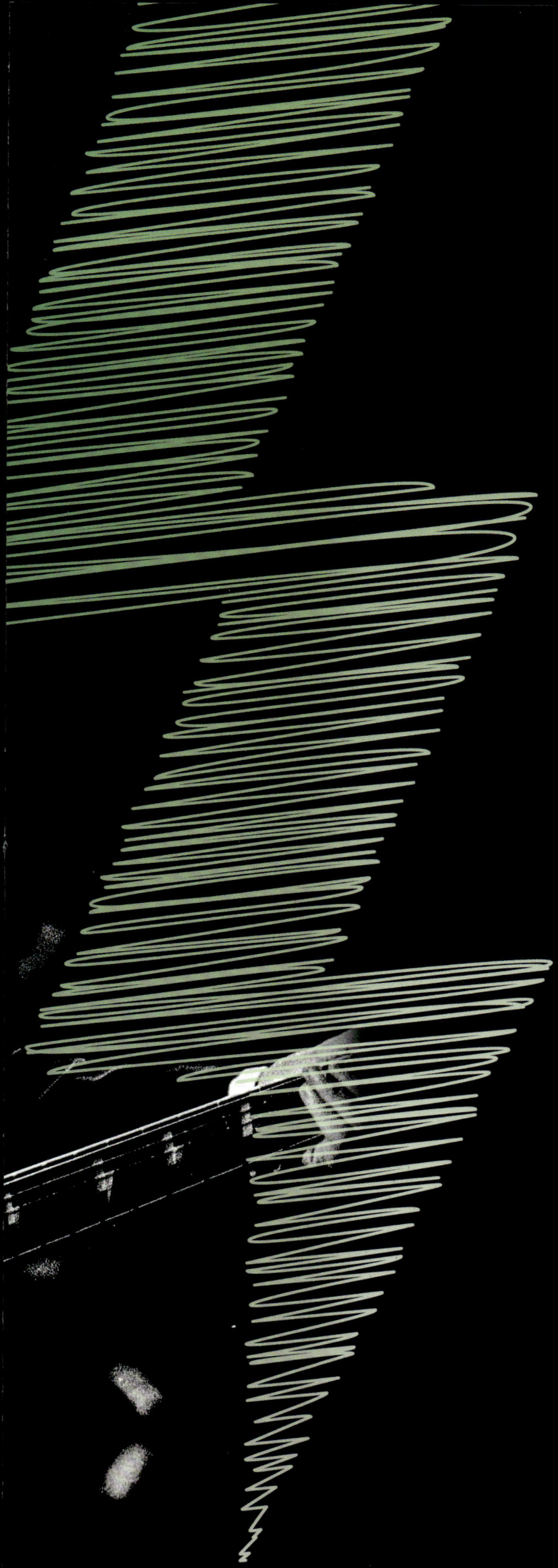

Monsters of Rock

"AC/DC are the real thing. What you've got here is one unbeatable rock 'n' roll band."

Rolling Stone

In the year in which AC/DC made the biggest rock album of all time, the biggest rock group in the world came to an end. The death of Led Zeppelin drummer John Bonham on September 25, 1980 came seven months after that of Bon Scott, and in similar circumstances. Bonham was a heavy drinker, and died in his sleep at the home of Zeppelin guitarist, Jimmy Page, near Windsor following rehearsals for a tour of North America. It was later revealed at the official inquest that Bonham had vomited and choked to death after consuming approximately forty shots of alcohol within twenty-four hours. The finding was accidental death. At thirty-two, Bonham was a year younger than Bon had been. For Led Zeppelin there was no way back. In December 1980 it was announced that the band had split. It was the end of the biggest rock band of them all, and with it the end of an era.

The rise of AC/DC and the fall of Led Zeppelin symbolized a changing of the guard in heavy rock music. By the end of 1980, many of the leading rock acts of the seventies were either finished, like Zeppelin, or in decline. Deep Purple had broken up way back in 1976, although the various ex-members had continued to flourish in new groups—Rainbow, Whitesnake, and Gillan. Black Sabbath had fired Ozzy Osbourne in 1979 and enlisted former Rainbow singer Ronnie James Dio, beginning a long and bitter feud between the two parties. Bad Company were on their last legs, and Status Quo were losing their edge. Among the many bands that AC/DC had opened for in the seventies, two of the big American rock acts were struggling. Aerosmith—once billed as "America's Rolling Stones"—had become mired in drug addiction, and guitarist Joe Perry, the AC/DC fan, had quit to form The Joe Perry Project, whose debut album in 1980 had a pointed title: *Let The Music Do The Talking*. Kiss had committed what many fans considered an act of heresy with the disco-influenced song "I Was Made For Lovin' You," and as a result the band's popularity plummeted.

As the giants fell, new rock 'n' roll heroes rose up. Once again, many of them were bands with whom AC/DC had shared stages.

With Aerosmith and Kiss on the slide, Van Halen had become the kings of American rock, with Eddie Van Halen a revolutionizing guitar hero, and singer David Lee Roth the fast-talking, high-kicking showman supreme. Rush had reinvented their sound for the new decade and had a huge hit with the modern rock anthem "The Spirit Of Radio." Judas Priest had a major breakthrough in the US with the 1980 album *British Steel*, and top twenty singles in the UK with "Breaking The Law" and "Living After Midnight." UFO, AC/DC's old drinking buddies, were still a major act despite the departure of guitarist Michael Schenker. Likewise, Thin Lizzy, who had lost Gary Moore, but still had a hit with the album *Chinatown*, even if, like Aerosmith, hard drugs were beginning to eat away at them. German band Scorpions were making waves. Motörhead—once famously described as "The Worst Band In The World"—made it big in 1980 with the album *Ace Of Spades* and the single of the same name. In their slipstream came the rising stars of the New Wave Of British Heavy Metal, led by Iron Maiden, Def Leppard, and Saxon.

Previous: **Angus Young on stage at the Donington Monsters of Rock Festival in the UK, 1981**

By the end of 1980, many of the giants of the of the seventies rock scene were falling: Aerosmith (opposite) **were addled by drug addiction; Led Zeppelin collapsed following the death of drummer John Bonham** (above), **and KISS** (left) **committed career suicide with some badly judged song choices.**

By early 1981, *Back In Black* had sold more than three million copies in the US, and with its success came another strange twist in the story of AC/DC and Bon Scott. As the album was selling millions around the world, demand for new AC/DC product skyrocketed. Consequently, on March 17, 1981, Atlantic Records gave a belated US release to the band's 1976 album *Dirty Deeds Done Dirt Cheap*—five years after it had been dismissed by Atlantic as unfit for public consumption.

It was in May, two months after the *Back In Black* tour ended, that Malcolm and Angus Young began writing and rehearsing songs for the next album. What they had was some typical AC/DC stuff—songs about sex, including the single-entendre "Let's Get It Up." There were two songs guaranteed to put a hair up the ass of the moral majority in America—"Evil Walks" and "C.O.D.," the latter an acronym for "Care Of The Devil." And there was an epic even bigger than "Hells Bells," similar in tone and feel, with a riff that Angus described as "deadly" and a title inspired by a book on Roman gladiators that Angus had read. The gladiators' motto, translated from Latin, was: "Hail, Emperor, those who are about to die salute you." AC/DC named their new anthem "For Those About To Rock (We Salute You)."

"AC/DC is still the best hard rock band in the world."

Sylvie Simmons

The rise of the new rock 'n' roll heroes. Van Halen (above left) **became the new kings of American rock, while the new wave of British heavy metal was ushered in by bands such as Iron Maiden** (above center) **and Saxon** (above right).

Such was the popularity of heavy music in 1981 that in June a new magazine was launched as an offshoot of *Sounds*, dedicated entirely to hard rock and metal, with an onomatopoeic title evoking the dissonance of a ringing power-chord: *Kerrang!* Edited by Geoff Barton, a key supporter of AC/DC in the past, the first issue had Angus on the cover in a close-up on-stage shot, bare-chested, mouth agape, long hair dripping with sweat. Inside was the 'Heavy Hundred', a list billed as "The All-Time Favourite HM Tracks as voted by readers of *Sounds*." And at number one—ahead of such classics as Led Zeppelin's "Stairway To Heaven," Rainbow's "Stargazer," Lynyrd Skynyrd's "Free Bird," Deep Purple's "Smoke On The Water," and Black Sabbath's "Paranoid"—was "Whole Lotta Rosie." It was both a tribute to Bon Scott and a confirmation of AC/DC's status. Five other AC/DC songs were in that list: "Let There Be Rock" at number eighteen, "Touch Too Much" at twenty-nine, "Highway To Hell" at thirty-nine, "Hells Bells" at forty-five, and "Walk All Over You" at one hundred. Angus recollected that he laughed when he first saw the magazine—thinking that "*Kerrang!*" was a pun on his nickname "Ang."

In July, it was back to the serious business, as AC/DC began recording in Paris, with Mutt Lange again installed as producer. They knew, all of them, that *Back In Black* was a hard act to follow, and from the outset it was Lange's aim to create an even bigger sound than before—as defined in "For Those About To Rock (We Salute You)," the album's title track and cornerstone, with its slow-rolling, gargantuan riff, monumental chorus, and a frenzied climax punctuated by deafening cannon fire. As Angus later told writer Sylvie Simmons: "It's a very inspiring song. It makes you feel powerful, and I think that's what rock 'n' roll's all about."

With Lange in pursuit of sonic perfection, work at Pathé-Marconi studios was called to a halt after just two weeks. Instead, the basic tracks were cut at a warehouse in a suburb of Paris, utilizing a mobile studio, with lead and backing vocals recorded at a different studio, Family Sound. It was a lengthy process, and a frustrating one for the band, who described a typical day as sitting around smoking while Lange worked obsessively in the control room. There was a point, Malcolm said, when it felt as if the life was getting sucked out of these songs.

A break from the studio came on August 22, when AC/DC

GOD
created
HARLEY-
DAVIDSON

returned to the UK to headline the Monsters of Rock festival at Donington Park in Leicestershire. This was the first festival of its kind, geared exclusively to denim-and-leather-clad headbangers. In 1980, the inaugural event had Rainbow topping a bill featuring Scorpions, Judas Priest, Saxon, April Wine, Riot, and Touch, and drew an audience of thirty-five thousand. In 1981, with AC/DC as the main attraction, the size of the audience almost doubled, to sixty-five thousand. The supporting cast featured Whitesnake, Blue Oyster Cult, Slade—who were enjoying a comeback long after their glory days in the seventies—plus Southern rockers Blackfoot, and new wave of British heavy metal band, More.

There was rain throughout the day and night, and recurring problems with the PA. But for AC/DC it was a landmark show—in a sense, a coronation. In the band's set there were no tasters of the forthcoming album. Instead, this show served as the late last stand of the *Back In Black* tour, and the band rolled out all the big guns: "Hells Bells," "Shot Down In Flames," "Sin City," "Back In Black," "Bad Boy Boogie," "The Jack," "What Do You Do For Money Honey," "Highway To Hell," "Whole Lotta Rosie," "Rocker," "T.N.T.," "Rock And Roll Ain't Noise Pollution," "You Shook Me All Night Long," and to finish, "Let There Be Rock."

Among the sixty-five thousand at Donington that day was AC/DC fan Joe Mackett, then aged sixteen. "I was transfixed by Angus," he said. "I couldn't keep my eyes off him. But the whole band seemed larger than life. They had an aura about them."

By the time the new album was completed in September, Peter Mensch was no longer the manager of AC/DC, although the band remained signed with Leber-Krebs. It was on November 21, ten days after a world tour began in Seattle, that *For Those About To Rock (We Salute You)* was released, with a single cannon pictured on the album's bronze-hued cover.

The sound in the title track, vast and granite-hard, carried throughout the album. This was AC/DC super-sized, exactly as Mutt Lange had intended. Only bigger did not mean better.

Left: **Eric Bloom and Buck Dharma of Blue Oyster Cult on stage at Donington, 1981**

Bottom: **Angus Young at Donington, 1981**

Opposite: **Brian Johnson on stage at the Donington Monsters of Rock Festival in the UK, 1981**

"A good-time cocktail of muscular musical simplicity, animal sexuality, a sweaty sense of spectacle, and an honest celebration of revelry, rebellion and teenage fantasy."

Garry Bushell, *Sounds*

Where *Back In Black* had a perfect balance of rock 'n' roll groove and heavy metal power, the scales tipped towards the latter on *For Those About To Rock (We Salute You).* While this album's title track demanded that kind of crunchy, metallic sound, there was a sense of overkill across the piece, and a clinical edge that proved Malcolm Young's instincts about over-production correct. There was a furious energy in the fastest track, "Snowballed," and a simmering intensity in the album's end song "Spellbound." But on the boogie numbers—"Let's Get It Up," "Evil Walks," and "C.O.D."—the band sounded a little heavy-handed, not swinging like they used to. Moreover, where *Back In Black* was a genuine all-killer-no-filler record, *For Those About To Rock (We Salute You)* had some generic, uninspired, throwaway numbers: "Inject The Venom," "Put The Finger On You," "Night Of The Long Knives," "Breaking The Rules."

The album received mixed reviews. The headline in *Sounds* was: "For Those About To Yawn." Writer Phil Bell awarded the album three out of five stars and described it as "downright samey, repetitive, tedious." Bell's conclusion was damning: "This record was worn out before I'd played it." *Rolling Stone*'s Kurt Loder took the opposite view, hailing *For Those About To Rock (We Salute You)* as "AC/DC's best album." In this, as with *Rolling Stone*'s review of *Back In Black*, was a sense that what Atlantic Records had lost with Led Zeppelin was found again in AC/DC. Loder stated: "AC/DC are the real thing, perhaps the purest major practitioners of hot and snotty rock since Led Zeppelin lumbered off the boards. All ten tunes are aimed straight at the group's testosterone-plagued audience. What you've got here is one unbeatable rock 'n' roll band."

It was a sentiment echoed by Sylvie Simmons in an on-the-road story for *Creem*. Simmons joined the AC/DC tour in Indianapolis on November 28, when the band played to seventeen thousand at the Market Square Arena. "AC/DC is still the best hard rock band in the world," she wrote. "And in a country where statistics show one American goes deaf every fifteen minutes, AC/DC got through a year's worth in one night."

Brian Johnson spoke to Simmons about the astonishing success of *Back In Black.* "I couldn't believe it," he said. "I thought, fucking hell, what have I done? Whatever I did I'm going to keep on doing it!" He also spoke of his pride in the new album's dirtiest song, "Let's Get It Up." "Filth," he said. "Pure filth! We're a filthy band." It was Angus who took the credit, or perhaps the blame, for the

Previous: **Angus Young** (left) **and Brian Johnson on tour in the UK, 1981**

Above: **Monsters of Rock headliners, AC/DC, 1981**

Opposite: **Angus Young live on stage with his Gibson SG guitar at the Cow Palace in San Francisco, USA, on February 16, 1982**

album's two potentially controversial songs, "C.O.D." and "Evil Walks." "I came up with 'Care of the Devil,'" he said cheerfully. "And with 'Evil Walks,' I said, 'Those chords sound dead evil.' It's just a catchy title. We're not black magic Satanists or whatever you call it. I don't drink blood. I may wear black underwear now and again but that's it." He laughed in the face of the moral majority: "They've been bothering us for years," he said. "Some people are sick. If they want to go God-bothering they should go God-bother the Pope. He needs it. We don't."

On December 2, when the tour reached New York City, a prediction made by Bon Scott back in 1979 became a reality. AC/DC headlined at Madison Square Garden for the first time. In the set that night were nine songs the band had made with Bon, and eight made with Brian—six from *Back In Black*, plus "For Those About To Rock (We Salute You)" and "Put The Finger On You." Another first for AC/DC, another career milestone, came at the end of the year. For all the millions that *Back In Black* had sold, and all the time that it had been in the US top ten, it never reached the top. On December 21, *For Those About To Rock (We Salute You)* was the number one album in America. In both the UK and Australia, it had made number three.

The tour rolled on for another year, with a three-month break in the spring of 1982. It was in September that the band returned to the UK, a little over a year since their appearance at Monsters of Rock. There were seventeen dates in the UK, including three in Newcastle, on Brian Johnson's home turf, and six nights in London, four at the Hammersmith Odeon and two more at Wembley Arena. The opening night at Birmingham NEC was reviewed by *Sounds'* Garry Bushell, who summed up the band's mass appeal: "A good-time cocktail of muscular musical simplicity, animal sexuality, a sweaty sense of spectacle, and an honest celebration of revelry, rebellion and teenage fantasy." He concluded, with tongue in cheek: "The Devil has still got all the best tunes!"

When the tour ended in Zurich, Switzerland on December 12, AC/DC were indisputably the biggest hard rock act in the world. *Back In Black* had raised them to the top. *For Those About To Rock (We Salute You)* kept them there. To an extent, the phenomenal success of *Back In Black* made AC/DC bulletproof, but it was also an album they could never match again, a once-in-a-lifetime triumph. And in the years that followed *For Those About To Rock (We Salute You)*, there would be troubled times for AC/DC, both professional and personal, starting with the exits of two hugely important figures—the producer who had done so much to transform AC/DC into superstars, and the drummer who had powered this band, through all the highs and lows, since 1975.

Opposite: **Malcolm Young playing live on stage with his favored Gretsch guitar at Donington, 1981**

FOR THOSE ABOUT TO ROCK (WE SALUTE YOU)

Released: November 23, 1981
Recorded: May–September 1981, Mobile One Studios, Paris and Family Sound Studios, London
Label: Albert Productions/Atlantic Records
Producer: Robert John "Mutt" Lange

All tracks written by Angus Young, Malcolm Young, and Brian Johnson.

SIDE ONE
"For Those About To Rock (We Salute You)"
"Put The Finger On You"
"Let's Get It Up"
"Inject The Venom"
"Snowballed"

SIDE TWO
"Evil Walks"
"C.O.D."
"Breaking The Rules"
"Night Of The Long Knives"
"Spellbound"

PERSONNEL
Brian Johnson—lead vocals
Angus Young—lead guitar
Malcolm Young—rhythm guitar, backing vocals
Cliff Williams—bass guitar, backing vocals
Phil Rudd—drums, percussion

For Those About To Rock (We Salute You) was the first AC/DC album to hit number one in America. In both the UK and Australia it made number three. It is the final AC/DC album to be produced by Robert John "Mutt" Lange.

Atlantic also released *Dirty Deeds Done Dirt Cheap* in 1981, five years after the original international release.

NIKE

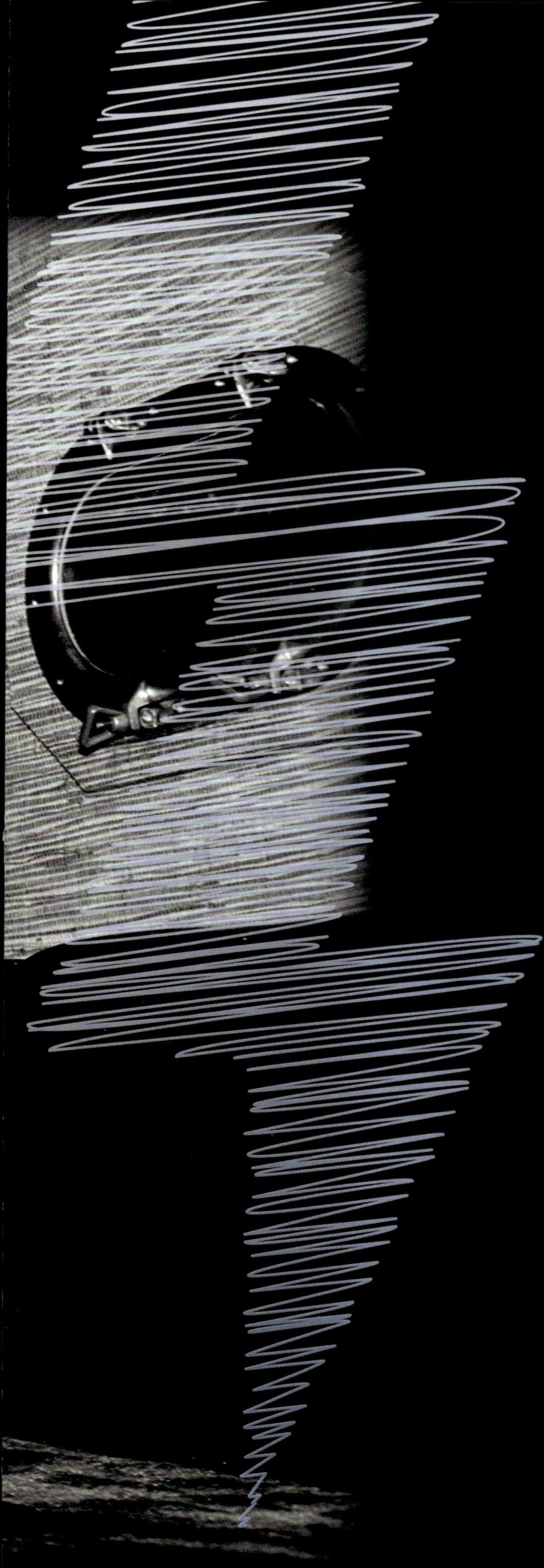

A Hard Road

"The lads got concerned. They'd seen Bon go, and I was fucking up. I knew I had to get it out of my system if I was ever to get back."

Malcolm Young

When AC/DC returned to Nassau and Compass Point Studios in early 1983, where *Back In Black* was recorded three years earlier, Mutt Lange was no longer a part of the team. The producer had delivered three huge hit albums for the band, but the last of them, *For Those About To Rock (We Salute You)*, had been too long in the making, and its sound too overblown, for Malcolm Young's liking. He wanted to get back to basics, to strip it all down and make a raw, no-frills rock 'n' roll record, like *Let There Be Rock* and *Powerage*. To this end, the new album was produced by the band—in effect, Malcolm. But in a smart move, he called in two old hands to help out. His big brother George Young and 'The Dutch Damager' Harry Vanda, the guys who had produced those early AC/DC albums, knew what Malcolm was after. And he got it.

The album was named *Flick Of The Switch*, and it was in its own way as pure and uncompromising a statement of artistic integrity as AC/DC ever made. In reaction to the albums that Lange had produced, *Flick Of The Switch* was, in Malcolm's words, "thrown together real quick." The songs were simplistic even by AC/DC's own standards—rough and tough, with choruses shouted out like a bunch of drunkards, the way they used to before Mutt polished up their act.

The production was bone-dry. The whole thing was brutal in its minimalism. And as AC/DC laid down this heavy statement of intent, a tense relationship between Malcolm Young and Phil Rudd was coming to a head.

Rudd was one of the best drummers in the business. He was to AC/DC what John Bonham was to Led Zeppelin, and what Charlie Watts was to The Rolling Stones. When he and Malcolm played, they were as tight as Charlie Watts and Keith Richards. However, by 1983 something had come between them—what was reported, euphemistically as "a personal issue." It was also rumored that Rudd had developed problems with alcohol and drugs. There was nothing wrong with his drumming, his playing on the album was rock solid, but with a tour of North America beginning in October, a decision had to be made. As Angus Young stated in a 1990 interview with *Kerrang!* writer Howard Johnson: "We were due to start in the States straight afterwards. He (Rudd) would have gone overboard and done something drastic to himself or to someone else."

With Phil Rudd out of the band, various auditions for a new drummer were held in the Bahamas, then in New York while the album was being mixed, and later in London. There were hundreds of applicants, and some big names were considered, including Simon Kirke of Free and Bad Company, and Paul Thompson of Roxy Music, but instead the job went to a relative unknown who was still a month away from his twentieth birthday. Simon Wright, born on June 19, 1963 in Oldham, Lancashire, had cut his teeth with two low-level heavy metal bands, A II Z and Tytan. While inexperienced, Wright came with no baggage and knew his place.

Previous: **Malcolm Young on the AC/DC tour bus, 1985**

Right: **With Phil Rudd out of the band, auditions for a new drummer included some big names, such as Simon Kirke of Free and Bad Company** (pictured).

Top: **Simon Wright** (left), **Phil Rudd's replacement and Brian Johnson, 1983**

Left: **Joe Elliott of Def Leppard during the first leg of their groundbreaking *Pyromania* tour in 1983**

Most important of all, he hit the drums hard. Rudd's departure was announced just before *Flick Of The Switch* was released on August 15, 1983. The cover art—a sketch of Angus in a literal interpretation of the album title—was indicative of the spartan music within.

A five-star review in *Sounds* described the album as "electrifying," but it was *NME* writer Barney Hoskyns who delivered a more telling verdict, placing this album, and the band, in a broader context. On one hand, Hoskyns praised AC/DC's single-minded vision: "What continues to impress is their simplicity and intrinsic modesty. Effectively they carry on working the same song year in year out and still something as titanically oafish as 'This House Is On Fire' lurches out of the maelstrom." On the other, he suggested that AC/DC were beginning to sound outdated. "It's the new super-rock producers who are modelling today's guitar sound," Hoskyns stated, citing Mutt Lange as the leading exponent. "On *Flick Of The Switch*, AC/DC are producing themselves, and the guitars are very boring." The real stinger was the comparison to a band that had once been AC/DC's support act, and had gone on to make, with Lange, one of the game-changing rock albums of 1983. "AC/DC's music," he said, "is now superseded by Def Leppard."

As Leppard singer Joe Elliott has frequently stated, the blueprint for his band was "AC/DC meets Queen." Leppard's first album with Lange, 1981's *High 'n' Dry*, had a sound and a riff-based attack that was heavily influenced by AC/DC and *Highway To*

AC/DC returned to Donington Park on August 18, 1984, for their second headlining appearance at the Monsters of Rock festival (above left). **The heavyweight bill also featured rising stars, Mötley Crüe** (above center: **Vince Neil of Mötley Crüe is pictured on the right, backstage) and Accept** (above right), **Germany's biggest heavy metal band since the Scorpions.**

Hell in particular. However, with the album *Pyromania*, released in January 1983, Leppard and Lange elevated hard rock to a new level, with a huge production utilizing cutting-edge technology, multi-tracked vocal harmonies, and pop hooks at every turn. Moreover, Def Leppard were not the only major rock act breaking new ground. ZZ Top had similar tastes to AC/DC's—rooted in the simple virtues of hard rock, boogie, and blues—but on the Texan trio's 1983 album *Eliminator* their signature sound was modernized to brilliant effect, with synthesizers and sequencers enhancing their gritty rock 'n' roll on hit songs such as "Gimme All Your Lovin'" and "Sharp Dressed Man."

What AC/DC had in *Flick Of The Switch* was a badass rock record with no hope of radio play. By the end of 1983, *Pyromania* had sold six million copies in the US, *Eliminator* five million. *Flick Of The Switch* reached number fifteen on the US *Billboard* chart, but sold just half a million. In the UK the album fared much better, peaking at number four. And while this was no *Back In Black*, it remains the band's most underrated album. A couple of tracks, "Landslide" and "Brain Shake," are no more than fillers. But the monumental appeal of "This House Is On Fire"—"titanically oafish," as Barney Hoskyns put it—carries through the title track, "Rising Power," "Deep In The Hole," and "Bedlam In Belgium." There is, in "Badlands," one of the meanest-sounding numbers the band have ever recorded. And there are two anthems in the classic AC/DC tradition—"Nervous Shakedown," with a great, wristy riff from Malcolm, and "Guns For Hire," its jolting intro played by Angus as if he had a cattle-prod up his backside.

It was business as usual as the band rolled through arenas in North America from October 11 to December 16. But there were no dates in Australia or Japan on the *Flick Of The Switch* tour, and it was only after a break of eight months that the tour was completed with a run of festivals and arena shows in Europe—among them, a return to Donington Park on August 18, 1984 for the band's second headlining appearance at Monsters of Rock.

It was a heavyweight bill: AC/DC, Van Halen, Ozzy Osbourne, Gary Moore, Y&T, Accept, and Mötley Crüe. Arguably, it was the strongest line-up ever assembled for Monsters of Rock. Mötley Crüe were rising stars, the self-proclaimed "Bad Boys of Hollywood," with an over-the-top glam image and a major hit album in *Shout At The Devil*. Accept were Germany's best and biggest heavy metal band since the Scorpions. San Franciscan hard rockers Y&T had made their name in the UK with kick-ass albums such as *Earthshaker* and *Black Tiger*. Gary Moore, a guitarist who bowed to no one, was riding high as a solo artist. Ozzy Osbourne, the legendary madman of rock, had now eclipsed his former band Black Sabbath. While Van Halen had risen to dizzying heights, having headlined the US Festival in California in 1983 before an audience of 350,000.

Ahead of the show, there was much talk in the UK rock press of an intense rivalry between AC/DC and Van Halen, and of a

"What continues to impress is their simplicity and intrinsic modesty."

Barney Hoskyns, *NME*

showdown between the guitar heroes, Angus and Eddie. Angus played it down when he spoke to Mat Snow of the *NME* "Van Halen competition?" Angus mused. "Nah. One guy makes a car, another makes a car. You've got a Rolls Royce, you got a Jaguar. I don't see that as competition—people just go out and buy 'em."

On the day, honors were even. In the afternoon, under a hot sun, Gary Moore, in a vivid red jumpsuit, laid down the gauntlet for the other guitarists to follow, playing explosively on "Rockin' And Rollin'," and beautifully on "Parisienne Walkways." Ozzy, the people's hero, threatened to upstage both Van Halen and AC/DC by sheer force of personality. Van Halen went off like a rocket with an opening double-whammy of "Unchained" and "Hot For Teacher," Eddie playing at superhuman level, David Lee Roth all swagger and razzle-dazzle. At times they blew hot and cold—losing momentum with a drum solo that came too early and a guitar solo that was too long—but peaking with the synth-powered hit "Jump," in which Roth's acrobatic leap from the drum riser drew a huge roar from the crowd.

Finally, with darkness closing in, the funny little guy in the school uniform appeared on a podium high above the stage, playing a manic solo to deafening cheers, then duckwalking down a ramp, firing off the intro to "Guns For Hire," and arriving center stage with perfect timing as the band locked into that meaty riff. It was a brilliant entrance, and from there on in it was like shooting fish in a barrel, as AC/DC rolled out the heavy artillery: "Shoot To Thrill," "Sin City," "Back In Black," "Bad Boy Boogie," "Rock And Roll Ain't Noise Pollution," "Flick Of The Switch," "Hells Bells," "The Jack," "Have A Drink On Me," "Highway To Hell," "Dirty Deeds Done Dirt Cheap," "Whole Lotta Rosie," "Let There Be Rock," "T.N.T.," and the grand finale, "For Those About To Rock (We Salute You)." For all the pre-match hype, AC/DC had not been outgunned at Monsters of Rock. What followed the festival was sobering; shows in France in September were far from sold-out.

With the final dates of the *Flick Of The Switch* tour set for January at the first Rock in Rio festival in Brazil, the band traveled to Montreux in Switzerland in October to resume work on the songs that had been written earlier in the year. Among the songs they banged out in Montreux, few would have made the cut for *Flick Of The Switch*, let alone the great albums that came before it.

It was also in October that Atlantic Records released archive material from AC/DC in the form of a mini-album, *'74 Jailbreak*, featuring five tracks from the early days with Bon that had never before been released outside Australia: "Jailbreak," "You Ain't Got A Hold On Me," "Show Business," "Soul Stripper," and "Baby, Please Don't Go." Work on the new album was delayed as the band took a break before the last stop on what had been a long, on-off tour.

Rock in Rio was a huge event spread over ten days, with AC/DC as one of the headline acts alongside Queen, Rod Stewart, and Yes. AC/DC performed two shows there, on January 15 and 19. On the first night, they played to fifty thousand people. On the second night, the size of the audience was estimated at a quarter of a million. It was a triumphant end to the tour.

Soon after, the band returned to Montreux to finish the new album at Mountain Studios. With Malcolm and Angus as co-producers, this album, titled *Fly On The Wall*, was in the same vein as *Flick Of The Switch*—hard, unrefined, nothing fancy. As writers, Malcolm and Angus were running on empty. Songs such as "Danger," "Stand Up," and "Hell Or High Water" were as tired and generic as their titles implied. A couple of dirty-joke numbers, "Sink The Pink" and "Playing With Girls," lightened the mood. Only one song, "Shake Your Foundations," had the kind of groove and big chorus that had come so easily to AC/DC in the past. There was an edge of desperation in the way that Brian Johnson screeched through this stuff. And in their role as producers, Malcolm and Angus made their band sound like a tribute act on a bad night.

Fly On The Wall was released in June 1985, and peaked at number seven in the UK and number thirty-two in the US, where it was eventually certified gold. A review of the album in *Rolling Stone*

Ahead of Monsters of Rock, there was much talk in the UK rock press of an intense rivalry between AC/DC and Van Halen. David Lee Roth's acrobatic leap on stage (above) **drew a huge roar from the audience, but Angus Young's manic guitar playing** (left) **proved that AC/DC still had the edge.**

by Tim Holmes offered praise, of a sort, for a band sticking to its guns by playing what he called "the dumbest, most irresistibly repetitive chords in the lexicon." When Malcolm Young spoke to me in 2003, all he could muster in defense of this record was the most backhanded of compliments. "Even though it might be one of our worst," he said, "it's still fucking okay."

Just five years since they had shaken the world with *Back In Black*, AC/DC sounded burned out with *Fly On The Wall*, and there was worse—much worse—to follow. In August 1985, on the eve of a US tour, the band's name made headlines in a story that shocked the world. Since June 1984, a killer named by the media as the "Night Stalker" had committed a series of brutal murders in and around Los Angeles and San Francisco. The man arrested in August 1985 and charged for these crimes was Richard Ramirez, aged twenty-five, from El Paso, Texas. In the newspaper reports that followed it was alleged by Ramirez that he had been influenced by the AC/DC song "Night Prowler." One headline read: "AC/DC MUSIC MADE ME KILL 16." It was also revealed that an AC/DC baseball cap was found in Ramirez's home after his arrest.

In an interview in 1991, Angus Young said to me: "Some people in America got real mad about the lyrics to 'Night Prowler.' Some guy claimed he was influenced by the song. But we didn't take it

so seriously." Malcolm Young and Brian Johnson also addressed this subject when I interviewed them in 2003. Malcolm voiced his contempt for Ramirez and for the newspapers that implicated AC/DC. "Your answer to that is, did you search his stomach for a McDonald's?" he said. "If you're a wacko, you're a wacko."

The band focused instead on the business at hand, the *Fly On The Wall* tour. The tour would run from September 1985 to February 1986 and if the album was a dud, AC/DC were still a big draw, playing all the major venues: Madison Square Garden, the LA Forum, and two nights at London's Wembley Arena. Then in May 1986 came a brand new single in which the band rediscovered their mojo.

"Who Made Who" was the title track from an unorthodox AC/DC album—the soundtrack to the horror movie *Maximum Overdrive*, written and directed by Stephen King, the bestselling author and devoted AC/DC fan. The album was in part a best-of collection, featuring classic tracks including "Hells Bells," "You Shook Me All Night Long," "For Those About To Rock (We Salute You)," and one deep cut from the Bon era in "Ride On." In addition, there were three previously unreleased tracks: "Who Made Who," plus the instrumentals "D.T." and "Chase The Ace." While the instrumentals were unremarkable except in novelty value, "Who Made Who" was a doozy, with a funky riff, and the kind of big-hitting chorus that was so sorely lacking on the previous album. Significantly, it was a track produced by Harry Vanda and George Young. In this, perhaps, a tacit admission from Malcolm and Angus of the mess they had made of *Fly On The Wall*. "Who Made Who"

Above: **AC/DC at the beach in Ipanema, Brazil during the South American leg of the *Fly On The Wall* tour, January 1985:** (L–R) **Brian Johnson, Cliff Williams, Simon Wright, Angus Young, Malcolm Young**

Opposite: **AC/DC on stage at the Rock in Rio music festival in January 1985**

was one of AC/DC's most successful singles, reaching number nine in Australia and number sixteen in the UK. The album was also a major hit, although the tour in support of it was limited to forty-three shows in North America.

In 1987, AC/DC laid low. It was only at the end of the year that the band set to work on a new album at Studio Miraval in the southeast of France. Yet, in their absence, AC/DC's influence remained powerful in two of the bands that defined hard rock music in that year. The Cult, with the album *Electric*, made a radical transformation from goth rock to full-on heavy metal, and in the album's opening track, "Wild Flower," was a riff lifted straight out of AC/DC's "Rock 'N' Roll Singer." Guns N' Roses, the wildest band to come out of Los Angeles since Mötley Crüe, cited AC/DC as an inspiration along with Aerosmith, the Stones, the Sex Pistols, and Hanoi Rocks. When they played their first UK shows in June 1987—three nights at the famous old Marquee Club, where AC/DC had performed back in 1976—they encored on the last night with "Whole Lotta Rosie." For Guns N' Roses singer Axl Rose, there would be a major part to play in AC/DC's story many years later. Likewise, Rick Rubin, the producer of The Cult's *Electric*, would be drawn into AC/DC's orbit in the nineties.

In February 1988, the release of a new AC/DC album, *Blow Up Your Video*, came with heightened anticipation. "Who Made Who" had promised a return to form. Moreover, this was the band's first album since *Powerage* to be produced by Vanda and Young. What the band delivered in *Blow Up Your Video* was solid enough: nowhere near *Powerage*, but a whole lot better than *Fly On The Wall*. The album began with a bang—the hard and fast "Heatseeker"—and the

Below: **Brian Johnson and Angus Young on stage at London's Wembley Arena in the UK on January 17, 1986 as part of the *Fly On The Wall* tour**

Above: **Angus doppelgangers on the video set of "Who Made Who," 1986**

Right: **Billy Duffy** (left) **and Ian Astbury of The Cult. Their 1987 album, *Electric* was heavily influenced by AC/DC, as were dangerous new band Guns N' Roses** (below) **who cited AC/DC as an inspiration.**

Right: **Malcolm Young backstage at London's Wembley Arena on the *Blow Up Your Video* tour, 1988**

band's rhythmic power was evident in tracks such as "Meanstreak," "Go Zone," "Some Sin For Nuthin'," and "That's The Way I Wanna Rock 'n' Roll." There were some songs that rang hollow—"Kissin' Dynamite," "Two's Up," "Ruff Stuff," "This Means War"—but a review in *Rolling Stone* accentuated the positives. Critic Jim Farber noted AC/DC's renewed "hip status," citing the band's influence in the records that Rick Rubin had produced for The Cult and rap-rock agitators the Beastie Boys. But as Farber declared: "The original riff masters still rule. In fact, the riffs here add up to the band's catchiest work since its classic album *Back In Black*."

Blow Up Your Video was a big hit—number two in the UK and Australia, number twelve in the US. Another huge world tour began in Australia with five sold-out shows in Perth, six in Melbourne, and five more in Sydney. However, when the band reached North America in May, Malcolm Young was not with them. After years of heavy drinking, he ended up in rehab. His replacement on the tour was his nephew, Stevie Young, whose group Starfighters had opened for AC/DC on the *Back In Black* tour. Speaking in 1991, Angus said: "We were already committed to touring the States, so we got Stevie in. He fitted right in after just ten days' rehearsal." Angus was also brutally honest in what he told me about Malcolm's struggle with alcoholism. "Over the years, Malcolm had given alcohol a hell of a beating," he said. "Finally he decided he wanted to dry out. He didn't want to become another casualty."

Malcolm himself was equally candid when I interviewed him in 2003, recalling the dark days of 1988, what had led him there, and how the shadow of Bon's death hung over him. He said of his decision to withdraw from the US tour in 1988: "You just don't see it coming. We'd have two Bloody Marys at the hotel in the morning, then straight to the airport and into the bar. On the plane you go, 'I'll have a screwdriver,' and you get two! We all went that way, except Ang, who was teetotal. It hit me big time." He also spoke of the effect that this had on those closest to him, and of the depths to which he had sunk. "The lads got concerned," he said. "They'd seen Bon go, and I was fucking up. I knew I had to get it out of my system if I was ever to get back."

FLICK OF THE SWITCH

Released: August 15, 1983
Recorded: April 1983, Compass Point Studios, Nassau, Bahamas
Label: Albert Productions, Atlantic, Sony
Producer: AC/DC

All tracks written by Angus Young, Malcolm Young, and Brian Johnson.

SIDE ONE
"Rising Power"
"This House Is On Fire"
"Flick Of The Switch"
"Nervous Shakedown"
"Landslide"

SIDE TWO
"Guns For Hire"
"Deep In The Hole"
"Bedlam In Belgium"
"Badlands"
"Brain Shake"

PERSONNEL
Brian Johnson—lead vocals
Angus Young—lead guitar
Malcolm Young—rhythm guitar, backing vocals
Cliff Williams—bass guitar, backing vocals
Phil Rudd—drums

Additional personnel
Brent Richardson—cover art, based on an original drawing by Angus Young

The cover art for *Flick Of The Switch* features a sketch of Angus in a literal interpretation of the album title and reflected the simple back-to-basics music within. *Flick of The Switch* was the last album to feature drummer Phil Rudd before his eleven-year break from the band.

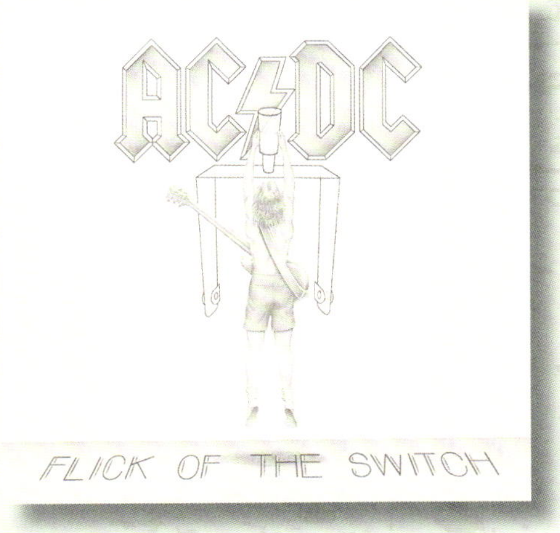

'74 JAILBREAK

Released: October 15, 1984
Recorded: 1974–76
Label: Atlantic
Producer: Harry Vanda, George Young

All tracks written by Angus Young, Malcolm Young, and Bon Scott

SIDE ONE
"Jailbreak"
"You Ain't Got A Hold On Me"
"Show Business"

SIDE TWO
"Soul Stripper" (Young, Young)
"Baby, Please Don't Go" (Big Joe Williams)

PERSONNEL
Bon Scott—lead vocals
Angus Young—lead guitar, rhythm guitar
Malcolm Young—rhythm guitar, lead guitar, backing vocals
George Young—bass guitar, backing vocals, drums
Rob Bailey—bass guitar
Mark Evans—bass guitar on "Jailbreak"
Phil Rudd—drums and percussion on "Jailbreak"
Tony Currenti—drums and percussion on "You Ain't Got A Hold On Me," "Show Business," and "Soul Stripper"
Peter Clack—drums and percussion on "Baby, Please Don't Go"

'74 Jailbreak is a mini-album featuring five tracks from the early days with Bon that had never before been released outside Australia.

FLY ON THE WALL

Released: June 28, 1985
Recorded: October 1984–February 1985, Mountain Studios, Montreux, Switzerland
Label: Albert Productions, Atlantic Records
Producer: Angus Young and Malcolm Young

All tracks written by Malcolm Young, Angus Young and Brian Johnson.

SIDE ONE
"Fly On The Wall"
"Shake Your Foundations"
"First Blood"
"Danger"
"Sink The Pink"

SIDE TWO
"Playing With Girls"
"Stand Up"
"Hell Or High Water"
"Back In Business"
"Send For The Man"

PERSONNEL
Brian Johnson—lead vocals
Angus Young—lead guitar
Malcolm Young—rhythm guitar, backing vocals
Cliff Williams—bass guitar, backing vocals
Simon Wright—drums, percussion

Additional personnel
Bob Defrin—art direction
Todd Schorr—cover illustration

WHO MADE WHO

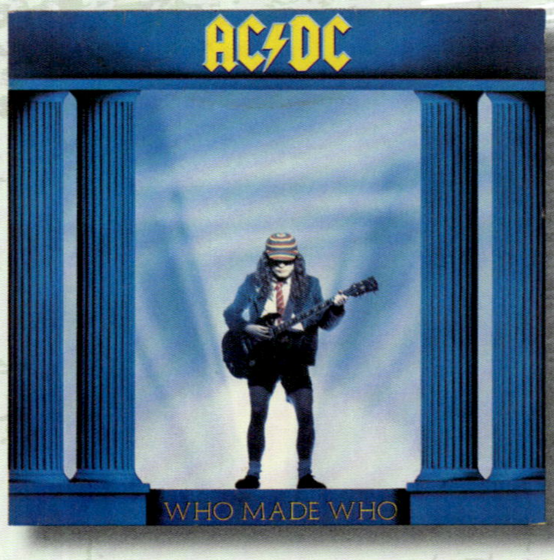

Released: May 24, 1986
Recorded: December 1985
Label: Albert Productions
Producer: Robert John "Mutt" Lange, Harry Vanda, George Young, Angus Young, Malcolm Young

All tracks written by Malcolm Young, Angus Young and Brian Johnson, except where noted.

Who Made Who is a soundtrack album to Stephen King's horror movie *Maximum Overdrive.*

SIDE ONE
"Who Made Who"
"You Shook Me All Night Long" (from *Back In Black*)
"D.T." (Young, Young; Instrumental)
"Sink the Pink" (from *Fly On The Wall*)
"Ride On" (from *Dirty Deeds Done Dirt Cheap*) Young, Young, Bon Scott

SIDE TWO
"Hells Bells" (from *Back In Black*)
"Shake Your Foundations" (from *Fly On The Wall*)
"Chase The Ace" (Young, Young; Instrumental)
"For Those About To Rock (We Salute You)" (from *For Those About To Rock (We Salute You)*

PERSONNEL
Brian Johnson—lead vocals
Angus Young—lead guitar
Malcolm Young—rhythm guitar, backing vocals
Cliff Williams—bass guitar, backing vocals
Simon Wright—drums
Bon Scott—lead vocals on "Ride On"
Phil Rudd—drums on "You Shook Me All Night Long", "Ride On", "Hells Bells" and "For Those About To Rock (We Salute You)"
Mark Evans—bass guitar and backing vocals on "Ride On"

Additional personnel
George Bodnar—cover photography

BLOW UP YOUR VIDEO

Released: January 18 1988, February 1, 1988 (US)
Recorded: August–September 1987, Miraval Studio, Le Val, France
Label: Albert Productions
Producer: Harry Vanda, George Young

All tracks written by Malcolm Young, Angus Young, and Brian Johnson.

SIDE ONE
"Heatseeker"
"That's The Way I Wanna Rock 'n' Roll"
"Meanstreak"
"Go Zone"
"Kissin' Dynamite"

SIDE TWO
"Nick Of Time"
"Some Sin For Nuthin'"
"Ruff Stuff"
"Two's Up"
"This Means War"

Above (L–R): **Brian Johnson, Simon Wright, Cliff Williams, Malcolm Young, and Angus Young in Australia 1988, where *Blow Up Your Video* was certified platinum**

PERSONNEL
Brian Johnson—lead vocals
Angus Young—lead guitar
Malcolm Young—rhythm guitar, backing vocals
Cliff Williams—bass guitar, backing vocals
Simon Wright—drums, percussion

Additional personnel
Bill Smith Studio—art direction
Gered Mankowitz—cover photography

Blow Up Your Video was the band's first album since *Powerage* to be produced by Vanda and Young.

I'm Like Two Different People—Sometimes Three!

"Once you go into being The Schoolboy it's pretty hard to come off it."

Angus Young

There were a number of a reasons why AC/DC decided to take a year out after the *Blow Up Your Video* tour ended on November 13, 1988. Despite lying low the previous year, the band had been on the album and tour treadmill for as long as they could remember. Brian Johnson was in the process of a divorce. Most significant of all, Malcolm Young was in recovery.

For drummer Simon Wright, still only twenty-five and full of ambition, it was frustrating to be out of action. He waited for the best part of a year before he accepted an invitation to play drums on an album by Dio, the band led by former Rainbow and Black Sabbath singer Ronnie James Dio. The album, *Lock Up The Wolves*, was recorded in Reno, Nevada, in late 1989. Wright subsequently decided to leave AC/DC and join Dio on a permanent basis.

Wright's replacement was Chris Slade, then in his early forties, and with a bald head to prove it. What he also had was an impressive pedigree.

Born on October 3, 1946 in the Welsh town of Pontypridd, Slade was just a kid of sixteen when he played in the sixties beat group Tommy Scott and The Senators, fronted by the singer who went on to worldwide fame as Tom Jones. In the seventies Slade was a member of Manfred Mann's Earth Band. In the eighties he worked with Uriah Heep, Gary Numan, and Pink Floyd's David Gilmour before joining the short-lived supergroup, The Firm, led by former Led Zeppelin guitarist Jimmy Page and ex-Free and Bad Company singer Paul Rodgers. Slade was a member of Gary Moore's band when the call came from AC/DC. It was an offer he could not refuse.

Previous: **AC/DC 1990. Chris Slade** (second right) **replaced Simon Wright as drummer.**

Left: **Malcolm Young performing live on home ground in Australia, 1991**

Slade was an upgrade on Simon Wright, with more of a natural feel for the kind of rock 'n' roll that AC/DC played. He joined a band that was rejuvenated after a lengthy hiatus. The songs that Malcolm and Angus had written were their strongest since *Flick Of The Switch*. They had also written all the lyrics, with Brian Johnson on temporary leave of duty due to complications in his divorce. There was one song that really stuck out. It was based on a fast-fingered guitar lick that came to Angus more by accident than design, while, in his words, "just fiddling with my left hand." Malcolm had a rhythm part that fitted just right, and from this a new epic was created. They named it "Thunderstruck." "It seemed to have a good ring to it," Angus explained. "AC/DC equals power." A chant of "Thunder!" was added to the intro for added dramatic effect. The song was destined to become an AC/DC classic.

The band had intended to stick with Harry Vanda and George Young as producers, but after George withdrew from the project due to personal issues, they turned instead to Canadian producer Bruce Fairbairn. In the preceding years, Fairbairn had worked on a number of multi-million-selling rock albums, including the two that made Bon Jovi a household name, *Slippery When Wet* and *New Jersey*, and those that revived Aerosmith's career, *Permanent Vacation* and *Pump*. In May 1990, AC/DC began recording their album, *The Razors Edge* at Little Mountain Sound Studios in Vancouver, Fairbairn's hometown. What came out of it was the best-sounding record the band had made since Mutt Lange was their producer.

It was front-loaded with four great tracks. "Thunderstruck" is a juggernaut, the most over-the-top AC/DC song since "For Those About To Rock (We Salute You)," the chanting reminiscent of the early classic "T.N.T.," and Brian Johnson singing in a manner that Angus once described to me as "like somebody dropped a truck on his foot". "Fire Your Guns" is an all-out attack at breakneck speed. "Moneytalks" is a catchy, freewheeling rock 'n' roll tune like something off *Back In Black*. While the album's title track has heaviness of a different kind, all bad vibes and dark power. Across the remaining eight tracks are some routine numbers such as "Rock Your Heart Out," "Shot Of Love," and "Are You Ready;" and a joke song, "Mistress For Christmas," that stinks like a wet dog. But there was enough in those first four songs, "Thunderstruck" especially, to make this AC/DC's biggest album in almost a decade.

Released on September 24, 1990, *The Razors Edge* hit number two in the US chart, and number four in the UK. The review of the album by *Rolling Stone*'s John Mendelsohn was withering in its accuracy: "In spite of the fact that guitarist Angus Young, the straw

Left: **Angus Young, mid-duckwalk, on stage in London during *The Razors Edge* tour, 1991**

Far left: **Still at the top of their game, AC/DC again headlined Monsters of Rock on August 17, 1991. Also on the bill were Metallica** (above left), **Mötley Crüe, Queensrÿche, and The Black Crowes** (above right).

that stirs AC/DC's drink, is over thirty now and Johnson is past forty, AC/DC can think of little to sing about but the joys of sex, rock 'n' roll and general loutishness. In fact, with *The Razors Edge*, AC/DC sets a new record for the longest career without a single new idea." However, for the band, these were badges of honor. Songs about sex, rock 'n' roll, and general loutishness were loved by millions of AC/DC fans around the world.

The Razors Edge tour was a twelve-month marathon in which the band experienced so many highs but also another heartbreaking tragedy. The tour's first leg began in North America on November 2 at the Worcester Centrum in Massachusetts. With Malcolm back in business, and Chris Slade on debut, there was another new face in the band that night—bass player Paul Gregg filling in for Cliff Williams, who was forced to miss a few gigs due to illness. The new opening number was "Thunderstruck," and in a twenty-one-song set list, alongside the staple tracks that would never be dropped were three more from *The Razors Edge*, recent hits "Who Made Who" and "Heatseeker," and two great old songs that had been out of the set for years, "Jailbreak" and "High Voltage."

It was on the second leg in North America that the tragedy occurred. During AC/DC's performance at Salt Lake City's Salt Palace arena on January 18, 1991, three fans were killed in a crush near the stage. All three were in their teens: Jimmie Boyd and Curtis Child both aged fourteen, and Elizabeth Glausi, nineteen. The sense of loss within the band was expressed in a message of "heartfelt sympathy" to the families of the victims. The tour continued as scheduled, but as Brian Johnson later said, the impact of what happened in Salt Lake City left him unable to sleep for a week.

In March and April, the band toured in Europe and the UK, playing to sold-out arenas, with three dates in Birmingham and in London. Some of these shows were recorded for a live album. The third and final leg in North America ran from May 24 to July 14. The biggest shows came in August and September, when AC/DC headlined a series of Monsters of Rock festivals, including a return to Donington Park on August 17, where they were joined by Metallica, Mötley Crüe, Queensrÿche, and The Black Crowes.

Ahead of the Donington show, I interviewed Angus for *Kerrang!* He began by talking about the frantic pace of his life, and how it had been that way ever since the band started. "For us," he said, "it's been rush, rush, rush. Last year, for the first time, I sat down and said, what happened to the last seventeen years?" He spoke of the physical toll of playing live, at full-tilt, night after night, for months on end. "We don't get much rest on the road," he explained, "with days running into the next. After a show I just wind down for a couple of hours. I try to hide, just in case somebody grabs me and says, 'Hey, you didn't play this song tonight!' I need time to relax. I wouldn't like to be the 'Angus Young on stage' all the time. I'd be burnt out inside a week. On the last American tour my weight went down to ninety-four pounds. I was a hundred and nine pounds when we started."

Angus admitted that he still got the shakes before a show. "Sometimes it is frightening," he said. "But you've got to psych yourself up a bit, give yourself a good kick up the ass. Being older, Malcolm is the best person to give me a kick. He'll just say to me, 'Those feet look a little slow tonight.' Usually, once I've got the uniform on, I'm okay. I'm on edge, nervous, but I'm not in a panic. At least I don't have to put on make-up. I sport my own pimples. But because of nerves, I've tripped over and even forgotten to do my zipper up a few times. I go for a pee and forget. Last thing before I go on stage, I always go for a piss and then have a cigarette. If you ever see my shorts smoking, you know I didn't put it out right!"

He described the euphoria of playing live. "On stage, I'm on my own little cloud. Adrenalin takes over. It's like when you take off in an aeroplane. It's exhilarating. When you're firing well, it's the best feeling in the world. And when it goes wrong, it's like someone's shoved a red hot poker up your backside." And he explained, with typically self-effacing humor, the reason for AC/DC's longevity. "People have said we've hung around long enough," he said. "But some bands fade when they try to adapt to what's current. We play rock music. It's a little bit late for us to do a ballad. Rock is what we do best. Sometimes I'm asked if I want to play music other than AC/DC. Sure, at home I play a little blues, but after five minutes I'm like, sod this! And I'm playing hard rock again."

What eighty thousand people saw in AC/DC's performance at Donington was a band still at the top of its game. All of the acts that preceded them were on a high. The Black Crowes, America's hottest new rock 'n' roll band since Guns N' Roses, were pushing their million-selling debut album *Shake Your Money Maker*. Queensrÿche, a leading band in American metal, dug into their brilliant concept album *Operation: Mindcrime* and finished with the Pink Floyd-inspired hit "Silent Lucidity." Mötley Crüe, survivors of what was loudly proclaimed their "decade of decadence," played the hits that had made them superstars—"Shout At The Devil," "Looks That Kill," "Girls, Girls, Girls," "Dr. Feelgood."

Metallica were performing at Donington for the third time, just as AC/DC were. They left the stage to a huge ovation—a band soon to become one of the biggest in the world. In the end though, it was AC/DC who ruled at Monsters of Rock.

"Thunderstruck" was a spectacular opener—Angus high up on a curving ramp as he peeled off that electrifying intro, and thousands of fans bouncing in delirium as the band built up a head of steam. The three songs that followed—"Shoot To Thrill," "Back In Black," and "Hell Ain't A Bad Place To Be"—left no one in doubt as to whose show this was. The home run was unbeatable—eight songs, all deathless classics, from "Hells Bells" through "High Voltage," "Whole Lotta Rosie," "You Shook Me All Night Long," "T.N.T.," "Let There Be Rock," "Highway To Hell," and "For Those About To Rock (We Salute You)."

It was AC/DC's greatest performance at Donington, but what followed on September 28, with the last of the Monsters of Rock shows, made Donington and even Rock in Rio look like small potatoes. On the vast, flat expanse of Moscow's Tushino Airfield, an audience of one and a half million gathered to see AC/DC, Metallica, The Black Crowes, rising American metal band Pantera, and the Russian group E.S.T. It was one of the biggest concert events ever staged.

After Moscow, there was one last run for *The Razors Edge* tour, back on home ground in Australia in October and November, with the final date in Auckland, New Zealand on November 16. On the guest list at that last show was Phil Rudd, who was at this point a resident of Auckland. He made his peace with Malcolm and Angus, having been out of the band for eight years.

Opposite: **The crowd at Moscow's Tushino Airfield on September 28, 1991, made Donington and Rock in Rio look small.**

Below: (L–R) **Cliff Williams, Malcolm Young, Chris Slade, Angus Young and Brian Johnson in Australia for the last run of *The Razors Edge* tour**

Right: **Angus Young and Brian Johnson, 1995**

Ten months down the line, in October 1992, I met again with Angus Young for another *Kerrang!* interview. A new AC/DC live album was being released, their second, and the first to feature Brian Johnson. Also released at this time was the *Live At Donington* video from the previous year's Monsters of Rock.

Dressed in blue jeans and matching denim jacket, drinking tea and chain-smoking, Angus was full of good humor during the hour that we talked. "I'm teetotal," he said. "Have been for a few years. But," he added with a laugh, "it's not a religious thing." Later on, he said dryly: "If I was out there paying money for a show, I'd want to see John Lennon resurrected for some of the prices."

The new album's prosaic title, *AC/DC Live*, lacked the fighting spirit of *If You Want Blood You've Got It*. Equally, this album lacked the raw intensity of what was captured on *If You Want Blood*—"the magic show," as Angus called it. What *AC/DC Live* did have, as a double album, was the best of the great songs the band had made since 1978, including "Highway To Hell," many from *Back In Black, For Those About To Rock (We Salute You),* and the latest classic, "Thunderstruck." Four songs had previously featured on *If You Want Blood*: "Whole Lotta Rosie," "The Jack," "Let There Be Rock," and "High Voltage." As Angus said to me: "We did have a twinge of conscience about that. But I don't think it would be an AC/DC live album without those songs. If they don't like it they can always put on *If You Want Blood*." He added: "Every kid I've ever met at our shows, the first thing they always ask is, 'When are we getting this live album you've been promising for eleven years?' Plus, Brian's been with us a long time and recorded a lot of strong stuff, the *Back In Black* album especially and *For Those About To Rock*, which still gives me goosebumps."

He talked about the blood and sweat that had gone into this album: "It's always a challenge every time you go on stage. I enjoy playing and that's what keeps me going." Of the *Live At Donington* video, he had a laugh about the moment in "The Jack" when he was doing his striptease and the crowd were shouting, "Get 'em off!" He said: "I thought they were singing 'Get 'im off!'"

There was more laughter as he talked about his schoolboy act and how he and the other guys in the band related to it—including the new guy in the band, Chris Slade. "Chris being new, to him I am a bit hilarious. He's always played in strict environments before, where music is sacrosanct. You know, some nights I look at Brian and crumble, you fall apart. I had to tell him, 'Don't make me laugh before I go on.' Some nights I'm in stitches when I'm trying to be The Schoolboy. For me, the shows go so quick. You're on and you're off, and then you have to go back to how you are as a person. That's the hard part, because once you go into being

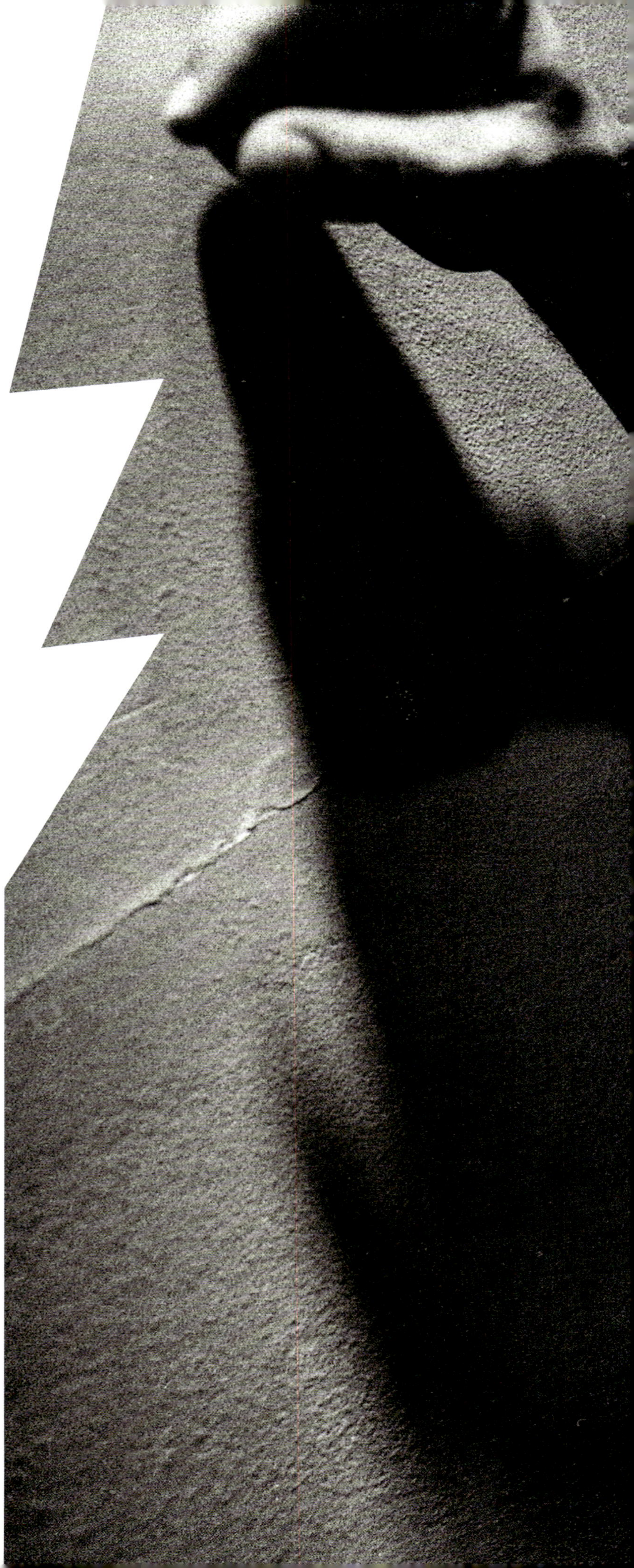

The Schoolboy it's pretty hard to come off it. I'm like two different people—sometimes three!" I asked him who was the third. "That's what I'm trying to figure out," he laughed. "I've been up there playing and thinking, what are those feet doing? I'm watching them to see which way they want to go. That's all I ever do, follow the feet and the guitar. The duckwalk came naturally."

Angus made fun of Brian Johnson. "That cap is his pride and joy," he said, smirking. "And I still have trouble understanding what he's talking about. In America he has to do a John Wayne imitation so they can understand him. If you haven't been around him in a while, it takes you a week to catch the drift again. Like Bon, Brian has a good sense of humour. He'll just go out and be himself. At this stage of the game, he'd look pretty silly up on stage going, 'Aren't I pretty?' Image isn't really one of our strong points."

He also talked in depth about music—the music he makes with AC/DC, and the old stuff that still inspired him. "It's a challenge to keep coming up with songs of the calibre of 'Let There Be Rock,' 'Highway To Hell,' and 'Back In Black,'" he said. "Every song we write has got to stand up. Most of our stuff is just about sex, as is most rock music. It's pretty hard to write a song about your dog. But I've never really found a sexual thing in music. I've never found anything sexy that was meant to be sexy. Now, that's a good Freudian thing. If you go back to the blues, that's the standard tempo in most of the strip joints, and that's what we rely on too. It has to be earthy. When I get in a car, the first thing that goes in is a Muddy Waters tape, even though I've played it four hundred times. I love that and Chuck Berry. Nowadays everything sounds so nice—buzz-free, hiss-free. I like that hiss! I like to hear the valves on the amplifier warming up. It's pure energy. I still spend

Above right: **Angus Young with Arnold Schwarzenegger on the set of the video for "Big Gun." The song was used on the soundtrack for the 1993 movie, *Last Action Hero*.**

Above left: **Rick Rubin. His work on the production of "Big Gun" led to him producing *Ballbreaker* for AC/DC.**

Opposite: **Phil Rudd** (second left) **back in the band**

> **"That's all I ever do, follow the feet and the guitar. The duckwalk came naturally."**
>
> **Angus Young**

hours sitting and listening to the sound Chuck Berry's guitar makes. There's not a day that goes by when I don't pick up a guitar. And I'm getting there—I've got two fingers going now!"

This last joke was one that said a lot about the man and his humility. While in Cologne, I spoke with the band's manager Stewart Young, who told me that when people said to Angus how great he is, Angus would shrug and say, "My brother's a good player."

AC/DC Live was a big seller, hitting number one in Australia, number five in the UK, fifteen in the US, and top twenty across Europe. The band's next release, in 1993, was the single "Big Gun," a rowdy song featured in the soundtrack to the Arnold Schwarzenegger movie *Last Action Hero*.

For the producer of "Big Gun," it was a dream come true to work with a band he had loved since he was a kid. Rick Rubin had become a hugely influential figure in music in the eighties, as co-founder of hip-hop label Def Jam Recordings, and producer of

SONOR

records that had defined the era, including Run-DMC's *Raising Hell* (featuring the groundbreaking collaboration with Aerosmith on a rap-rock version of "Walk This Way"), The Beastie Boys' *Licensed to Ill*, and thrash metal band Slayer's *Reign In Blood*, arguably the heaviest album ever made.

Rubin had been in the frame to produce *The Razors Edge* before the band settled on Bruce Fairbairn. His work on "Big Gun" secured him the job of producing AC/DC's next album. Recording began in October 1994, at the Power Station Studios in New York City. While Rubin was the new guy on the team, a familiar face was back in the band. When Phil Rudd had reunited with Malcolm and Angus in Auckland in 1991, an offer was made. Rudd was told he could rejoin the band. In early 1994, Chris Slade decided to jump before he was pushed. According to Malcolm, having Rudd back in the band was "pure magic." But at the time, no official announcement was made. A more pressing concern for the band was the sound of the tracks laid down in the early sessions at the Power Station. The live ambience that Malcolm wanted was not coming through. After ten weeks in New York, the operation was moved to Los Angeles and Ocean Way Recording studios in early 1995. But even then, it was a struggle to get this album made.

Rubin's methodology was as painstaking as Mutt Lange's. Reportedly, he had the band running through as many as fifty takes of a single song. It was, in a sense, *For Those About To Rock (We Salute You)* all over again. And when, after five long months in LA, the album was at last finished, so was Rick Rubin's working relationship with AC/DC.

The album was aptly named: *Ballbreaker*. And much the same as *The Razors Edge*, it turned out half great, half not so great. With Phil Rudd anchoring the band as only he can, "Hard As A Rock" has a deep groove, "The Furor" oozes power, the album's title track is an out-and-out bruiser, and "Boogie Man" is a dirty, grinding blues number, AC/DC's best since "Ride On," with Brian Johnson savoring the sleaziness of it all.

Ballbreaker was released on September 22, 1995, its dramatic cover art portraying Angus atop a giant wrecking ball and lit up with bolts of electricity. The album was afforded a degree of grudging admiration in a review by *Rolling Stone* writer Jancee Dunn: "Have AC/DC written another 'You Shook Me All Night Long?' No. Do they deliver guilty-pleasure metal like no other hard-rock band? Yup. Their longevity can be credited to two factors: nostalgia and the fact that AC/DC still view the world through the mind of a horny 15-year-old. God knows there's more than enough of them to go around."

Left: **Brian Johnson sits astride a giant wrecking ball during AC/DC's *Ballbreaker* tour at the Forum in Inglewood, California on February 21, 1996.**

"There's not a day that goes by when I don't pick up a guitar."

Angus Young

And so there were. The album reached number four in the US and six in the UK. On the tour that followed, running from January 12, 1996 through to November 30, a new stage prop was featured along with the bell, for "Hells Bells," and the cannons in "For Those About To Rock (We Salute You)"—a wrecking ball that smashed through part of the staging as the band opened the show with "Back In Black," and from which Brian Johnson gamely swung while singing "Ballbreaker." It was pantomime stuff that the fans enjoyed. It was also a thrill for them to see Phil Rudd back, the band restored to full power, with the line-up that made *Back In Black*.

AC/DC's last release of the 1990s was a monument to the past. Bon Scott had once said to Malcolm in a lighthearted moment: "If I ever make it big and they want me to do a solo album, I'll call it Bonfire." Fittingly, this became the title of the AC/DC box set released on November 18, 1997, seventeen years after Bon's death. Across five CDs was a wealth of rare and previously unreleased material from the seventies: the much sought-after 1977 recording *Live From The Atlantic Studios*; the two-disc soundtrack to the band's concert movie *Let There Be Rock*, recorded in Paris in '79; and *Volts*, a collection of assorted rarities, which featured among its highlights an early draft of "Whole Lotta Rosie," named "Dirty Eyes," and a blistering live version of "She's Got Balls" from a 1977 gig at the Bondi Lifesaver in Sydney. The fifth disc was the *Back In Black* album. If this appeared incongruous in a package that celebrated the life and work of Bon Scott, there was poignancy in what *Back In Black* represented to the band: their tribute to the singer who never lived to see it become the biggest rock album of all time.

THE RAZORS EDGE

Released: September 24, 1990
Recorded: Windmill Lane Studios, Dublin, Ireland and Little Mountain Studios, Vancouver, BC, Canada
Label: Atco Records
Albert/EMI (AUS/NZ)
Producer: Bruce Fairbairn

All tracks written by Angus Young and Malcolm Young.

SIDE ONE
"Thunderstruck"
"Fire Your Guns"
"Moneytalks"
"The Razors Edge"
"Mistress For Christmas"
"Rock Your Heart Out"

SIDE TWO
"Are You Ready"
"Got You By The Balls"
"Shot Of Love"
"Let's Make It"
"Goodbye & Good Riddance To Bad Luck"
"If You Dare"

PERSONNEL
Brian Johnson—lead vocals
Angus Young—lead guitar
Malcolm Young—rhythm guitar, backing vocals
Cliff Williams—bass guitar, backing vocals
Chris Slade—drums, percussion

Additional personnel
Mike Fraser—engineer and mixing

The Razors Edge hit number two in the US chart, and number four in the UK, helping the band return to its former glory. Worldwide, the album has sold between ten and twelve million copies, making it the fourth highest selling AC/DC album (after *Dirty Deeds Done Dirt Cheap, Highway To Hell* and *Back In Black,* and ahead of *Who Made Who*).

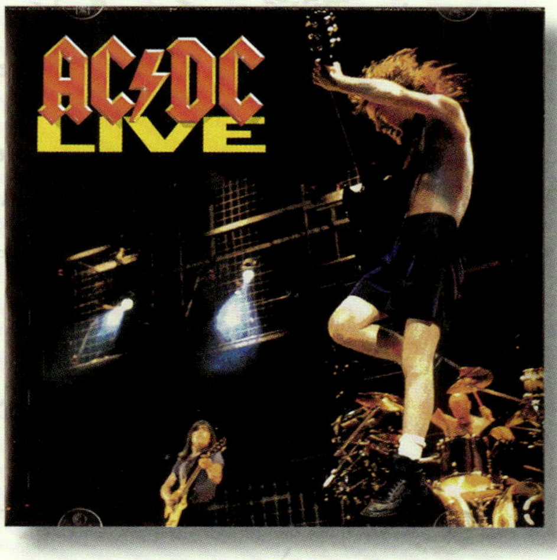

Released: October 27, 1992
Recorded: 1991
Label: Albert Productions, Atco
Producer: Bruce Fairbairn
The recordings on this live album are taken from several shows from AC/DC's 1991 *The Razors Edge* tour: Glasgow, Edmonton, Birmingham, and the Donington and Moscow Monsters of Rock shows.

All tracks written by Angus Young, Malcolm Young, and Brian Johnson, except where noted.

VINYL 2 LP "COLLECTOR'S EDITION"

SIDE ONE
"Thunderstruck" (Young, Young; recorded at Donington Park, Leicestershire, England, August 17, 1991)
"Shoot To Thrill" (NEC, Birmingham, England; April 23, 1991)
"Back In Black" (Donington Park, Leicestershire, England; August 17, 1991)
"Sin City" (Young, Young, Scott; recorded at NEC, Birmingham, England, April 23, 1991)
"Who Made Who" (NEC, Birmingham, England; April 23, 1991)
"Fire Your Guns" (Young, Young; recorded at Donington Park, Leicestershire, England, August 17, 1991)

SIDE TWO
"Jailbreak" (Young, Young, Scott; recorded at NEC, Birmingham, England, April 23, 1991)
"The Jack" (Young, Young Scott; recorded at Tushino Airfield, Moscow, Russia, September 28, 1991)
"The Razors Edge" (Young, Young; recorded at NEC, Birmingham, England, April 24, 1991)
"Dirty Deeds Done Dirt Cheap" (Young, Young, Scott; recorded at NEC, Birmingham, England, April 23, 1991)

SIDE THREE
"Hells Bells" (Northlands Coliseum, Edmonton, Alberta, Canada; June 22, 1991)
"Heatseeker" (NEC, Birmingham, England; April 23, 1991)
"That's The Way I Wanna Rock 'n' Roll" (place and date of recording unknown)
"High Voltage" (Young, Young, Scott; unknown recording)
"You Shook Me All Night Long" (Donington Park, Leicestershire, England; August 17, 1991)

SIDE FOUR
"Whole Lotta Rosie" (Young, Young, Scott; recorded at Tushino Airfield, Moscow, Russia, September 28, 1991)
"Let There Be Rock" (Young, Young, Scott; recorded at S.E.C.C., Glasgow, Scotland, April 20, 1991)
"Highway To Hell" (Young, Young, Scott; recorded at S.E.C.C., Glasgow, Scotland, April 20, 1991)
"T.N.T." (Young, Young, Scott; recorded at NEC, Birmingham, England, April 23, 1991)
"For Those About To Rock (We Salute You)" (Northlands Coliseum, Edmonton, Alberta, Canada; June 22, 1991)

PERSONNEL
Brian Johnson—lead vocals
Angus Young—lead guitar
Malcolm Young—rhythm guitar, backing vocals
Cliff Williams—bass guitar, backing vocals
Chris Slade—drums, percussion

Additional personnel
Bob Defrin—art direction
Larry Busacca—photography

BALLBREAKER

Released: September 22, 1995
Recorded: 1994-5 at Record Plant Studios, New York City, and Ocean Way Recording, Los Angeles
Label: East West, Albert Productions, Epic
Producer: Rick Rubin, Mike Fraser

All tracks written by Angus Young and Malcolm Young.

SIDE ONE
"Hard As A Rock"
"Cover You In Oil"
"The Furor"
"Boogie Man"
"The Honey Roll"
"Burnin' Alive"

SIDE TWO
"Hail Caesar"
"Love Bomb"
"Caught With Your Pants Down"
"Whiskey On The Rocks"
"Ballbreaker"

PERSONNEL
Brian Johnson—lead vocals
Angus Young—rhythm and lead guitars
Malcolm Young—rhythm guitar, backing vocals
Cliff Williams—bass guitar, backing vocals
Phil Rudd—drums, percussion
With Phil Rudd back in the band, this album resurrects the original *Back In Black* line-up.

Additional personnel
Bob Defrin—original art direction
SMAY design—reissue design
Phil Heffernan at **Colorspace** and **David McMacken**-cover illustration
Robert Ellis—cover photography

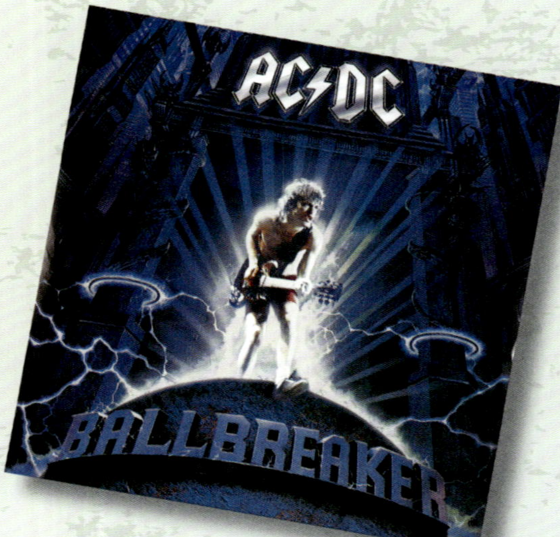

BONFIRE

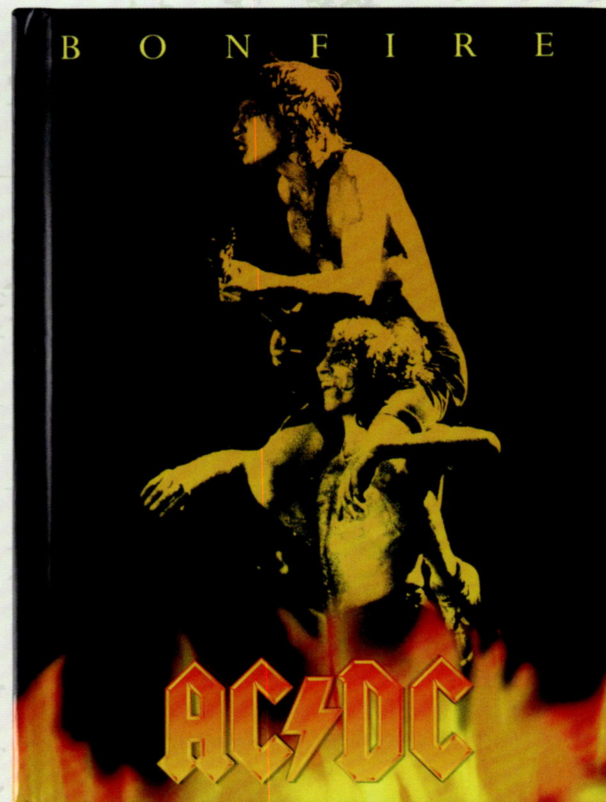

Released: November 18, 1997
Recorded: 1974-1980
Label: East West
Producer: Harry Vanda, George Young, Mutt Lange

This Bon Scott tribute featured the much sought-after 1977 recording *Live From The Atlantic Studios*; the two-disc soundtrack to the band's concert movie *Let There Be Rock*, recorded in Paris in '79; and *Volts*, a collection of assorted rarities and *Back In Black*.

PERSONNEL
Bon Scott—lead vocals (disc 1,2,3)
Brian Johnson—lead vocals (discs 4, 5)
Angus Young—lead guitar
Malcolm Young—rhythm guitar
Cliff Williams—bass guitar
Phil Rudd—drums

Additional personnel
Jim DeBarros—art direction
Georges Amann—cover photography

DISC ONE: LIVE FROM THE ATLANTIC STUDIOS

Recorded live on December 7, 1977 at Atlantic Studios, New York.

All tracks written by Angus Young, Malcolm Young, and Bon Scott.

"Live Wire" *(T.N.T.)*
"Problem Child" *(Dirty Deeds Done Dirt Cheap)*
"High Voltage" *(T.N.T.)*
"Hell Ain't A Bad Place To Be" *(Let There Be Rock)*
"Dog Eat Dog" *(Let There Be Rock)*
"The Jack" *(T.N.T.)*
"Whole Lotta Rosie" *(Let There Be Rock)*
"Rocker" *(T.N.T.)*

DISC TWO AND THREE: LET THERE BE ROCK: THE MOVIE–LIVE IN PARIS

Recorded live on December 9, 1979 at the Pavillon de Paris, Paris, France.

All tracks written by Angus Young, Malcolm Young, and Bon Scott.

DISC TWO

"Live Wire" *(T.N.T.)*
"Shot Down In Flames" *(Highway To Hell)*
"Hell Ain't A Bad Place To Be" *(Let There Be Rock)*
"Sin City" *(Powerage)*
"Walk All Over You" *(Highway To Hell)*
"Bad Boy Boogie" *(Let There Be Rock)*

DISC THREE

"The Jack" *(T.N.T.)*
"Highway To Hell" *(Highway To Hell)*
"Girls Got Rhythm" *(Highway To Hell)*
"High Voltage" *(T.N.T.)*
"Whole Lotta Rosie" *(Let There Be Rock)*
"Rocker" *(T.N.T.)*
"T.N.T." *(T.N.T.)*
"Let There Be Rock" *(Let There Be Rock)*

DISC FOUR: VOLTS

All tracks written by Angus Young, Malcolm Young and Bon Scott, except where noted.

"Dirty Eyes" (First title and lyrics to riffs of "Whole Lotta Rosie")
"Touch Too Much" (Same title as the track on *Highway To Hell*, different lyrics and music)
"If You Want Blood (You've Got It)" (First recording)
"Back Seat Confidential" (First title and Lyrics to the riffs of "Beatin' Around The Bush")
"Get It Hot" (Same title as the track on *Highway To Hell*, different lyrics and music)
"Sin City" (Live 1978 from *The Midnight Special*)
"She's Got Balls" (Live 1977 from The Bondi Lifesaver, Sydney)
"School Days" (Chuck Berry; from *T.N.T.*, not previously released outside Australia)
"It's A Long Way To The Top (If You Wanna Rock 'n' Roll)" (Longer version from *T.N.T.*)
"Ride On" (*Dirty Deeds Done Dirt Cheap*, followed by brief interviews)

DISC FIVE: BACK IN BLACK

All tracks written by Angus Young, Malcolm Young, and Brian Johnson.

"Hells Bells"
"Shoot To Thrill"
"What Do You Do For Money Honey"
"Given The Dog A Bone"
"Let Me Put My Love Into You"
"Back In Black"
"You Shook Me All Night Long"
"Have A Drink On Me"
"Shake A Leg"
"Rock And Roll Ain't Noise Pollution"

"If I ever make it big and they want me to do a solo album, I'll call it Bonfire."
Bon Scott

GRETSCH
Gibson

You Don't Go to the Butcher for Brain Surgery

"The greatest thing I've ever done with this band was smoke The Rolling Stones into the weeds."

Phil Rudd

The more things change, the more they stay the same. The new songs that Malcolm and Angus Young wrote in 1998 were as old school as the little guy's cap and shorts. There was a greasy boogie number named "Stiff Upper Lip," a riff in "Satellite Blues" that was pure Keith Richards, and in "Can't Stop Rock 'n' Roll" a song that picked up where they had left off with "Rock And Roll Ain't Noise Pollution." While Brian Johnson was no longer writing lyrics—a job he had ceded to Malcolm and Angus since *The Razors Edge*—the filthy innuendos that littered songs such as "Stiff Upper Lip," "Meltdown," and "Come And Get It" had a little of that flavor that Bon Scott had instilled into the band.

The plan was for AC/DC to record this material in late 1999 with Bruce Fairbairn, the producer who had been instrumental in getting the band back on track with *The Razors Edge*. Certainly, they had a better understanding with Fairbairn than they had with Rick Rubin on *Ballbreaker*. However, on May 17, 1999, there was shocking news for the band, when Bruce Fairbairn was found dead at his home in Vancouver. Aged forty-nine, Fairbairn had been working at that time on an album with progressive rock band Yes. The cause of his death was unknown.

After Malcolm and Angus attended the funeral in Vancouver, they turned to the producer they trusted more than any other, their big brother, George Young. At the time, George was effectively retired, but with the band in such difficult circumstances, he agreed to produce the new album, albeit without his old partner Harry Vanda. Instead, George was assisted by Mike Fraser, who had engineered and mixed *The Razors Edge* and co-produced *Ballbreaker*, and had also worked with Fairbairn on Aerosmith's *Permanent Vacation* and *Pump*.

It was in Vancouver that the AC/DC album was recorded, at The Warehouse Studio, a facility owned by the city's most famous son, rock superstar Bryan Adams. They started in September and were done by the end of October, with eighteen tracks in the can, of which twelve made the cut. The album, titled *Stiff Upper Lip*, was released on February 28, 2000, and amid all the fuss about the dawn of a new millennium, in AC/DC's world nothing had changed. *Stiff Upper Lip* could have been made at any point in the preceding twenty years. The sound was reminiscent of *Flick Of The Switch*—real bare-bones stuff. The band played the same old song and dance.

The review that really nailed this album was in *MOJO*, by long-time AC/DC supporter Sylvie Simmons. "This is AC/DC back in business, and business is good," she wrote. "On *Ballbreaker*, there was an almost parodic approach—exuberantly young-and-dumb Beavis and Butt-Head songs with an obsessional, teenage Rick Rubin production. This time, there's less rabble-rousing. Songs are often sparer and more low-key. And producer George Young thought to turn down the bludgeon and abrasion knobs on Brian Johnson's psycho-force-feeding-Tweety-Pie-steroids-before-torturing-it-with-a-dentist's-drill vocal once in a while, allowing him more freedom to actually *sing*. The overall impression is of a band deconstructing its music to its basic elements—the Chuck Berry rock 'n' roll of 'Can't Stand Still;' the metal blues of 'Meltdown;' the ZZ Top boogie of 'Come And Get It'—and having a lot of fun putting it all back together."

Previous: **AC/DC backstage at the United Arena, Chicago, Illinois, April 8, 2001:** (L–R) **Malcolm Young, Brian Johnson, Angus Young, Cliff Williams, and Phil Rudd**

Above right: **Guns N' Roses guitarist Slash, who supported AC/DC on the opening leg of their *Stiff Upper Lip* tour, with his band at the time, Snakepit**

Opposite: **Angus Young live on stage in front of "Junior"—an enormous replica of the bronze statue of him that was used as the cover image on *Stiff Upper Lip***

Stiff Upper Lip is not a classic AC/DC album. Only the title track ranks alongside the band's very best, but the album was a big hit—number three in Australia, seven in the US, twelve in the UK, and top ten all over Europe. The *Stiff Upper Lip* tour was another marathon, extending from August 1 all the way through to the following summer. The image on the album's cover—Angus as a bronze statue, with fist raised in triumph—was replicated in an enormous stage prop that the band jokingly named "Junior."

The opening leg in North America ran smoothly, with a support act led by another famous AC/DC fan—former Guns N' Roses guitarist Slash, with his band Snakepit. It was on the opening night of a European tour that tragedy struck again. On October 14, as AC/DC performed at the Flanders Sports Arena in the Belgian city of Ghent, thirty-eight year-old Isidoor Theunissen was fatally injured after falling twenty-three feet on to a concrete floor. Nine years after the deaths of three fans during the band's concert in Salt Lake City, it was another dark day in the history of AC/DC. There had been many.

The tour reached the UK in November, with the first date at the NEC in Birmingham being reviewed in *The Guardian* by Keith Cameron. "Nobody else plays deafeningly loud nuts-and-bolts basic rhythm and blues like AC/DC," he stated. "They are so constrained by their own legend that half of this two-hour set picks itself. Fortunately, just as Van Gogh painted the same vase of flowers a hundred times without diminishing the wonder of his art, so AC/DC make a virtue out of endlessly re-ploughing the same gnarly furrow, each time unearthing hitherto unimagined nuggets of base wisdom."

In January and February 2001, the band played in Australia and Japan. From March through to May, they were back in North America, where, on April 12, they returned to Salt Lake City for the first time since the terrible events of 1991. The tour finished with fifteen stadium shows in Europe in the summer. The first was in the UK at the National Bowl in Milton Keynes on June 8, where the bill featured punk stars The Offspring, thrash metal survivors Megadeth, and a rising American band that would go on to huge success in later years, Queens of the Stone Age. At this show, AC/DC delivered all that was expected, and more besides. They opened with "Stiff Upper Lip," the only song drawn from that album. Following that, the first big surprise, with "You Shook Me All Night Long" dropped in much earlier than usual. Then, while much of the set list was written in stone, the band pulled out three other songs to delight the connoisseurs among the audience: "Problem Child," the one that Bon Scott wrote about Angus; "What Do You Do For Money Honey," a deep cut from *Back In Black*; and most thrilling of all, "Up To My Neck In You," that riotous number from *Powerage*, which the band had last played live with Bon back in 1978.

Previous: **AC/DC performing live at London's Wembley Arena complete with stage-set cannons**

The last leg of the *Stiff Upper Lip* tour played out over fifteen stadium shows in Europe; the first at the National Bowl in Milton Keynes in the UK on June 8, with punk stars The Offspring (below), **thrash metal group Megadeth** (far left), **and rising American band Queens of the Stone Age** (left).

There was an even bigger surprise for the eighty-thousand-strong audience at the show at the Stade de France in Paris on June 22. After the tumultuous finale of "For Those About To Rock (We Salute You)," with the smoke from the cannon fire still lingering in the air, many fans were streaming out of the venue when the band reappeared on the stage dressed in France football shirts. Brian Johnson said simply, "This is a Bon Scott song," and what they played was "Ride On," a song that AC/DC had never before performed live, the one in which Bon had really bared his soul, and which Brian sang with tenderness and reverence for the man whose life was so deeply connected to his own.

The last stop on the *Stiff Upper Lip* tour was in Cologne in Germany on July 8. At the end of that year came two major announcements. First, AC/DC were named as inductees into the Rock and Roll Hall of Fame, alongside The Police, The Clash, Elvis Costello, and the Righteous Brothers. Secondly, it was announced that AC/DC had, after almost thirty years, severed ties with the Warner Music group to sign a new deal with Sony Music. A major

RENAULT CLIO
RENAULT

reissue campaign of the band's back catalog was scheduled for 2003—a year that turned out to be one of the best they ever had.

In February, Malcolm and Angus were invited to jam with a band they had loved since the days when Angus wore a school uniform because he had to. The Rolling Stones were in Australia ahead of a series of stadium shows on their *Forty Licks* tour, and for fun they played an intimate gig at the two-thousand-capacity Enmore Theatre in Sydney on February 18. The Stones were an hour into their set, having just finished "Start Me Up," when Mick Jagger gave the cue for Malcolm and Angus to join them for a run through the old blues standard "Rock Me Baby." The brothers took up their customary positions on stage, Angus up front with Keith Richards, Malcolm hanging back near the drum riser with Ronnie Wood. If Angus looked unfamiliar in jeans and T-shirt, his hair cut short, by the time he took a solo he was up to his old tricks, duckwalking just the same as he always did, and shaking his ass at the audience as Keith Richards looked on with a broad smile. Malcolm and Angus had a blast. Playing the blues with the Stones was a moment to savor.

By contrast, the Rock and Roll Hall of Fame was not their kind of scene. The induction ceremony on March 10 in

Above: **The Rolling Stones:** (L–R) **Mick Jagger, Ronnie Wood, Charlie Watts, and Keith Richards, who invited AC/DC to jam with them on their *Forty Licks* tour**

Left: **Brian Johnson pictured in a France football shirt with Angus Young on stage at the Stade de France in Paris on June 22, 2001**

Brian Johnson accepting AC/DC's induction into the Rock and Roll Hall of Fame (above) **and performing with Aerosmith's Steven Tyler** (opposite top) **at the Waldorf-Astoria Hotel on March 10, 2003, in New York City**

Opposite bottom: **Brian Johnson and Angus Young on stage at Columbiahalle, Berlin; a smaller venue than usual**

the ballroom of the Waldorf-Astoria hotel in New York City played to an audience of music industry high rollers, many in tuxedos, all seated at tables. This was not AC/DC's natural habitat. It was an old friend, Steven Tyler of Aerosmith, who gave the induction speech: "Thank God for the power chord," Tyler said. "That thunder from Down Under that gives you the second most satisfying surge that can run through your body. There is no greater purveyor of that power chord than AC/DC." When the band walked on, it was Brian Johnson who spoke for them, beginning by quoting lines from "Let There Be Rock" before introducing Bon's nephews, Paul and Daniel, who accepted the award. Brian gave thanks to record companies past and present, but stated emphatically: "This award is for the fans all over the world who have stuck by us through thick and thin." Finally, the band performed two songs, "Highway To Hell" and "You Shook Me All Night Long," with Tyler joining them for the latter.

"Thank God for the power chord. There is no greater purveyor of that power chord than AC/DC."

Steven Tyler, Aerosmith

On April 1, it became evident that when Malcolm and Angus had jammed with the Stones, a little business was going on behind the scenes. AC/DC were confirmed as special guests for the Stones' three open-air shows in June in the German cities of Oberhausen, Leipzig, and Hockenheim. AC/DC had not opened for another act since 1979, but their respect for the Stones, and a reported $4m on the table, sealed the deal. Around those shows, AC/DC played two of their own, in small venues, the first at the three-thousand-capacity Columbiahalle in Berlin on June 9, the second at the slightly bigger Circus Krone in Munich on June 17.

I was present in Berlin to see the show and to interview the band for Q magazine. In the moments before the band took to the stage, the buzz of anticipation in that audience was mixed with a sense of disbelief at the prospect of seeing AC/DC in such a small venue. When the house lights dimmed, the noise from those three thousand people was deafening. In the darkness, a single tiny point of light was visible—the red glow from Phil Rudd's cigarette as he moved into place behind the kit. Then, in a blaze of white light, the band were up and running, straight into "Hell Ain't A Bad Place To Be." Standing beside me were Pete Flatt, the band's British PR, and Jerry Ewing, a friend and journalist for *Metal Hammer*, whose love for AC/DC is declared in the tattoo on his forearm: "Bad

Boy Boogie." All around us, people were bouncing, headbanging, punching the air. Disbelief had turned to pure joy.

What I witnessed that night in Berlin, as numerous beers were sunk, was the best AC/DC show I had ever seen. They played all the songs that would go into their seventy-minute set at the Stones' gigs: the anthems—"Back In Black," "Thunderstruck," "Bad Boy Boogie," "The Jack," "Hells Bells," "Dirty Deeds Done Dirt Cheap," "T.N.T.," "Highway To Hell," "Whole Lotta Rosie," "You Shook Me All Night Long," "Let There Be Rock," and "For Those About To Rock (We Salute You)"—and also two cult classics in "Rock 'n' Roll Damnation" and "If You Want Blood (You've Got It)." But in this show, on their own time, they also banged out two more big numbers from *Back In Black*, "Shoot To Thrill" and "Rock And Roll Ain't Noise Pollution," and dug deep into the *Powerage* album with their funkiest song, "Gone Shootin'," and another groover, "What's Next To The Moon." When it was all over, Pete Flatt turned to Jerry and I and said: "I've never seen two journalists enjoy a gig as much as you did."

It was on the following afternoon that I met up with Angus, Malcolm, and Brian in a suite at the Four Seasons hotel, where the plush surroundings seemed at odds with the three guys in jeans and T-shirts. Although I had met Angus before, I was struck by how short all of them were. Equally, I was impressed by their lack of ego. They appeared more like blue-collar workers on their lunch break than world famous rock 'n' roll stars. Brian had a sore throat from the gig, rendering his Geordie accent almost incomprehensible. "It were fuckin' hot last night," he wheezed. The interview was for a feature entitled "Cash For Questions," in which the readers of Q were invited to ask whatever they wanted to know from the band. The room filled with cigarette smoke and laughter as all manner of questions came their way . . .

AC/DC have not supported another band for twenty odd years, so why play second fiddle to The Rolling Stones in Germany? Was the money too good to refuse?

Malcolm Young: "They've offered it a few times over the years. We'd never really met them but when they played in Sydney, Ron Wood asked me

On July 30, 2003, AC/DC and the Rolling Stones played together again at a huge benefit concert in Toronto. Angus Young is pictured here with Mick Jagger (above left) **and Keith Richards** (left). **Also at the concert was pop star Justin Timberlake, pictured center with AC/DC** (opposite top).

Opposite bottom: (L–R) **Malcolm Young, Brian Johnson, Angus Young, and Cliff Williams—the final show of 2003 at the Apollo Hammersmith in London, UK on October 21, 2003**

GIRLS gone WILD

Marshall

STIFF UPPER LIP

Released: February 28, 2000
Recorded: September–October 1999, The Warehouse Studio, Vancouver, British Columbia, Canada
Label: East West
Producer: George Young

All tracks written by Angus Young and Malcolm Young.

SIDE ONE
"Stiff Upper Lip"
"Meltdown"
"House Of Jazz"
"Hold Me Back"
"Safe In New York City"
"Can't Stand Still"

SIDE TWO
"Can't Stop Rock 'n' Roll"
"Satellite Blues"
"Damned"
"Come And Get It"
"All Screwed Up"
"Give It Up"

PERSONNEL
Brian Johnson—lead vocals
Angus Young—lead guitar
Malcolm Young—rhythm guitar, backing vocals (lead guitar on "Can't Stand Still")
Cliff Williams—bass guitar, backing vocals
Phil Rudd—drums

Additional personnel
Mike Fraser—engineering and mixing
Alli—art direction
Mista Dean Karr—statue concept and photography
Mark Alfrey and Stan Lok of SMG Effects—statue scuplture

and Angus to jam with them. We played a twelve-bar blues and Angus and Jagger were duckwalking, taking the mickey out of each other."

Angus Young: "I know I was in Mick's spot, but that was by accident."

Angus, you're forty-four years old—isn't it time to retire the schoolboy's uniform?

Angus: "Nah! When I put the uniform on, I'm ready. The legs start shaking . . . "

Every AC/DC album sounds the same . . .

Malcolm: "Same band! That's the good thing about us. It's just loud rock 'n' roll wham, bam, thank you ma'am!"

Angus: "You don't go to the butcher for brain surgery."

Where do you get your flat caps, Brian?

Brian: "New York, now. I used to get them from this old bag lady . . . no, not a bag lady, this old fucking bag what was a lady . . . "

Angus: "It gets worse by the minute!"

Brian: "She was a miserable old fucker. Had a stall in Kensington Market. The hats were five pounds—never changed. She used to make the peaks with cardboard, so when I got sweaty, this big lump would come up like a big dick on top of me head. I said to her once, 'Do you remember me? I must be your most regular customer.' And she went, 'Pick up your cap and fuck off.' She must be dead now—the stall's there but there's no hats on it."

Three days after that interview, the band played the first show with the Stones, in Oberhausen, where Malcolm and Angus jammed with them again on "Rock Me Baby." Repeat performances followed in Leipzig and Hockenheim. On July 30, the Stones and AC/DC played again at a huge benefit concert in Toronto, to aid a city that had suffered a disastrous decline in tourism following a major outbreak of the SARS virus. The concert also featured pop star Justin Timberlake and two famous Canadian rock groups—The Guess Who and Rush. The audience was close to half a million and for all the camaraderie between AC/DC and the Stones, there was also a sense of rivalry, as Phil Rudd revealed when he recalled this show in a 2005 interview with *Drum* magazine. "The greatest thing I've ever done with this band was smoke The Rolling Stones into the weeds in Toronto in front of four hundred and eighty thousand people," Rudd said. "We got into the van off stage and went, 'Yeah, fucking follow that!'"

AC/DC's final show of 2003 was on October 21 at a place they knew well—the Carling Apollo Hammersmith, better known as the Hammersmith Odeon. The band had last played in this theater in 1982. The set list was much the same as in Berlin, minus five numbers. The reaction from the audience was exactly the same, outright euphoria.

For AC/DC the year had ended on a high. Such was the energy within the group, generated on stages big and small, Malcolm and Angus had already begun writing songs for a new album. Only this album would be a long time coming. And while it would turn out to be one of the peaks in the band's career, it would also be the last for the man who had led AC/DC from the very start.

Opposite: **AC/DC in 2003:** (L–R) **Malcolm Young, Brian Johnson, Angus Young, Phil Rudd, and Cliff Williams**

Bruce Fairbairn was originally lined up to produce *Stiff Upper Lip*, but on May 17, 1999, he was found dead at his home in Vancouver. George Young stepped in to help, producing his last album for AC/DC before his death in 2017.

In Australia, New Zealand, and Europe, a special two-disc tour edition of *Stiff Upper Lip* was released by Albert Productions in January 2001. As well as the *Stiff Upper Lip* disc, this edition includes a bonus disc with a non-album track, five live tracks recorded from a concert at Plaza de Toros de Las Ventas, Madrid, Spain in 1996, and three music videos.

"**Cyberspace**" (Non LP track)
"**Back In Black** (Live, Plaza de Toros, Madrid, 1996") (Young, Young, Johnson)
"**Hard As A Rock** (Live, Plaza de Toros, Madrid, 1996")
"**Ballbreaker** (Live, Plaza de Toros, Madrid, 1996")
"**Whole Lotta Rosie** (Live, Plaza de Toros, Madrid, 1996") (Young, Young, Bon Scott)
"**Let There Be Rock** (Live, Plaza de Toros, Madrid, 1996") (Young, Young, Scott)
"**Stiff Upper Lip**" (Music video)
"**Safe In New York City**" (Music video)
"**Satellite Blues**" (Music video)

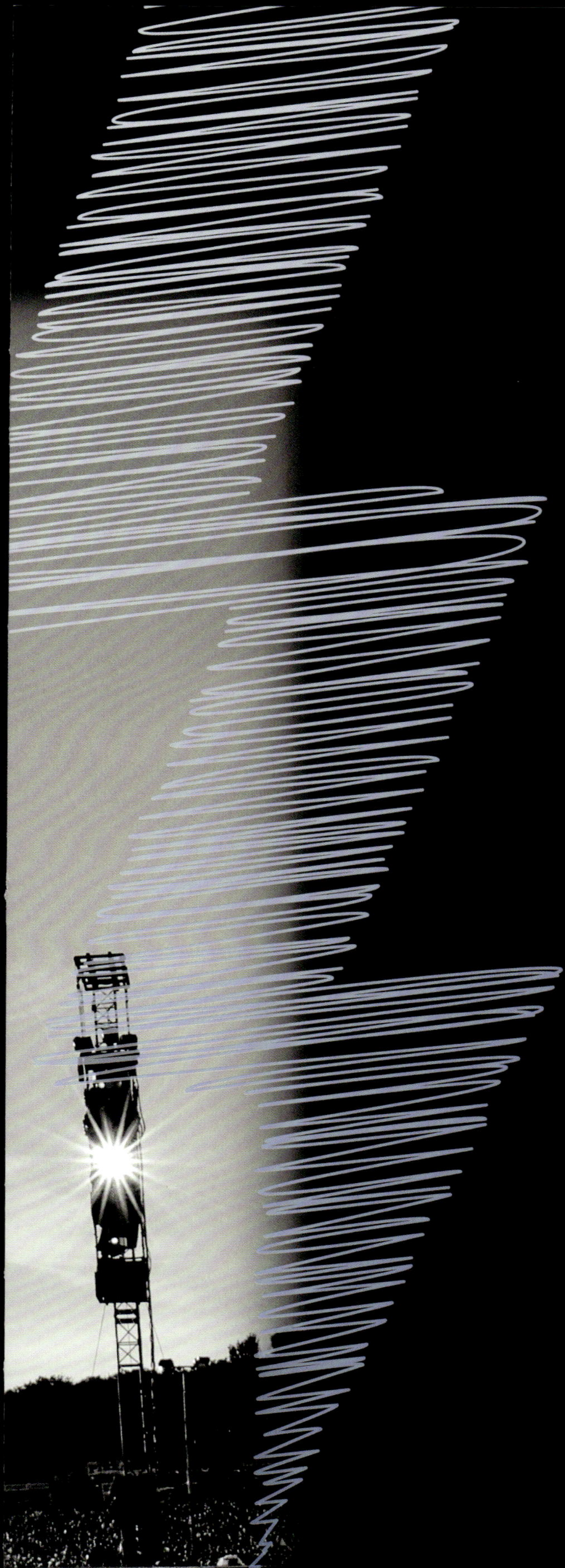

The Long Goodbye

"Age catches up on you. I don't want for people to see me on stage and say, 'Oh, poor old fucker, the band's carrying him!'"

Brian Johnson

AC/DC

There were eight years between the release of *Stiff Upper Lip* and AC/DC's next album, *Black Ice*, in 2008. In the band's early days, they banged out nine in eight years, from the original *High Voltage* through to *For Those About To Rock (We Salute You)*. In this late stage of their career, it was all so different from the "rush, rush, rush" that Angus Young had described to me in 1991. Even so, the recording of *Black Ice* was relatively quick, completed within two months in the spring of 2008 at The Warehouse Studio in Vancouver where the band had made *Stiff Upper Lip*.

There was a touch of irony in their choice of producer. Brendan O'Brien, originating from Atlanta, Georgia, had earned his stripes working for Rick Rubin's Def American label as engineer on The Black Crowes' *Shake Your Money Maker* and as producer of two records by British heavy metal band, Wolfsbane. O'Brien went on to produce some of the biggest rock albums of the nineties by acts such as Pearl Jam, Rage Against the Machine, Stone Temple Pilots, and Korn, and in the following decade three albums for Bruce Springsteen. His approach with AC/DC was quite unlike Rubin's. It was more of a throwback to the days of Vanda and Young, with most of the tracks cut live in the studio, with only minimal overdubs. Assisting O'Brien, as engineer and mixer, was Mike Fraser, a guy who knew this band inside out.

As a result, *Black Ice* had a real vibe to it, a feeling of

Previous: **Brian Johnson, Download Festival, 2010**

Left: **Brian Johnson leads AC/DC on stage during their *Black Ice* tour opener, October 28, 2008, in Wilkes-Barre, Pennsylvania, USA.**

Mike Fraser (below left) **and Brendan O'Brien** (below right) **oversaw production of AC/DC's 2008 album, *Black Ice*.**

spontaneity that had been lacking on previous albums. The sound of it was huge, better than any AC/DC record since *The Razors Edge*. With fifteen tracks, *Black Ice* has the longest running time of any AC/DC studio album, just short of an hour, and perhaps a little overlong, with a few songs, such as "Money Made" and "Smash 'n' Grab," just making up the numbers. Nevertheless, the album's opening track, "Rock 'n' Roll Train," stands tall as a genuine AC/DC classic. With its crunching riff and reach-for-the-sky chorus, it would not sound out of place on *Back In Black*. Among the great songs that follow, there is heavy thunder in "War Machine," strutting boogie in "Big Jack," dirty funk in the title track. There is even a nod to Slade, and to Brian Johnson's glam rock days, in the freewheeling "Anything Goes," and in "Rock 'n' Roll Dream"—the closest thing to an AC/DC ballad since "Love Song" back in '75—Brian's raspy voice has a soulful edge.

The review of *Black Ice* by *Rolling Stone*'s Brian Hiatt hailed the purity of AC/DC's ethos. "No one this side of Chuck Berry has written so many great rock 'n' roll songs about rock 'n' roll, and no band short of the Ramones has so militantly refused to reach beyond the basics of the form. *Black Ice* is their best argument in years—maybe decades—that evolution is for suckers."

Black Ice hit number one in twenty-nine countries, including Australia, the UK, the US, and throughout Europe. In terms of chart positions, not sales, it was the highest performing album of AC/DC's entire career. The *Black Ice* world tour was also a landmark for the band. It was their longest tour, running for all of twenty months from October 28, 2008 to June 28,

Opposite top: **Brian Johnson performing live on the *Black Ice* tour at London's Wembley Stadium on June 27, 2009**

Left: **A hometown show for Malcolm and Angus Young at Glasgow's Hampden Park, Scotland, on June 30, 2009**

Below: **Brian Johnson, whose other passion is fast cars, pictured at Silverstone race track**

2010, and the highest grossing, with an actual gross reported at approximately $441,000,000. Only three acts have grossed more on a single tour—U2, The Rolling Stones, and Roger Waters, formerly of Pink Floyd.

The first leg of the *Black Ice* tour played in arenas in North America, with "Rock 'n' Roll Train" installed as the raise-the-roof opener. In Europe, from February 2009 into the summer, the shows were arenas and then stadiums, including London's Wembley Stadium on June 28, and two days later a hometown show for Malcolm and Angus Young at Glasgow's Hampden Park.

A few days after the Glasgow show, I interviewed Brian Johnson in London for *Classic Rock* magazine. He spoke about his forthcoming autobiography, *Rockers and Rollers*, based on his twin passions for rock 'n' roll and fast cars, and admitted that he would like to devote more time to car racing. "The years are flashing past and I don't want to be sitting in hotel rooms," he said. "I want to go racing again!"

Brian said that he was enjoying every moment on stage. "We've been out on the road since October but it never gets boring. They're just the best rock band, and just to listen to them every night, it gets me. Every time they kick in, you think, What the

"No one this side of Chuck Berry has written so many great rock 'n' roll songs about rock 'n' roll."

Brian Hiatt, *Rolling Stone*

fuck! You're on again and you're thinking: This is ridiculous! I'm still grooving!" Yet at the age of sixty-one, Brian was beginning to feel it. He insisted that he remained fully committed to AC/DC, but said, "It's a tough one. It's not me—it's just my age. Age catches up on you. I try to keep myself fit, and I love it being in this band. But it's not just me—Cliff is knocking on a bit more than the others. The other lads are in their early fifties. I'm the old dog in the regiment. It's a purely selfish thing. I don't want to look a prat if I try to push it too far. I don't want for people to see me on stage and say, 'Oh, poor old fucker, the band's carrying him!'"

I asked Brian how long he thought he and the band could continue. He laughed and recalled a recent conversation with Malcolm: "We were talking about the end of the tour and I said, 'We're finishing in March and that's me done!' But Malcolm said,

Previous: **Brian Johnson on stage at Telenor Arena in Oslo, Norway—the first European show of the *Black Ice* tour**

Above: **The crowd at the 2003 Circus Krone show in Munich. The live recording was included on *Backtracks*—AC/DC's second box set released on November 10, 2009.**

Right: **AC/DC play the first night at the Download Festival (formerly Monsters of Rock) in 2010 on a custom-built stage**

AC/DC
AC/DC

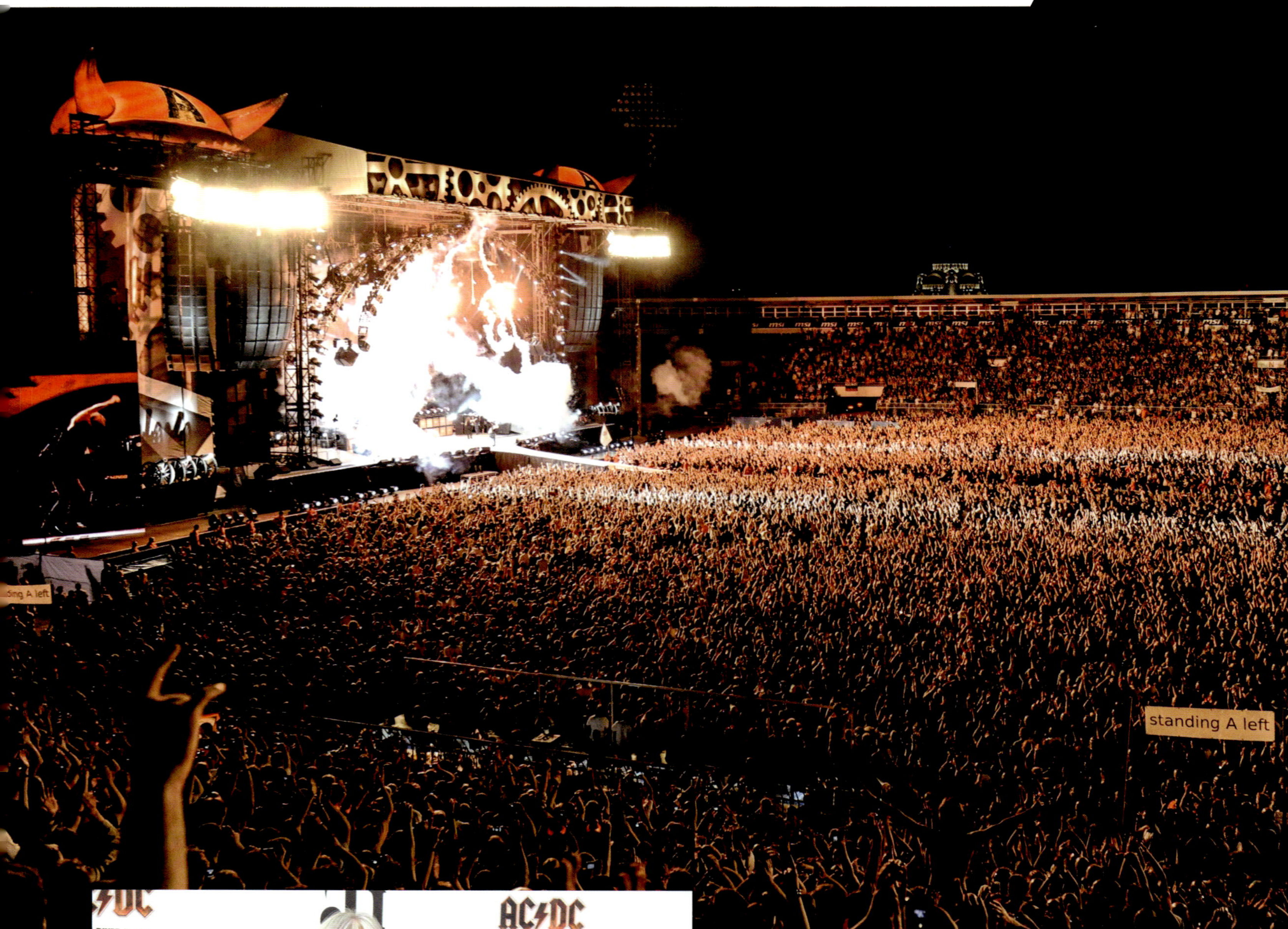

"I'll keep going till I can't."

Malcolm Young

'What are you talkin' about? We're not gonna let you retire!' And now they're talking about next year. I'm going, 'What do you mean next year? We're finishing in March in Japan, I'll be tired!' And they said, 'Well, we've been offered some festivals . . . ' We just keep selling tickets and I'm just going, Jesus Christ!"

At the end of July, AC/DC returned to the US for another three months. On November 10, the band's second boxed set was released, named *Backtracks*, and issued in deluxe format with three CDs, two DVDs, a vinyl LP, and hardback book; and a cheaper standard format with two CDs and one DVD. As with *Bonfire*, the onus was on rare and previously unreleased material, which included great old songs from the Bon Scott era such as "R.I.P. (Rock In Peace)" and "Crabsody In Blue," live and studio tracks originally issued as B-sides, promo videos not included on the 2005 DVD *Family Jewels*, and the 2003 live performance filmed at the Circus Krone in Munich.

At the end of November, AC/DC ventured down to South America. The first show in Brazil, at the Estádio do Morumbi in São Paulo, drew an audience of sixty-nine thousand. It was followed by three nights at the River Plate Stadium in the Argentinian capital of Buenos Aires on December 2, 4, and 6. It was there, on the second night, that the *Black Ice* tour was recorded in all its glory for the album and DVD *Live At River Plate*, released in 2012. Rock fans in South America have long been known for their excitability, and with more than seventy thousand inside this huge auditorium, the band played to an electrifying atmosphere. The reaction to the first bars of "Rock 'n' Roll Train" was so intense—thousands of bodies bouncing in unison, voices singing along to the riff—that Brian Johnson was seen in close-up cheering back at the crowd, his fists clenched with the adrenalin coursing through him. Moments later, he was singing the chorus along a ramp running out from the stage into the heart of the arena, flanked on both sides by a sea of raised hands. Angus followed him out there, duckwalking as he played the solo, and doffing his school cap in salute. In the two hours that followed, the level of energy, from band and audience, never dipped.

The tour was extended, just as Brian had indicated to me in the summer. The last run came in May and June with a series of huge open-air shows in Europe. On June 11 there was a return to Donington Park, where AC/DC had headlined

Opposite top: **The *Black Ice* tour finished with a series of open-air shows across Europe. Pictured here, Partizan Stadium, Belgrade, Serbia, on May 26, 2009**

Opposite bottom: **At the premiere of AC/DC's—*Live At River Plate* in London:** (L–R) **Malcolm Young, Cliff Williams, Angus Young, and Brian Johnson**

Left: **Angus Young, fifty-five and still dynamite on stage**

three Monsters of Rock shows in the past. The event had since been rebranded as the Download Festival, and expanded from one day to three. AC/DC played on the first night, using a gigantic, custom-built stage, positioned beside the one where Rage Against the Machine and Aerosmith topped the bill on the following nights. One hundred thousand people were in attendance as AC/DC blasted away, from "Rock 'n' Roll Train" to the smoke-and-thunder finale of "For Those About To Rock (We Salute You)."

The final date on the *Black Ice* tour came seventeen days later, at the San Mamés Stadium in Bilbao, Spain. This tour was, on every level, the biggest that AC/DC had ever played. Thirty years after *Back In Black*, the band's power was undiminished. However, away from the spotlight, all was not as it seemed.

At fifty-five, Angus Young was still the same human dynamo. For two hours a night on stage he was running his socks off, rolling around and picking up bruises, sweating off the pounds from his already tiny frame. As Metallica's James Hetfield said to me in 2009, with an air of incredulity: "You look at Angus now and he's still going strong—it's unbelievable. You'd think that guy's head would have fallen off—it's swiveled so hard! You'd think he would have just fallen apart."

Brian Johnson had admitted to me that age was creeping up on him, but he was still belting it out after all those years of singing like a truck had been dropped on his foot. He and Angus were holding up just fine. Likewise, Cliff Williams and Phil Rudd. It was Malcolm Young who was struggling, and had been ever since he and Angus started writing the songs for *Black Ice*.

As Angus later revealed in an interview with *ABC News Australia*: "When we were making *Black Ice*, when we were writing songs together, me and him, it was noticeable—just strange things, memory things. Malcolm was always very organized, and for the first time I saw him confused about a lot of things. That's when it hit me, that something's not right with him." It was at that point that Malcolm Young was diagnosed with dementia. With a world tour ahead of the band, Angus had asked his brother: "Do you want to keep doing this?" Malcolm replied: "I'll keep going till I can't."

When I interviewed Brian Johnson in the summer of 2009, he had been covering for Malcolm when he said it was Malcolm who would not let him retire. This much was evident in what Brian later said of the *Black Ice* tour to *ABC News*: "Malcolm started to rehearse the songs that he played every day for thirty years—before he did a show."

Malcolm Young was tough. He had beaten alcoholism. But this was a battle he could not win. After he had walked off the stage in Bilbao on June 28, 2010, there was no way back.

Clockwise from opposite top: **Phil Rudd, Cliff Williams, Brian Johnson and Malcolm Young on the *Black Ice* tour; the last for Malcolm.**

BLACK ICE

Released: October 20, 2008
Recorded: March 3–April 25, 2008, The Warehouse Studio, Vancouver, British Columbia, Canada
Label: Columbia
Producer: Brendan O'Brien

All tracks written by Angus Young and Malcolm Young.

SIDE ONE
"Rock 'n' Roll Train"
"Skies On Fire"
"Big Jack"
"Anything Goes"

SIDE TWO
"War Machine"
"Smash 'n' Grab"
"Spoilin' For A Fight"
"Wheels"

SIDE THREE
"Decibel"
"Stormy May Day"
"She Likes Rock 'n' Roll"
"Money Made"

SIDE FOUR
"Rock 'n' Roll Dream"
"Rocking All The Way"
"Black Ice"

PERSONNEL
Angus Young—lead guitar, slide guitar on "Stormy May Day"
Malcolm Young—rhythm guitar, backing vocals
Brian Johnson—lead vocals
Cliff Williams—bass guitar, backing vocals
Phil Rudd—drums, percussion

Additional personnel
Mike Fraser—engineer and mixing
Joshua Marc Levy—art direction and illustrations using vector graphics by You Work For Them LLC

With fifteen tracks, *Black Ice* has the longest running time of any AC/DC studio album, just short of an hour. It hit number one in twenty-nine countries, including Australia, the UK, the US, and throughout Europe, making it—in terms of chart positions, not sales—the highest performing AC/DC album ever.

Black Ice is the final album to feature the *Back In Black* era line-up of AC/DC, with founding rhythm guitarist Malcolm Young leaving the band in September 2014 following a diagnosis of dementia.

BACKTRACKS

Released: November 10, 2009
Recorded: 1974–2009
Label: Columbia

CD 1—STUDIO RARITIES

DISC ONE
All tracks written by Angus Young, Malcolm Young, and Bon Scott, except where noted.

"High Voltage" (deluxe edition only)
"Stick Around"
"Love Song"
"It's A Long Way To The Top" (deluxe edition only)
"Rocker" (deluxe edition only)
"Fling Thing" Young, Young
"Dirty Deeds Done Dirt Cheap" (deluxe edition only)
"Ain't No Fun (Waitin' Round To Be A Millionaire)" (deluxe edition only)
"R.I.P. (Rock In Peace)"
"Carry Me Home"
"Crabsody In Blue"
"Cold Hearted Man"
"Who Made Who Special Collector's Mix" (Young, Young, Johnson; deluxe edition only)
"Eye" (Young, Young, Johnson)
"Borrowed Time" (Young, Young, Johnson)
"Down On The Borderline" (Young, Young, Johnson)
"Big Gun" (Young, Young)
"Cyberspace" (Young, Young)

CDS 2 AND 3—LIVE RARITIES

DISC TWO

All tracks written by Angus Young, Malcolm Young, and Bon Scott, except where noted.

"Dirty Deeds Done Dirt Cheap" (Live at the Festival of Sydney, Haymarket, Australia, January 30, 1977)
"Dog Eat Dog" (Live at the Apollo, Glasgow, Scotland, April 30, 1978)
"Live Wire" (Live at the Hammersmith Odeon, London, November 2, 1979)
"Shot Down In Flames" (Live at the Hammersmith Odeon, London, November 2, 1979)
"Back In Black" (Young, Young, Johnson; live at the Capital Centre, Landover, Maryland, December 21, 1981)
"T.N.T." (Live at the Capital Centre, Landover, Maryland, December 21, 1981)
"Let There Be Rock" (Live at the Capital Centre, Landover, Maryland, December 21, 1981)
"Guns For Hire" (Young, Young, Johnson; live at the Joe Louis Arena, Detroit, Michigan, November 18, 1983)
"Sin City" (Live at the Joe Louis Arena, Detroit, Michigan, November 17, 1983 - deluxe edition only)
"Rock And Roll Ain't Noise Pollution" (Young, Young, Johnson; live at the Joe Louis Arena, Detroit, Michigan, November 18, 1983)
"This House Is On Fire" (Young, Young, Johnson; live at the Joe Louis Arena, Detroit, Michigan, November 18, 1983)
"You Shook Me All Night Long" (Young, Young, Johnson; live at the Joe Louis Arena, Detroit, Michigan, November 18, 1983)
"Jailbreak" (Live at the Reunion Arena. Dallas, Texas, October 12, 1985)
"Shoot To Thrill" (Young, Young, Johnson; live at Castle Donington, Leicestershire, England, August 17, 1991; deluxe edition only)
"Hell Ain't A Bad Place To Be" (Live at Castle Donington, Leicestershire, England, August 17, 1991; deluxe edition only)

DISC THREE

All tracks on the deluxe edition only, except where noted. All tracks written by Angus Young, Malcolm Young, and Bon Scott, except where noted.

"High Voltage" (Live at Castle Donington, Leicestershire, England, August 17, 1991)
"Hells Bells" (Young, Young, Johnson; live at Castle Donington, Leicestershire, England, August 17, 1991)
"Whole Lotta Rosie" (Live at Castle Donington, Leicestershire, England, August 17, 1991)
"Dirty Deeds Done Dirt Cheap" (Live at Castle Donington, Leicestershire, England, August 17, 1991)
"Highway To Hell" (Live at the Tushino Airfield, Moscow, September 28, 1991; standard edition also)
"Back In Black" (Young, Young, Johnson; live at the Tushino Airfield, Moscow, September 28, 1991)
"For Those About To Rock" (Young, Young, Johnson; live at the Tushino Airfield, Moscow, September 28, 1991; standard edition also)
"Ballbreaker" (Young, Young; Live at the Plaza de Toros de Las Ventras, Madrid, July 10, 1996)
"Hard As A Rock" (Young, Young; live at the Plaza de Toros de Las Ventras, Madrid, July 10, 1996)
"Dog Eat Dog" (Live at the Plaza de Toros de Las Ventras, Madrid, July 10, 1996)
"Hail Caesar" (Young, Young; live at the Plaza de Toros de Las Ventras, Madrid, July 10, 1996)
"Whole Lotta Rosie" (Live at the Plaza de Toros de Las Ventras, Madrid, July 10, 1996)
"You Shook Me All Night Long" (Young, Young, Johnson; live at the Plaza de Toros de Las Ventras, Madrid, July 10, 1996)
"Safe In New York City" (Young, Young; live at the American West Arena, Phoenix, Arizona, September 13, 2000; standard edition also)

FAMILY JEWELS DISC (DVD)

"Big Gun"
"Hard As A Rock"
"Hail Caesar"
"Cover You In Oil"
"Stiff Upper Lip"
"Satellite Blues"
"Safe In New York City"
"Rock 'n' Roll Train"
"Anything Goes"

Bonus videos:

"Jailbreak"
"It's A Long Way To The Top (If You Wanna Rock 'n' Roll)"
"Highway To Hell"
"You Shook Me All Night Long"
"Guns For Hire"
"Dirty, Deeds Done Dirt Cheap (live)
"Highway To Hell" (live)

Bonus features:

"The Making of 'Hard As A Rock'"
"The Making of 'Rock 'n' Roll Train'"
"Live at the Circus Krone" 2003 [edit]

LIVE AT THE CIRCUS KRONE DVD

DELUXE EDITION ONLY

Introduction
"Hell Ain't A Bad Place To Be"
"Back In Black"
"Stiff Upper Lip"
"Shoot To Thrill"
"Thunderstruck"
"Rock 'n' Roll Damnation"
"What's Next To The Moon"
"Hard As A Rock"
"Bad Boy Boogie"
"The Jack"
"If You Want Blood (You've Got It)"
"Hells Bells"
"Dirty Deeds Done Dirt Cheap"
"Rock 'n' Roll Ain't Noise Pollution"
"T.N.T."
"Let There Be Rock"
"Highway To Hell"
"For Those About To Rock (We Salute You)"
"Whole Lotta Rosie"

RARITIES 180 GRAM LP

SIDE ONE

"Stick Around"
"Love Song"
"Fling Thing"
"R.I.P (Rock In Peace)"
"Carry Me Home"
"Crabsody In Blue"

SIDE TWO

"Cold Hearted Man"
"Snake Eye"
"Borrowed Time"
"Down On The Borderline"
"Big Gun"
"Cyberspace"

"You look at Angus now and he's still going strong—it's unbelievable. You'd think that guy's head would have fallen off—it's swiveled so hard!

James Hetfield, Metallica

PERSONNEL

Angus Young—lead guitar,
Malcolm Young—rhythm guitar
Brian Johnson—lead vocals
Cliff Williams—bass guitar,
Phil Rudd—drums, percussion
Bon Scott—lead vocals on "Jailbreak," "It's A Long Way To The Top (If You Wanna Rock 'n' Roll)," "Highway To Hell"
Mark Evans—bass guitar on "Jailbreak," "It's A Long Way To The Top (If You Wanna Rock 'n' Roll)"
Simon Wright—drums on "Guns For Hire"
Chris Slade—drums on "Big Gun," "Dirty Deeds Done Dirt Cheap (live)," Highway To Hell (live)"

Additional personnel

Phil Yarnell and **John Jackson**—art direction,
Phil Yarnell SMAY DESIGN—cover art

Left: **Duckwalking, Angus Young still going strong on the *Black Ice* tour, 2010 at Cartuja Olympic Stadium in Seville, Spain**

LIVE AT RIVER PLATE

Released: November 19, 2012
Recorded: December 4, 2009, River Plate Stadium, Buenos Aires, Argentina
Label: Columbia

All tracks written by Angus Young, Malcolm Young, and Bon Scott; except where noted.

DISC ONE

"Rock 'n' Roll Train" (Young, Young)
"Hell Ain't A Bad Place To Be"
"Back In Black" (Young, Young, Johnson)
"Big Jack" (Young, Young)
"Dirty Deeds Done Dirt Cheap"
"Shot Down In Flames"
"Thunderstruck" (Young, Young)
"Black Ice" (Young, Young)
"The Jack"
"Hells Bells" (Young, Young, Johnson)

DISC TWO

"Shoot To Thrill" (Young, Young, Johnson)
"War Machine" (Young, Young)
"Dog Eat Dog"
"You Shook Me All Night Long" (Young, Young, Johnson)
"T.N.T."
"Whole Lotta Rosie"
"Let There Be Rock"
"Highway To Hell"
"For Those About To Rock (We Salute You)" (Young, Young, Johnson)

DISC THREE (SATURN.DE EXCLUSIVE EDITION)

"Rock And Roll Ain't Noise Pollution" (Young, Young, Johnson—incorrectly credited on packaging as Young, Young, B. Scott; live at the Circus Krone, Munich, June 17, 2003)
"If You Want Blood (You've Got It)" (Live at the Circus Krone, Munich, June 17, 2003)
"What's Next To The Moon" (Live at the Circus Krone, Munich, June 17, 2003)"

PERSONNEL

Brian Johnson—lead vocals
Angus Young—lead guitar, backing vocals in "T.N.T." and "Dirty Deeds Done Dirt Cheap"
Malcolm Young—rhythm guitar, backing vocals
Cliff Williams—bass guitar, backing vocals
Phil Rudd—drums

Additional personnel

Mike Fraser—engineer and mixing
Michelle Holme and **Josh Cheuse**—art direction
C. Taylor Crutners—photography

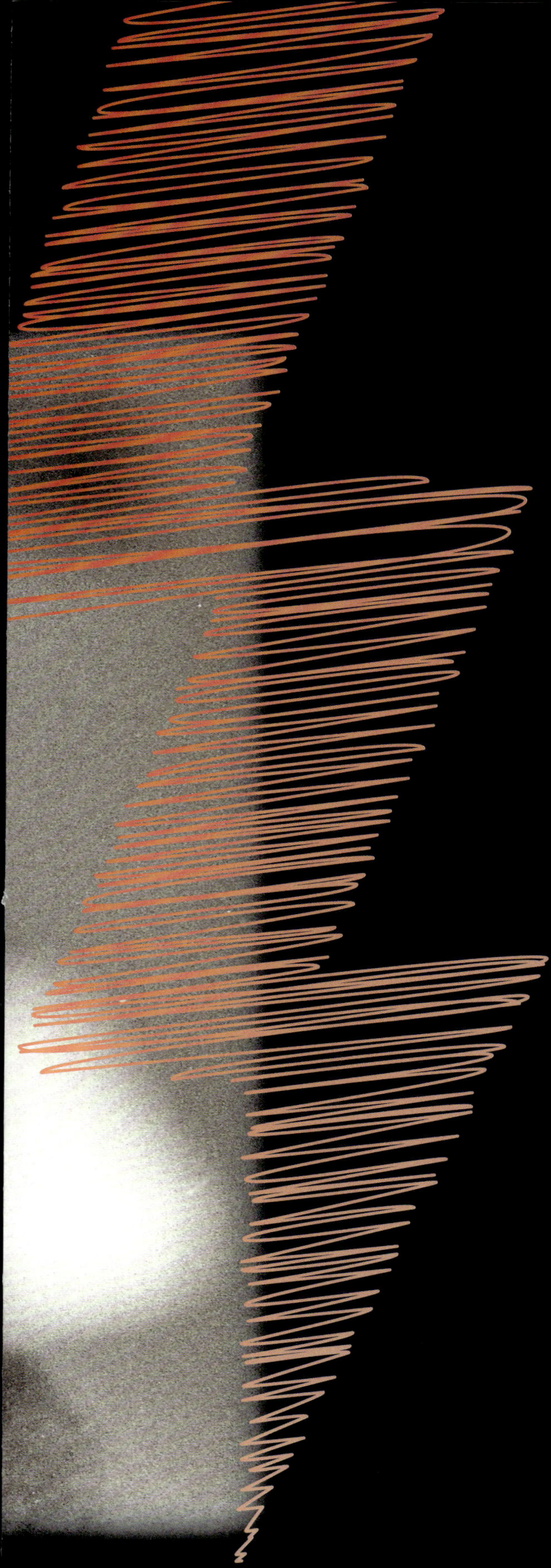

Last Man Standing

"Malcolm was an inspirational leader. He said, 'Keep making music. Just keep doing it.' If Ang said, 'I can't do it without Malcolm,' I'd have understood perfectly."

Brian Johnson

It was in 2014, in the months leading up to the release of AC/DC's album *Rock Or Bust,* when the truth about Malcolm Young was made public. First, in April, came a statement from the band: "After 40 years of life dedicated to AC/DC, guitarist and founding member Malcolm Young is taking a break from the band due to ill health. Malcolm would like to thank the group's die-hard legions of fans worldwide for their never-ending love and support. In light of this news, AC/DC asks that Malcolm and his family's privacy be respected during this time. The band will continue to make music." In July, Brian Johnson revealed to *Classic Rock* magazine that Malcolm had been absent from the recording of the album and was being treated in hospital for an unspecified condition. "We miss Malcolm obviously," Brian said. "He's a fighter. We've got our fingers crossed that he'll get strong again. He's such a strong man. He's a small guy but he's very strong. He's proud and he's very private, so we can't say too much. But fingers crossed he'll be back."

It was not to be. A statement from AC/DC's management in September confirmed: "Unfortunately, due to the nature of Malcolm's illness, he will not be rejoining the band. Stevie Young, nephew of founding members Angus and Malcolm Young, plays guitar on *Rock Or Bust* and will accompany the band on tour." Just days later, *The Sydney Morning Herald* revealed the nature of Malcolm's condition. The report stated: "Malcolm Young has been moved into full-time care in a nursing home facility in Sydney's eastern suburbs specializing in dementia, sources connected to the Young family have said. He has a complete loss of short-term memory. His wife, Linda, has put him in full-time care."

The sense of loss within the band was profound. What kept them going were the words Malcolm had said to them when he realized he could no longer be a part of the band. As Brian told *ABC News Australia:* "Malcolm was an inspirational leader. He said, 'Keep making music. Just keep doing it.' That's the way he talked." Brian also revealed that the decision for AC/DC to continue was made by the man who knew Malcolm best. "To me," he said, "it was always up to Angus. If Ang turned round and said, 'I can't do it without Malcolm,' I'd have understood perfectly."

History was repeating. After the death of Bon Scott, it was Bon's father who urged Malcolm and Angus to carry on, as Bon would have wanted. Thirty-four years later, AC/DC honored the words that Malcolm had said to them.

The ten songs they recorded for *Rock Or Bust* were credited to Malcolm and Angus. As Angus told *ABC News Australia:* "Mal kept writing up until he could do it no more." Stevie Young was perhaps the only player who could have come into the band at such a difficult time. He was family. He had stood in for Malcolm before, during the *Blow Up Your Video* tour, when Malcolm was

in rehab. Stevie was also only two years younger than Angus, his uncle. As Angus had told me in 2003: "Stevie's like Malcolm, a real rhythm player, like Keith Richards, Ike Turner, Pete Townshend. There aren't many like them today."

Rock Or Bust was recorded at the same place where *Black Ice* was made, The Warehouse Studio in Vancouver, and with the same producer and engineer, Brendan O'Brien and Mike Fraser. The album was cut in a little over two months, from May 3 to July 12. Brian said to *ABC News* that making a record without Malcolm was "a strange feeling," but added, "On this album there was a special togetherness."

It was just three weeks before the album's release that another crisis hit the band. On November 6, Phil Rudd was arrested following a police raid on his home in Tauranga, on New Zealand's North Island. Rudd was charged with attempting to procure a murder, threatening to kill, possession of methamphetamine, and possession of cannabis. While the charge of attempting to procure a murder was withdrawn on the following day, AC/DC's management had by then issued a statement regarding Rudd: "Phil's absence will not affect the release of our new album *Rock Or Bust* and upcoming tour next year."

The album was released on November 28, with a lenticular cover design in which the band logo was exploding rock. That much was classic AC/DC. On the inside cover though, was an image of great

Previous: **Malcolm Young in 1995**

Far left: **Brian Johnson and Angus Young pictured together in 2014, a year before Brian's departure from AC/DC**

Left: **Malcolm and Angus's nephew, Stevie Young, played guitar on *Rock Or Bust* and then toured with the band.**

When Phil Rudd (top) **was arrested, Chris Slade** (right), **was reappointed to play drums on the *Rock Or Bust* tour.**

poignancy: a sepia photograph of two guitars, Angus's Gibson SG and Malcolm's Gretsch, resting together against a Marshall amplifier stack, with a line from the song "Rock Or Bust" printed above: "In rock we trust." On the cover of the CD booklet was a black-and-white picture of vintage AC/DC badges on a worn denim jacket, one badge emblazoned with "Bon Scott, RIP, 1980." A final message was printed on a black page opposite a close-up shot of that Gretsch guitar: "And most important of all, thanks to Mal, who made it all possible."

In a sense, *Rock Or Bust* was as much a tribute to Malcolm as *Back In Black* was to Bon. Brian Johnson had wanted to name the album "Man Down," in salute to Malcolm, but *Rock Or Bust* was a better fit for what this album represented—in the words that Malcolm once said to me, "just loud rock 'n' roll—wham, bam, thank you ma'am!" And if this was not as great an album as many that had come before it, in the circumstances it was good enough.

There were some dissenting voices. Andrew Stafford wrote in *The Guardian*: "Without Malcolm Young, AC have, in effect, lost their DC, the man that made them a true rock *and* roll—as distinct from a mere rock—band." Nevertheless, most reviews celebrated the grit in *Rock Or Bust*—in the music and in the band's determination to soldier on. *Classic Rock*'s Rob Hughes stated: "*Rock Or Bust*, the product of AC/DC's own uncertain times, is a towering retort to any notion that they might be finished. As the name suggests, it's an album that places its faith at the feet of rock 'n' roll, both as a restorative force and also as a vaccine against all ills. Nowhere is this more explicitly stated than on the title track, which heaves along on the kind of monolithic riff Angus Young patented sometime around the Stone Age." *In Rolling Stone*, writer Kory Grow hailed AC/DC as "hard rock's masters of déjà vu."

The album hit number one in Australia, number three in the US and the UK, and top ten all around the world. With Phil Rudd out of the band, Chris Slade was reappointed as AC/DC's drummer, a safe pair of hands. The *Rock Or Bust* tour began in April 2015 with a two-night stand at the Coachella Valley Music and Arts Festival in California, where the band played to one hundred thousand people each night. From May through to July, there were stadium shows in Europe, including Berlin, Paris, Madrid, Glasgow, and London. In the classic AC/DC tradition, the shows opened with a new song, "Rock Or Bust," and ended with "For Those About To Rock (We Salute You)." The band was rock solid, even without Malcolm and Phil Rudd. As *The Guardian*'s Michael Hann stated in a review of the London show at Wembley Stadium on July 4: "It's a different band that takes to the stage from the one that played this

Right: **AC/DC at Coachella 2015 where they kicked off their *Rock Or Bust* tour with a two-night stand**

AC/DC

same stadium almost exactly six years ago. Age has withered them, a little. But the essence of AC/DC remains utterly unchanged. It is, of course, magnificent. It's too loud, the sound is imperfect, and Angus Young's solo during 'Let There Be Rock' seems to last—as it always does—several eternities. But it is also wonderful: rock 'n' roll reduced to its purest essence, in doses of flavour so concentrated they seem to set the world alight."

It seemed as if the band's troubles were behind them, but in early 2016, another crisis came. It resulted in Brian Johnson's exit from AC/DC, and following that, the most bizarre episode in the band's career.

It was on the last run of US dates, after a show in Kansas City, Missouri on February 28, that Brian Johnson withdrew from the tour on medical advice after sustaining ear damage. A statement on the band's website, posted on March 7, confirmed the news: "AC/DC are forced to reschedule the ten upcoming dates on the US leg of their *Rock Or Bust* World Tour. AC/DC's lead singer, Brian Johnson, has been advised by doctors to stop touring immediately or risk total hearing loss." And to this, the statement added: "Tomorrow's show in Atlanta through Madison Square Garden in New York in early April will be made up later in the year, likely with a guest vocalist." There were also dates in Europe to be rescheduled.

AC/DC fans were stunned by the news and there was widespread speculation as to who would replace Brian Johnson as "guest vocalist" on the AC/DC tour. Among the names mentioned were Jimmy Barnes and Angry Anderson. Then came the rumor that Guns N' Roses singer Axl Rose was in line for the job. At first it appeared to be a hoax. Only two months earlier, it had been announced that two members of the classic Guns N' Roses line-up—Slash and bassist Duff McKagan—had rejoined the band, marking the end of a bitter twenty-year feud between Axl and Slash. Guns N' Roses were headlining at Coachella on April 16 and 23, and there would be a major tour to follow. In purely logistical terms, it seemed unlikely that Axl could perform with two bands in the same time frame. Equally, Axl's persona did not seem a natural fit for AC/DC. He was renowned as a prima donna who frequently kept audiences waiting for hours before a show. That was not how AC/DC operated. Nonetheless, on March 28—three days after Guns N' Roses announced the *Not In This Lifetime...Tour*,

The shock announcement that Brian Johnson (pictured bottom left singing at his last show for AC/DC) **was leaving the band sparked widespread speculation as to who would replace him. Suggestions included Angry Anderson** (right) **and Jimmy Barnes of Cold Chisel** (below right).

beginning with twenty-one stadium shows in North America—the website TMZ posted a photo of Axl exiting an Atlanta rehearsal space with Angus Young and AC/DC's bassist and drummer, Cliff Williams, and Chris Slade. What had been jokingly named "AXL/DC" was suddenly a very real possibility.

With no subsequent statement from AC/DC, or from Brian Johnson, the situation with Axl Rose was further complicated when he sustained an injury on stage with Guns N' Roses at the Troubadour club in Los Angeles on April 1, the band's first show since the return of Slash and Duff McKagan. Axl broke bones in his foot after jumping off the drum riser, but another rock star came to Axl's rescue. Foo Fighters leader Dave Grohl had broken his leg during a tour, but had managed to keep the show on the road by performing while seated in a custom-made "throne" decorated with an array of guitar necks. It was from this throne that Axl sang when Guns N' Roses played in Las Vegas on April 8 and 9.

A week later, just hours before Guns N' Roses took to the stage at Coachella, came an announcement from AC/DC in which the rumors about Axl were confirmed: "AC/DC band members would like to thank Brian Johnson for his contributions and dedication to the band throughout the years. We wish him all the best with his hearing issues and future ventures. As much as we want this tour to end as it started, we understand, respect and support Brian's decision to stop touring and save his hearing. We are dedicated to fulfilling the remainder of our touring commitments to everyone that has supported us over the years, and are fortunate

that Axl Rose has kindly offered his support to help us fulfill this commitment." And at Coachella there was a taste of what was to come. An hour into Guns N' Roses' set, Axl told the audience: "Since I can't run around for you, we're gonna bring out a friend . . . " Angus Young appeared, in full schoolboy regalia, to join the band for a blast through the AC/DC classics "Whole Lotta Rosie" and "Riff Raff." Twenty-nine years after Axl had sung "Whole Lotta Rosie" with Guns N' Roses at the Marquee, he proved again that he could still nail it.

In the same month, Brian Johnson broke his silence with a statement in which he said he was "personally crushed" by his enforced exit from the AC/DC tour. "I was having difficulty hearing the guitars on stage and because I was not able to hear the other musicians clearly, I feared the quality of my performance could be compromised." The statement continued: "I wish to assure our fans that I am not retiring. My doctors have told me that I can continue to record in studios and I intend to do that. I am hoping that in time my hearing will improve and allow me to return to live concert performances. While the outcome is uncertain, my attitude is optimistic."

With AC/DC's US dates rescheduled for August and September, Axl Rose's first show with the band was on May 7 at the Passeio Marítimo de Algés stadium in the Portuguese capital of Lisbon. Before an audience of sixty thousand, Rose delivered, from his throne, what *Classic Rock* writer Fraser Lewry called "an astonishing, tour-de-force performance". At one point during the show, the audience began chanting "Axl! Axl!" He responded, smiling, "You mean Angus." Lewry hailed this performance as a victory for Axl. "On this showing, it really feels like it could work. And he did it from a chair . . . "

Another critic who witnessed the Lisbon show was *The Guardian*'s Michael Hann, who had described AC/DC as "a different band" when they played in London the previous summer without Malcolm Young and Phil Rudd. With Axl in place of Brian Johnson, the band had changed almost beyond recognition. But as Hann stated: "The triumph lies in the renditions of the songs AC/DC wrote and recorded when Bon Scott was still alive. Whereas the Johnson-era material tended towards boozy bonhomie, Scott was often a malevolently misanthropic writer and singer, concealing a slightly terrifying rage behind apparent good humor.

Previous: **Slash and Angus Young share the stage at Coachella 2016 where the newly reformed Guns N' Roses were headlining.**

Opposite: ***The Rock Or Bust* tour continued with Axl Rose** (left) **taking up Brian's role as singer.**

Left: **Brian Johnson was "personally crushed" by what he saw as his enforced exit from AC/DC.**

Rose, who is familiar with both malevolence and misanthropy, delivers those songs perfectly, giving them fresh menace. "Dirty Deeds Done Dirt Cheap" loses its cartoonish aspect, and becomes the bar-room chatter of a psychopath; he introduces "Shot Down in Flames" as "the story of my life" and convinces you it's true. His voice, too, is brilliant: no matter how high, every note is hit, and sustained. And he keeps it up for two hours."

By the time the tour reached Vienna on May 19, Axl was able to stand again. While the band rolled on without him, Brian Johnson gave an interview to SiriusXM radio in the US in which he explained how the damage to his hearing originated. He had been racing cars at an event in Watkins Glen, New York in 2008 when he wore a new helmet and neglected to use protective earplugs. "Off I went, and after about thirty-five minutes, my left ear just let out a little pop," he said. "And I went, 'What the heck was that?' All that happened was I suffered tinnitus for about six or seven months, but unfortunately, on stage, you don't have any defense . . . that industrial noise every night on stage . . . I mean, you're in a rock 'n' roll band. What the hell do you expect?" What Johnson said at the end of that interview was an admission that his time with AC/DC was finished. "I'm lucky. I'm sixty-nine this year. I've had a pretty good run. I've been in one of the best bands in the world. I had so many good times with the boys. I've had such a lucky and great life."

The *Rock Or Bust* tour carried on through Europe until June 15. Eight days later, Axl was back with Guns N' Roses for their US stadium shows. Before Axl hooked up with AC/DC again on August 27 to see out the tour with the last ten dates in America, there was one more bombshell for AC/DC fans. In early July, Cliff Williams told American magazine *Gulfshore Life* that he was leaving the band at the end of the tour. "It's been what I've known for the past forty years," Cliff said. "But after this tour I'm backing off of touring and recording. Losing Malcolm, the thing with Phil and now with Brian, it's a changed animal. I feel in my gut it's the right thing."

On August 1, Angus Young spoke to *Rolling Stone*'s David Fricke about the tumultuous events in AC/DC's recent history. Angus said of his brother Malcolm's condition: "It's hard to communicate.

But I let him know there are a lot of people missing him." He said of Brian Johnson: "It was becoming too hard for him." Of Axl Rose: "He's more in the Bon style—the rock 'n' roll character." He said of the man who had played bass with AC/DC since 1977: "Cliff made it known before we'd even started touring—this would be his last." And of his future, and that of the band, Angus admitted: "At this point, I don't know. We were committed to finishing the tour. Who knows what I'll feel after?"

Brian Johnson (left) **and Cliff Williams** (below), **in their last performances for AC/DC. While Brian's exit was unforeseen, Cliff was always certain that he would call it quits at the end of the *Rock Or Bust* tour.**

The end of the tour came on September 20 at the Wells Fargo Arena in Philadelphia. At the climax of "For Those About To Rock (We Salute You)," Cliff Williams stepped forward to take his final bow. And when the smoke cleared from the stage, Angus Young was all that was left of the band that made the biggest rock album of all time. The little guy in the shorts had become the last man standing.

In the year that followed, there was no official statement from AC/DC regarding the future of the band. Angus Young laid low. A rare public appearance came on October 9, 2017 when he saw

"The bond we had was unique and very special."

Angus Young

The Rolling Stones play in Düsseldorf and was photographed backstage with Keith Richards.

Brian Johnson was more visible. He fronted the TV series *Brian Johnson's A Life On The Road,* in which he interviewed other famous rock stars—former Led Zeppelin singer Robert Plant, Pink Floyd drummer Nick Mason, Sting, Joe Elliott of Def Leppard, and Metallica drummer Lars Ulrich. More surprising was Johnson's return to the stage. On May 14, 2017, when former Free and Bad Company singer Paul Rodgers performed at the New Theatre in Oxford, Johnson and Robert Plant got up to sing with Rodgers on a cover of the Barrett Strong classic "Money." And on August 27, at The Reading Festival, Brian made a guest appearance with British rock band Muse, singing an AC/DC song, "Back In Black." He sang it the way he always did, full-tilt. While there was a broad smile on his face, the words in the song took on a deeper meaning: "I've been too long, I'm glad to be back . . . "

AC/DC fans responded with calls for Brian's return to the band. But there was another singer who had already indicated that he had unfinished business with AC/DC. In September 2016, during the latter stages of the *Rock Or Bust* tour, Axl Rose had been interviewed alongside Angus Young and Cliff Williams for Brazilian TV show *Fantástico.* Axl said of his role with AC/DC: "I take pride in doing it. I'll do that as long as Angus wants to do it."

Phil Rudd also spoke of his desire to rejoin the band. Since his departure in 2014, the drummer had served eight months on home detention and also suffered a heart attack in 2016. Following the release of his solo album, aptly named *Head Job*, Rudd told *Classic Rock* in April 2017: "I'm always available for Angus. He knows that. I miss being in AC/DC. I've no idea what's going on with them. It's all because of my own stupidity, and of course I regret that. But I am a changed man."

What happened in the last months of 2017 was devastating for Angus Young. On October 20 came the news that George Young had passed away, aged seventy. The big brother who had done so much to inspire Malcolm and Angus and to define the sound of AC/DC was mourned in a statement from the band which read: "It is with pain in our heart that we have to announce the passing of our beloved brother and mentor."

Less than a month later, on November 18, it was announced that Malcolm Young had died at the age of sixty-four. A statement from the band read: "It is with deep heartfelt sadness that AC/DC has to announce the passing of Malcolm Young. Malcolm, along with Angus, was the founder and creator of AC/DC. With enormous dedication and commitment he was the driving force behind the band. As a guitarist, songwriter and visionary he was a perfectionist and a unique man. He always stuck to his guns and did and said exactly what he wanted. He took great pride in all that he endeavored. His loyalty to the fans was unsurpassed." Malcolm

Opposite: **Brothers Angus and Malcolm Young in 2010**

Left: **A fan holds a photograph of Malcolm Young at his funeral in Sydney. Malcolm passed away on November 18, 2017 after suffering from dementia for several years.**

Young's family issued a separate statement in which it was said that he had died peacefully, with his family at his side. From Angus there was this moving dedication: "As his brother it is hard to express in words what he has meant to me during my life, the bond we had was unique and very special. He leaves behind an enormous legacy that will live on forever. Malcolm, job well done."

In the days that followed, there were tributes from leading figures in rock, many of whom had shared stages with AC/DC. From Eddie Van Halen: "It is a sad day in rock 'n' roll. Malcolm Young was my friend and the heart and soul of AC/DC. I had some of the best times of my life with him on our 1984 European tour. He will be missed and my deepest condolences to his family, bandmates and friends." From Def Leppard's Joe Elliott: "I'm sad to hear of the passing of Malcolm Young. It was great to get the opportunity to open for AC/DC on the *Highway To Hell* tour and we certainly learned a thing or two. He was an incredible guitar player and the glue for that band onstage and off. RIP Malcolm, say hi to Bon." And from Slash of Guns N' Roses: "Malcolm Young was one of the best ever rhythm guitarists in rock 'n' roll. He was a fantastic songwriter and he had a great work ethic too. I toured with AC/DC on their *Stiff Upper Lip* tour. I found Malcolm to be a really cool, down to earth fellow. The entire rock 'n' roll community is heartbroken by his passing."

Brian Johnson told *Rolling Stone*: "Malcolm would have been absolutely stunned at the outpouring of tributes and grief. He didn't think of himself in that way, that he was great and all that. I learned the team spirit from Malcolm. You are just a cog in a well-oiled machine. If we all pulled together at the same time, you get this amazing thing happening. And it worked, you know. Mal is not here anymore, but if I ever have a problem I stop and go, 'What would Mal do?' He just always seemed to do the right thing."

In the aftermath, it was Angus alone who would decide the future of AC/DC. He still had his nephew Stevie with him, and also Chris Slade. He could find another bass player. He could go with Axl again. He could reconcile with Brian Johnson, and with Phil Rudd. He could get one last album out of AC/DC, one last tour.

Angus could do the hardest thing of all, and just let go of the band to which he had dedicated his life. Or he could do what Malcolm had asked of him, just as Bon Scott's father had so many years before. Ride on.

ROCK OR BUST

Released: November 28, 2014
Recorded: May–July 2014, The Warehouse Studio, Vancouver, British Columbia, Canada
Label: Columbia
Producer: Brendan O'Brien and Mike Fraser

All tracks composed by Angus Young and Malcolm Young.

"Rock Or Bust"
"Play Ball"
"Rock The Blues Away"
"Miss Adventure"
"Dogs Of War"
"Got Some Rock & Roll Thunder"
"Hard Times"
"Baptism By Fire"
"Rock The House"
"Sweet Candy"
"Emission Control"

PERSONNEL

Brian Johnson—lead vocals
Angus Young—lead guitar, backing vocals
Stevie Young—rhythm guitar
Cliff Williams—bass guitar, backing vocals
Phil Rudd—drums

Additional personnel

Josh Cheuse—art direction
James Minchin III—photography
Istvan at Chaotic Atmospheres—cover art

The album features a lenticular cover design in which the band logo is exploding rock. The inside cover is a sepia photograph of two guitars, Angus's Gibson SG and Malcolm's Gretsch, resting together against a Marshall amplifier stack, with a line from the song "Rock Or Bust" printed above: "In rock we trust."

The cover of the CD booklet is a black-and-white picture of vintage AC/DC badges on a worn denim jacket, one badge emblazoned with "Bon Scott, RIP, 1980." A final message is printed on a black page opposite a close-up shot of Malcolm's Gretsch guitar: "And most important of all, thanks to Mal, who made it all possible."

Left: **Angus Young, AC/DC's last man standing**

ACKNOWLEDGMENTS

Thanks to Phil Sutcliffe, Sylvie Simmons, Malcolm Dome, Geoff Barton, Phil Alexander, Paul Brannigan, Jerry Ewing, Pete Flatt, Paul Sticca, Ben Mitchell, Chris Ingham, Howard and Louise Johnson, Tony Stewart, Joe Mackett, Rick Fell, Geoff Layne, Andy Hunns, Mark Blake, Sian Llewellyn, Scott Rowley, Joe Elliott, Keith Richards, Gary Rossington, James Hetfield, Slash, Pete Way, Jo Rippon, and Rob Nichols.

Special thanks to Angus Young and Brian Johnson.

This book is dedicated to George and Audrey, and to Pete and Sorcha.

Malcolm Young, Rock In Peace.

PICTURE CREDITS

B: Bottom, **C:** Center, **L:** Left, **R:** Right, **T:** Top

Alamy: 12 Dundee Photographics/Alamy Stock Photo; 14-15, 16TL, 16B, 142-3C Pictorial Press Ltd/Alamy Stock Photo; 16TR Granamour Weems Collection/Alamy Stock Photo; 18 INTERFOTO/Alamy Stock; Photo; 19R, 114-5, 120 Trinity Mirror/Mirrorpix /Alamy Stock Photo; 26 Lewton Cole/Alamy Stock Photo; 47B Jeff Morgan 10/Alamy Stock Photo; 57B, 85, 101, 139, 153, 158T (ticket) CBW/Alamy Stock Photo; 83L David Fowler/Alamy Stock Photo; 130TL Gonzales Photo/Alamy Stock Photo; 130TR Pete Jenkins/Alamy Stock Photo; 138 Martyn Goddard/Alamy Stock Photo; 157B MediaPunch Inc/Alamy Stock Photo; 214B WENN Ltd/Alamy Stock Photo; **Camera Press:** 74, 75 Steve Emberton/Camera Press London; **Getty Images:** 4-5, 36-37, 45, 49, 50-51, 51, 53, 108-109 Dick Barnatt/Redferns; 6, 92 Larry Hulst/Michael Ochs Archives/Getty; 7, 95 Michael Marks/Michael Ochs Archives/Getty Images; 8-9 Ron Pownall/Getty Images; 13L, 32 GAB Archive/Redferns; 13R Gunter Zint/K & K Ulf Kruger OHG/Redferns; 17 Keystone/Getty Images; 31 Stephen Lovekin/Getty Images; 33, 48, 63, 128-129B, 169T, 172-173, 177 Bob King/Redferns; 36TL Val Wilmer/Redferns/Getty Images; 36TR Ron Pownall/Corbis via Getty Images; 37 Gus Stewart/Redferns; 42, 46-47 Martyn Goddard/Corbis via Getty Images 44, 67, 70, 98-99, 112, 122, 130-131, 133, 134, 146, 148-149, 150 Michael Putland/Getty Images; 54, 158L, 158-159C Erica Echenberg/Redferns; 55 The Sydney Morning Herald/Fairfax Media via Getty Images; 58, 60-61, 62, 142, 143, 144 Michael Ochs Archives/Getty Images; 64T, 64B Ellen Poppinga-K & K/Redferns; 65 Estate Of Keith Morris/Redferns; 66, 68T Waring Abbott/Getty Images; 68B, 107, 154 Ebet Roberts/Redferns; 69, 126, 157T Chris Walter/WireImage; 77, 80-81 Richard McCaffrey/Michael Ochs Archive/Getty Images; 78L Ed Perlstein/Redferns/Getty Images; 78-79 Jon Sievert/Getty Images; 79 Pete Cronin/Redferns; 86-87, 104L, 123, 145 Fin Costello/Redferns; 100 David Corio/Redferns; 109 Paul Kane/Getty Images; 110 GREG WOOD/AFP/Getty Images; 119R Fairfax Media/Fairfax Media via Getty Images; 121, 174-175B Ian Dickson/Redferns; 124 Janet Knott/The Boston Globe via Getty Images; 129T, 188 Paul Natkin/Getty Images; 136-137 Koh Hasebe/Shinko Music/Getty Image; 144-145C Virginia Turbett/Redferns; 151 Clayton Call/Redferns; 156 Paul Natkin/WireImage; 159R Jazz Archiv Hamburg/ullstein bild via Getty Images; 162T Dave Hogan/Hulton Archive/Getty Images; 164 Peter Still/Redferns; 165C Lynn Goldsmith/Corbis/VCG via Getty Images; 170 Terry O'Neill/Getty Images; 174L, 175R, 214 Brian Rasic/Getty Images; 174-175T, 194-195 Mick Hutson/Redferns; 178-179, 222-223 Martyn Goodacre/Getty Images; 180L Lisa Haun/Michael Ochs Archives/Getty Images; 181 Patrick Ford/Redferns; 182-183 Jim Steinfeldt/Michael Ochs Archives/Getty Images; 190 SGranitz/WireImage; 192-193 Hayley Madden/Redferns; 195, 217T, 229T Martin Philbey/Redferns; 196-197 Alain BENAINOUS/Gamma-Rapho via Getty Images; 198 Kevin Kane/WireImage; 199T Frank Micelotta/Getty Images; 199B Dagmar Scherf/ullstein bild via Getty Images; 200T, 200B, 201T, 206-207 KMazur/WireImage; 202 Jo Hale/Getty Images; 207C Stuart Mostyn/Redferns; 207R, 224L Mike Coppola/Getty Images for SiriusXM; 210-211 Sara Johannessen/AFP/Getty Images; 212T Bernd Muller/Redferns; 214-215 Morena Brengola/Redferns; 216L, 216R Neil Lupin/Redferns; 217B Michael Hurcomb/Corbis via Getty Images; 224R Brill/ullstein bild via Getty Images; 225T Marty Melville/AFP/Getty Images; 225B Francesco Castaldo/Pacific Press/LightRocket via Getty Images; 226-227, 230-231 Frazer Harrison/Getty Images for Coachella; 228, 234-235 Jason Squires/WireImage; 233 HANS KLAUS TECHT/AFP/Getty Images; 236 Colin McConnell/Toronto Star via Getty Images; 237 PETER PARKS/AFP/Getty Images; **IconicPix Music Archive:** 72, 165T George Bodnar Archive/IconicPix; 76, 97 Alan Perry/IconicPix; 83R Philippe Hamon/Dalle/IconicPix; 88, 102 Eric Mistler/Dalle/IconicPix; 90-91 Kevin Estrada/Iconicpix; 93 Bob Alford/Cache Agency/Dalle/IconicPix; 127, 166, 201B George Chin/IconicPix; 161L PG Brunelli/IconicPix; 161R Eddie Malluk/IconicPix; 208T Zaine Lewis/IconicPix; **Peter Anderson:** 2, Peter Anderson; **Rex Shutterstock:** 10, 20, 22, 24-25, 38-39, 52, 111 Philip Morris/Rex/Shutterstock; 19L Ray Stevenson/REX/Shutterstock; 28-29 Chris Capstick/Rex/Shutterstock; 30 Mazel/Sunshine/Rex/Shutterstock; 34-35 Ltd/Newspix/REX/Shutterstock; 96 Richard Young/REX/Shutterstock; 104-105 Jeff Blackler/REX/Shutterstock; 116 Dezo Hoffmann/REX/Shutterstock; 118B, Ian Dickson/REX/Shutterstock; 118-119C Brian Moody/REX/Shutterstock; 128T Benjamin Lozovsky/BFA/REX/Shutterstock; 140-141, 147l, 147R, 152, 180TR Andre Csillag/REX/Shutterstock; 162-163B Images/REX/Shutterstock; 165B Peter Brooker/REX/Shutterstock; 176 Massimo Alabresi/AP/REX/Shutterstock; 191 Franco Greco/Epa/REX/Shutterstock; 194L Achmad Ibrahim/AP/Rex/Shutterstock; 197T Andrew Murray/REX/Shutterstock; 204 Rob Monk/Classic Rock Magazine/Rex/Shutterstock; 208-209C Angus Blackburn/REX/Shutterstock; 209R Ebry/LAT/REX/Shutterstock; 212-213, 229B Kevin Nixon/Class Rock Magazine/REX/Shutterstock; 221L Jose Manuel Vidal/REX/Shutterstock; 232 Will Ireland/Classic Rock magazine/REX/Shutterstock; 235R Rex/Shutterstock; 238 Amy Harris/REX/Shutterstock

Every effort has been made to trace and acknowledge the copyright holders. If any unintentional omission has occurred, we would be pleased to add an appropriate acknowledgement in any future edition of the book.

ALBUM COVERS: 40 *High Voltage* (Australia) Chris Gilbey, (Albert Productions) cover concept; 41 *TNT* Albert Productions; *56 High Voltage* (International) Michael Putland cover photography; 57L *Dirty Deeds Done Dirt Cheap* (Australia) Kettle Art Productions; 57R *Dirty Deeds Done Dirt Cheap* (International) Hipgnosis; 71L *Let There Be Rock* (Australia) Colin Stead; 71R *Let There Be Rock* (International) Bob Defrin art direction, Keith Morris cover photography; 84 *Powerage* Bob Defrin art direction, Jim Houghton, cover photography; 85 *If You Want Blood (You've Got It)* Bob Defrin art direction, Jim Houghton cover photography; 101 *Highway To Hell* Bob Defrin art direction, Jim Houghton cover photography; 139 *Back In Black* Bob Defrin art direction; 153 *For Those About To Rock (We Salute You)* Atlantic Records; 167L *Flick Of The Switch* Brent Richardson cover art, based on an original drawing by Angus Young; 167R *'74 Jailbreak* Atlantic Records; 168T *Fly On The Wall* Bob Defrin art direction, Todd Schorr cover illustration; 168B *Who Made Who* George Bodnar cover photography; 169 *Blow Up Your Video* Bill Smith Studio art direction, Gered Mankowitz cover photography; 184 *The Razors Edge* ATCO Records; 185 *AC/DC Live*, Bob Defrin art direction, Larry Busacca photography; 186L *Ballbreaker* Bob Defrin original art direction, SMAY design reissue design, Phil Heffernan at Colorspace and David McMacken cover illustration, Robert Ellis cover photography; 186-187 *Bonfire* Jim deBarros art direction, Georges Amann cover photography; 203 *Stiff Upper Lip* Alli art direction, Mista Dean Karr, statue concept and photography, Mark Alfrey and Stan Lok of SMG Effects, statue sculpture; 218L *Black Ice* Joshua Marc Levy art direction and illustrations using vector graphics by You Work For Them LLC; 218R-210 *Backtracks* Phil Yarnell and John Jackson art direction, Phil Yarnell SMAY DESIGN cover art; 211 *Live At River Plate* Michelle Holme and Josh Cheuse art direction, C. Taylor Crutners, cover photography; 239 *Rock Or Bust* Josh Cheuse art direction, James Minchin III, photography, Istvan at Chaotic Atmospheres cover art.

SOURCES

Magazines and newspapers *Sounds, Kerrang!, Classic Rock, Q, MOJO, Rolling Stone, Record Mirror, Creem, Melody Maker, N.M.E., The Guardian.*

Books

Walker, Clinton. *Highway to Hell: The Life and Times of AC/DC Legend Bon Scott*: Pan Macmillan, 1994

Engleheart, Murray and Durieux, Arnaud. *AC/DC: Maximum Rock & Roll*: HarperEntertainment, 2006